What's Wrong with China

Paul Midler

WILEY

Published by John Wiley & Sons, Inc., Hoboken, New Jersey
Published simultaneously in Canada

No part of this publication may be reproduced, stored in a retrieval system, or transmitted in any form or by any means, electronic, mechanical, photocopying, recording, scanning, or otherwise, except as permitted under Section 107 or 108 of the 1976 United States Copyright Act, without either the prior written permission of the Publisher, or authorization through payment of the appropriate per-copy fee to the Copyright Clearance Center, 222 Rosewood Drive, Danvers, MA 01923, (978) 750-8400, fax (978) 646-8600, or on the Web at www.copyright.com. Requests to the Publisher for permission should be addressed to the Permissions Department, John Wiley & Sons, Inc., 111 River Street, Hoboken, NJ 07030, (201) 748-6011, fax (201) 748-6008, or online at www.wiley.com/go/permissions.

Limit of Liability/Disclaimer of Warranty: While the publisher and author have used their best efforts in preparing this book, they make no representations or warranties with the respect to the accuracy or completeness of the contents of this book and specifically disclaim any implied warranties of merchantability or fitness for a particular purpose. No warranty may be created or extended by sales representatives or written sales materials. The advice and strategies contained herein may not be suitable for your situation. You should consult with a professional where appropriate. Neither the publisher nor the author shall be liable for damages arising herefrom.

For general information about our other products and services, please contact our Customer Care Department within the United States at (800) 762-2974, outside the United States at (317) 572-3993 or fax (317) 572-4002.

Wiley publishes in a variety of print and electronic formats and by print-on-demand. Some material included with standard print versions of this book may not be included in e-books or in print-on-demand. If this book refers to media such as a CD or DVD that is not included in the version you purchased, you may download this material at http://booksupport.wiley.com. For more information about Wiley products, visit www.wiley.com.

Library of Congress Cataloging-in-Publication Data

Names: Midler, Paul, 1968- author.
Title: What's Wrong with China / by Paul Midler.
Description: Hoboken, New Jersey : John Wiley & Sons, Inc., [2018] | Includes index. |
Identifiers: LCCN 2017043469 (print) | LCCN 2017048361 (ebook) | ISBN 9781119213727 (pdf) | ISBN 9781119213734 (epub) | ISBN 9781119213710 (cloth)
Subjects: LCSH: Economic development—China. | China—Commerce. | China—Economic policy. | China—Civilization—21st century. | China—Social conditions—21st century.
Classification: LCC HC427.95 (ebook) | LCC HC427.95 .M53 2018 (print) | DDC 330.951—dc23
LC record available at https://lccn.loc.gov/2017043469

Cover Design & Image: Emily Mahon

Printed in the United States of America

10 9 8 7 6 5 4 3 2 1

CONTENTS

What's Wrong with China

The problem of China is largely pathological, and very slightly political.

—Putnam Weale (1925)

Don't try to give the American people the whole truth about China. In the first place they wouldn't believe you, and in the second place their stomachs are too weak.

—Hallett Abend (1931)

To understand China at all, it must first be very clearly understood, no matter what the Chinese say of themselves in public, that all but an infinitesimal fraction of the Chinese people are convinced that there is nothing fundamentally wrong with China.

—Rodney Gilbert (1926)

CHAPTER 1

The Pirate Ship

Two weeks before boarding my first flight to Asia, a friend of my mother's wished me well, letting me know she was jealous.

"You're so *lucky*," she told me. "Wish *I* was going."

She had never been to the Far East but was enamored by its ideas and traditions, especially medicine.

"Just think about it," she said. "They've been practicing medicine for thousands of years. They know *all kinds* of things we don't."

It was an unintended send-off as I found her words echoing back to me two weeks later in Taipei. I had been invited to join a group of office workers on a day trip their company had planned, and on the return—at the drop-off point—I managed to get my hand smashed in the door of their van.

"*Duibuqi!*" cried the woman who injured me.

I was frozen in pain. A colleague offered that she had something. "Chinese medicine," she said enthusiastically, before bolting.

A glass jar was presented, upon which were some handwritten Chinese characters. The lid was removed, revealing a dark, viscous liniment. And as it was applied to my hand, I held out hope.

Three women stood around me now, concentrating fully on my paw and taking turns offering commentary.

"That's better," one assured.

"Much better," another confirmed.

While everyone stood around waiting for something to happen, my hand continued to throb and a strange thought entered my head: *Was this Chinese traditional medicine? Was this how these people thought the human body worked? Broken bones healed in a jiffy with a magic salve?*

I was in my twenties then and somewhat embarrassed to have such rude thoughts. But the scene struck me as comical, and I had to suppress the urge to laugh. Thanking everyone for an otherwise lovely afternoon, I lied and told them I was feeling better. I then made my way to an area hospital, where I received a set of X-rays for the hand, which luckily had not suffered any fractures.

It was a strange beginning to a career in Asia, and perhaps an unproductive one. Westerners in it for the long haul were supposed to arrive mesmerized—enchanted at least—and that condition was meant to carry them through the several years it took to pick up the language. The bloom would come off the rose eventually, but it was meant to do so only after a fair amount of time had passed.

The effect of having my bubble burst almost upon arrival put me in an odd disposition: Chinoiserie and other Orientalia now struck me as daffy. I had little interest in studying anything Chinese in the traditional sense, and along with that ennui went any intention of taking my time in this part of the world seriously.

Thankfully I was young—this was twenty-five years ago—and I didn't need much of an excuse to stick around. A reliable old motorcycle, a rooftop apartment in the mountains outside of the city, an assortment of colorful characters for friends, and the odd job would suffice. I spent no time on language training and managed to pick up a fair amount of Mandarin in spite of myself. Wrapping up three years in Taiwan, I returned to the United States and entered a graduate school program that began by sending me to Beijing for the summer.

And that was how I wound up in my first proper Chinese language course with a woman named Miss Zhang.

In our first one-on-one session, Miss Zhang tossed me what she must have thought was a softball question: "Why are you still in China?" She was taking the American government's dubious view (it was Beijing's as well) that the years I lived in Taiwan should be clocked as time spent in the People's Republic of China, and she asked because few nonnatives ever returned after a stint.

Although foreigners were arriving in significant numbers, when they finally went home, they rarely boomeranged back.

Why had *I returned?*

In making my way to graduate school—it was a business program with an international component—I had to explain in an application why I had wanted to study such things as discounted cash flow and conjoint analysis. On this other motivation, I was drawing somewhat of a blank.

On the surface, Miss Zhang appeared a serious woman. She considered me for the briefest moment and then broke the silence between us by saying, "You know what you should tell people when they ask you that question?" Then she giggled. "You should tell them, '*Wo shangle zeichuan.*' I'm on the pirate ship."

It was a twist on an old idiom, one that suggested it is easier to jump on a tiger's back than to dismount. I got the reference but wondered: *Was the ship meant to be China? Who were the pirates?* In the back of my mind, a light bulb went off, one that would take me years to identify. Only later would I conclude that Miss Zhang had picked up on something—that I was lost—and what she ultimately offered me was not a conversation starter but a hint of where I ought to be looking for inspiration.

Not long after graduating from the University of Pennsylvania, I moved to Guangzhou, a sprawling metropolis located two hours north of Hong Kong, and from there I began a career representing American companies that had manufacturing interests in the region. The work put me in contact with Chinese factory bosses who were indeed pirate-like in their approach to commerce. And I appreciated that they shared a similar brand of humor to Miss Zhang's.

In the middle of the boom in export manufacturing, I found myself riding a train in Guangdong, seated facing two questionable-looking characters who were dressed head-to-toe in black. My reputation as a fixer was established by this time, and they easily appeared to be the sort who traded merchandise for a living.

Almost as soon as we pulled out of the station, the man seated by the window began eyeballing me, so I thought I would break the ice.

"*Nimen cong nali laide?*" I asked him.

"You wouldn't know the place," he said.

"I've been around. Try me."

"It's a small city," he demurred.

"*Ni shuo ba*," I insisted. "Where are you from?"

"Chaozhou," he said, finally. "We are from Chaozhou."

I had worked in Chaozhou, with a factory there that made majolica-style pottery. It was an out-of-the-way place, and though I had never experienced trouble there myself, I was familiar with its nasty reputation. Putting on an air of familiarity, I told him that I knew his fair city well—because I had once been swindled there.

"*Wo zai nimen Chaozhou bei pianle,*" I said, deadpan.

He caught the joke and laughed. That a foreigner would be cheated in his roughneck city was a given. That the *laowai*—outsider—should take such abuse as the normal course of events made it hilarious.

His partner, who wore a cap, was considerably less amused.

"Cheated in Chaozhou?" he said, sounding incredulous. "That is impossible. The people of my city would never cheat a fine foreigner such as yourself. Whatever the circumstances of your dealings, surely there must have been some misunderstanding."

His partner, the fellow by the window, was no longer smiling. I couldn't quite catch the relationship between the two but knew at least which one could be trusted. China was a rough-and-tumble world all right, and there were those who were frank about the place and those who put on airs and graces. You appreciated the ones who gave it to you straight, because you knew that you could work with them. The other sort was nothing but trouble. Imagine standing under an awning in the middle of a downpour, commenting on the weather, only to have some stranger next to you respond: "Rain? What rain?"

China brought many meaningful lessons, but only in great retrospect. It takes time for the subconscious to process the unfamiliar. Patterns form only slowly, and then you have to wait as certain realizations bubble to the surface and become points of aware-ness. Along the way to enlightenment, it is also necessary to let go of preconceived cultural notions, which often impede understanding.

A few years ago, wandering around Hong Kong, I had the idea to buy a new pair of shoes. This was in Tsim Sha Tsui, in the days before they ripped down the Hyatt Regency Hotel on Nathan Road, replacing it with the popular commercial center iSquare. There used to be a small shop just behind the hotel right off Peking Road, and in the storefront window I spotted a sign saying that it was an official reseller of a popular American walking shoe. It sounded like the perfect replacement, and after trying on a pair and immediately paying for them, I asked the shopkeeper to throw away my old shoes, explaining that I would just walk out with the new ones.

I almost immediately regretted the move. Within an hour, my feet were feeling pinched, and by the time I got back to my apartment in Guangzhou I was in agony. This confused me, because the shoe brand had such a strong reputation, and I wondered if the shoes were not somehow counterfeit. Just over the border from Hong Kong was Guangdong province, where the vast majority of the world's shoes were being produced. It made bootlegging easy, but this was an internationally known brand that I had purchased and the vendor had been officially licensed. It seemed unlikely that the shop would sell a bootlegged product, yet I had the feeling I had purchased shoes that were illegitimate.

An acquaintance in Guangzhou who was in the shoe game lived not far from me, and as I had not seen him in a while, I offered to drop by his office and say hello.

Taking up one of the shoes, he removed the insole and showed me evidence of a bad glue job. He then pointed out poor stitching and some odd stamp marks. It was not the work of a big-brand company.

"These are fake, for sure," he said.

"But the shop is an official reseller," I said. "How can they get away with selling knockoffs?"

The next few words out of his mouth would shift my perspective on the Chinese economy in a dramatic way.

"They probably sell both."

"Both?" I asked, not quite wanting to understand.

"Well, to keep their license, they sell some real shoes. Then, on the side, they sell a few fakes."

The scales fell from my eyes. Not only did I understand what he meant by such a hybrid business model, but I immediately also recognized that I had been seeing it for years—and that I had even run into a version of it during my first attempt at product sourcing.

After graduating from business school, I took what I called my *Four H's Trip*—a train journey that took me through Hunan, Hubei, Henan, and Hebei provinces—a bisection of the country from south to north. My final destination was Beijing, and a friend in the States who knew I would be there asked if I would help him purchase a volume of costume jewelry in the wholesale market there.

I didn't know much about trinkets, but a contact in Beijing offered to make a formal introduction to a woman named Bei Bei, who operated a store within the Hongqiao Pearl Market. "Do not stop at any of those other shops," I was warned, because Bei Bei was the only plain dealer in the multistoried bazaar.

Seated at a table in Bei Bei's showroom, I went over samples with an assistant, taking photos and making a note of the prices, which seemed more than fair. The work went fast, and after two hours, I excused myself to take a break. On the way to the front door, I passed by an older European man who was also evaluating merchandise.

"How much for that one?" I asked, pointing to a piece he had been inspecting that was identical to an item I had been shown. I had no actual interest in comparing prices and was just making small talk, but the man peered up at me over a pair of bifocals and, smiling, he mentioned the figure he was about to pay. It was three times what I was quoted and, save for some unseen difference in quality, the variance in pricing seemed... unusual.

When I got back to the shop, I said nothing to the gentleman and walked straight to the room Bei Bei occupied in the back.

She had a small window that looked out onto the showroom. "What's going on out there?" I asked, gesturing with a thumb toward the old man.

"You needn't worry about him," she said, confirming my suspicion that a fleecing was in progress.

This made no sense to me, at least not at the time. How could I be treated fairly while another customer was being taken advantage of *in the very same shop?* Many of us have a preconceived notion that there are only two kinds of service providers: the good and the bad. You have the reputable mechanic and the dishonest one, the fair attorney and the predatory one.

Chinese business operators instinctively understand how a hybrid model achieves the highest level of economic returns. Businesses that offer a fair deal to everyone leave too much money on the table, but those that cheat indiscriminately risk entirely losing their reputation. The key is to provide a fair deal to those customers who provide a key benefit, such as large volume or a link to a reputation network, while squeezing mercilessly those who do not bring such advantages. Chinese business owners split their customer base in much the way a farmer separates his milking cows from those bound for the slaughterhouse.

Mainland Chinese are sometimes described as *morally agnostic*, which is a way of saying that they choose to do "whatever" in a given business situation. But this is not what usually takes place. Chinese business operators who seek a hybrid business model look to lift profitability to a theoretical maximum. As though on a search for the Holy Grail, they pursue every possible strategy that has a hope of increasing profits. Business operators will use methods that appear haphazard, nonsensical, or even unscrupulous in their constant search for that *economically optimal point*.

Once you recognize this sort of thing is taking place, all kinds of previously unfathomable business models used in China suddenly make better sense. I once booked a room in a fashionable-looking hotel, but stepping inside I was surprised to find something from the Mao era: carpeting pockmarked with cigarette burns, wallpaper peeling at the corners, and, between two rock-hard twin beds, an antiquated-looking console with knobs and switches that no longer worked.

A manager eventually explained that there were two types of rooms on offer and that the refurbished rooms were located only on the seventh floor and above. I had seen an advertisement for the nicer type of room but had not taken care to book the one shown. This was not a bait-and-switch strategy but rather an odd hybrid with a four-star hotel situated above one of the same name that rated only two stars. In the United States, we would call this a branding nightmare, but Chinese are not bothered by the scheme. Quite the opposite—they welcome the flexibility. Taking a cheaper room, they might allow their friends to think incorrectly that they were staying at a luxury property.

Chinese economic behavior fascinates me in a way that traditional culture never could. Before they ripped down the Xiangyang Market in Shanghai, I enjoyed going there on occasion to bargain for merchandise that was obviously counterfeit. North Face knockoffs were especially popular, and walking past a vendor, you might be told that a jacket was being offered for 300 yuan. If you picked up the item and put it back on the rack, the price would immediately drop, and you soon learned there was a natural floor at 150 yuan—or one-half of the original asking price.

It was supposed to be an open secret among tourists, but after visiting the market for years, an old China hand revealed to me that most merchandise could actually be had for only one-third of the originally quoted price. "One-half is for the tourists," he explained.

How utterly efficient, I thought, that these vendors would have worked out such an informal system of price discrimination that placed all buyers into one of three buckets: the foolish naïf, the ambitious tourist, and the savvy local. It was certainly a good deal more efficient than the Arab souk, where sellers start by asking for an astronomically high price and buyers open with an equally ridiculous bid, with the two working out the difference slowly over several cups of tea and perhaps a game of backgammon.

The oddest thing about the market benchmark is that it has been in use for ages. In *Understand the Chinese*, published in 1934, William Martin wrote about these market vendors: "He asks for twenty dollars; you offer a third of it, as a rule."

A few years ago, interested in finding a new freight forwarder, I acted on a tip from a trader I knew in Guangzhou. "Call these guys," he said, handing me a business card. "They are the cheapest."

Ringing the company the following morning, I spoke with the receptionist, who asked me first where the goods would be shipping to. When I told her the United States, she gave me a different number to phone. At the other number, I was given a quote that was laughably high and threw the business card in the trash. I didn't even think about the exchange until I ran into the acquaintance who made the original link.

He asked me how it had gone, so I told him.

"Your freight forwarder is crap," I said.

"What are you talking about? They're the best."

Relaying my experience in detail, I explained that I had rung the company and was told to call their other office.

"That's strange," he said. "The freight forwarder is owned by my friend. He doesn't have any second office."

The receptionist, it turned out, fancied herself an entrepreneur, and while collecting a steady paycheck from her employer, she sent occasional leads to an outside company in exchange for a commission. This was another sort of hybrid model common to China, a combination of working faithfully for one company while quietly leveraging that position in order to earn a margin for oneself in an outside venture.

Chinese philosophy speaks of the *doctrine of the mean*, a principle that emphasizes midpoint solutions. When two people are arguing a case, for example, neither is judged as wholly right or wrong; truth is meant to lie somewhere in between. In a similar way, there is a tendency to recognize that absolute loyalty to a company (or a person) is not ideal, because utter fidelity is rarely a utility-maximizing proposition.

An American private equity company that I have worked with bought a sporting goods manufacturer based in China. The seller of the business, an enterprising Shanghainese, received forty million dollars in cash and, as part of the deal, he remained CEO on an annual salary of one million dollars. On top of that, he had an opportunity to earn bonuses and he retained a twenty-five percent equity stake in the business. But despite every incentive to play it straight, he quietly set up a separate, competing trading company and started redirecting new orders there. This was naturally in contravention of a noncompete agreement in place, so his business partners sued him.

The Americans involved presumed that it was the goal of the enterprising CEO to trash his original company entirely—to put it under while wholly supporting the new competing entity he had created. But that was not his plan at all, because such a move would not have been economically optimal. The separate business was nothing more than a backup, an auxiliary channel for reducing personal risk while increasing personal income by some small additional amount. Chinese operators enjoy hybrid models because they fit in with their mindset, which views incrementalism as a core strategy. The goal is always to establish a new foundation, and then from this starting position nibble one's way toward greater levels of advantage.

CHAPTER 2

A Mania
for Money

A few years ago, I wrote a book called *Poorly Made in China*, in which I attempted to explain the destructive practices I had witnessed in manufacturing. Factories were discreetly degrading the quality of their products by manipulating raw inputs. It was more than corner-cutting, because the fooled party—the foreign buyer—commonly gave explicit instructions on what was supposed to be produced. Manufacturers were sly about this quality fade and went as far as tricking third-party testing agencies into assuring their products were top-notch.

Manipulation took place in secret, and if the factory's moves went undetected, the degradation would usually worsen over time. You could get a producer to return to a better quality standard, but first you had to uncover the scheme, and then you had to browbeat the operator into doing the right thing.

It was gamesmanship, and it was annoying. It seemed prevalent, yet no one was talking about it. My work took me to different manufacturing sectors, and because I saw the same pattern in various corners of the economy, it struck me that this could be some kind of national characteristic. I even had the temerity to think that I might be the first to write publicly about the phenomenon. I read a lot but had never run across any description of

China in this light. As it turned out, I just wasn't looking far back enough.

In 1855, French Catholic priest Abbé Huc published a two-volume account entitled *A Journey Through the Chinese Empire* in which he described his intrepid adventures through the interior provinces. Assigned a lower-level official to meet their needs and ensure their safety, Huc's travel party paid a considerable sum to a mandarin to ensure that the expedition would be a smooth one. Only after covering some ground did they realize that they were increasingly being taken advantage of.

At first, they were put up in palaces and "treated in all things like mandarins of the first degree." But as the trip wore on, the money that the missionaries provided was applied to fewer comforts. Lodgings became increasingly poor until they found that they could not bear to spend the night in them.

In those days, there were no roads, and the best routes were little more than stony footpaths. The sedan chair was the way to go, and while it might seem like a burden to the men who made a living carrying these chairs, the weight of one rider when distributed among four sturdy laborers was not all that much. Huc wrote that though they had paid for new sedan chairs of the sort used by officials, they were in fact given old, narrow chairs that were uncomfortable for any length of time. And though they had covered the expense of four sedan chair bearers, the official who handled their affairs contracted only three coolies, pocketing the salary of the fourth. All of this done, Huc said, "in order to squeeze a little more profit out of us."

China's economy has risen fast, so we presume that any witnessed fixation on money must surely be a byproduct of the current go-go business climate. "His whole life is materialism put into action" is how we might describe a young Shanghainese of today who is monomaniacal about getting ahead. "Lucre is the sole object on which his eyes are constantly fixed" sounds like an accurate description of factory owners you currently deal with in Guangdong. To read these exact descriptions by Huc of Chinese people he met 150 years ago is curious. And he was not the only traveler of the era to make such observations.

"All they talk about is money," quipped Edwin Joshua Dukes, another Christian missionary, in 1887. If clergymen of the nineteenth century were put off by native materialism, it was at least partially because such values presented an obstacle to their proselytizing. Chinese appeared to need an economic incentive for conversion, so the disparaging term *rice Christians* gained popular usage. Reverend George Smith claimed in all seriousness that he was sometimes asked, "How many dollars a month shall we obtain if we become Christians?"

Yet another fed-up missionary, Reverend E. J. Hardy, decried in his 1905 book, *John Chinaman at Home*, the emphasis that materialism was given over matters of the spirit. "After the day's business, the shopkeeper counts his cash with great care, and the click of his little calculating machine brings music to what he is pleased to call his soul." The machine to which he alludes is, of course, the abacus.

"The Chinese are by no means the only people in whom the instance of the pursuit of gain is highly developed," wrote Reverend Arthur Smith in 1888, "but with them it is carried to a higher pitch, more uniformly exercised, and operates as a more potent force than with most other races."

Alexis Krausse may have been ahead of his time when he suggested in 1900 that a local would "sell his grandmother for a profit of a few cash." The Baptist missionary William Edgar Geil took denunciations of the Chinese furthest when he suggested in 1904 that "the desire for money is as strong in them as in any other people, not even excepting the Jews."

That is quite a statement, and perhaps we should wonder how the Chinese managed to avoid a reputation for money-grubbing during subsequent years when anti-Semitism was fueled by negative impressions of precisely the same sort.

Chinese have such a penchant for thrift that it has been highlighted as a contributing factor in modern-day food safety crises. We were reminded of this recently when thousands of infected pigs were found floating down the Yellow River. Accompanying reports highlighted locals seen pulling carcasses out of the water for their salvage value. The past has a way of echoing back to us. During England's first trade mission to China in 1793, George Macartney observed the same scene as his party floated down a river on their way out of China. Inhabitants were seen fishing a dead pig, "obviously diseased," from the same waters in which they were traveling.

Chinese today are concerned over food safety because they understand the lengths to which many are willing to go in order to generate a profit. Stories about fake beef and fake mutton are commonplace today, and it's easy to find information on the chemical processes required to create these dangerous counterfeits. Should we be surprised to discover that this was also a nineteenth-century problem? William Henry Wilkinson in 1855 described a dinner hosted by Western Christians in Peking. Two of his guests—natives of the city—had only one request of their missionary hosts: that they not be served beef, because any meat advertised as such was more than likely "horse or donkey re-christened."

That China as a nation habitually produces shoddy items is not a new story by any measure. A century ago, foreigners had a saying related to the many roads then being built in the country: "Good for ten years, bad for ten thousand." It is a pattern with which many are familiar today. Chinese buildings and infrastructure projects almost always appear impressive when they are unveiled, but sooner than expected, they fall into disrepair.

China has built so much in recent years, and the development has inspired awe among outsiders. Americans have even shamed themselves by comparing China's gleaming structures to their own crumbling infrastructure. It is an unfair comparison. Mainland buildings have shorter life spans than those in the United States, in part because the Chinese build for maximum flash. They prefer to take out smaller loans (or no loan at all) in order to minimize the payback period, and this often means deemphasizing longevity and concentrating more on the face that is created at the grand opening. As a result, no one sheds a tear when a fifteen-year-old building is torn down in China. The economics of a fast-growing economy support a build-it-up-and-tear-it-down strategy. But that model will reveal flaws when growth slows and it becomes too expensive to replace a building and too impractical to refurbish it.

Quality issues may appear trivial, yet we can say that they have contributed significantly to major wars fought by China. The Anglo-Chinese War (1839–1842) and the Arrow War (1856–1860) have been called the "Opium Wars" by historians and as such are portrayed exclusively as having been motivated by England's desire to force a dangerous narcotic onto an unsuspecting Chinese populace.

Such a view overlooks more important contributing factors behind the two nineteenth-century wars, namely, increased smuggling and the collapse of the Canton System. As for the drug itself, we acknowledge that pure-grade opium is not nearly as harmful as many presume.

Nineteenth-century advocates for the opium trade argued that lying down to a civilized pipe was not much different than joining a friend for a couple glasses of brandy. Charles Dickens was a known opium eater, and for all we know, some of his best work may have been done under the influence. Samuel Taylor Coleridge's habit, taken in the form of laudanum, is also well-documented. Jonathan Spence, the famed Harvard sinologist, noted that some Chinese who sat for the notoriously difficult civil service examination smoked opium during the exams.

We have conflicting images of opium use and abuse. On the one hand, smoking appeared to be a genteel custom popular among the wealthy and scholar-officials—the emperor himself was said to have indulged in the habit. But on the other, there is clear evidence that it was devastating to the general population. One late-nineteenth-century author provides a possible reason behind the contradiction: "Should the victim be rich," wrote John Arthur Turner in 1894, he "does not seem much the worse" for his habit. It is a meaningful clue that helps explain contrasting portrayals.

In an obscure book called *Formosa*, written by J. D. Clark and published in 1896, I found the following description of opium that was then available for sale on the island: "In Formosa, for the adulteration of opium, two varieties of 'cake' are used. One is called 'Tientsin cake,' an abominable mixture of buffalo, horse, pig, or other skins boiled down to a liquid—burnt skin having a smell similar to that of Opium smoke—to which some kind of medicine is added and a small quantity of Native Opium, either pure or obtained by boiling refuse pods of the poppy plant."

The other kind Clark references was called Hankow cake. Made from sesame seeds, this second variety contained no opium whatso-ever, and apparently smokers could not tell the difference between these fake offerings and the genuine article—both in taste and in effect.

Abbé Huc mentioned that British opium suffered "much adulteration before it reaches the pipe of the smoker," so who knows where to assign blame? If the counterfeiting of opium was as widespread as writers suggest—and knowing that fakes almost always involve a loss in quality—we are led to wonder about the real source of ill effects.

Historians are so hell-bent on blaming the West for everything that went wrong with China in the nineteenth century that they have no room for an investigation into the serious possibility that the nation may have actually poisoned itself. If adulteration caused more harm to health than opium, then we might see the government's efforts to stop the opium trade less as an honest attempt to solve a drug problem and more as a desperate attempt to blame the British for what was essentially a Chinese failing.

CHAPTER 3

Blush of Shame

American sentimentalists—*panda huggers* is another term—show not only a willingness to defend China against claims that there is something wrong, but they go one step further by suggesting that the country's biggest problems are somehow the fault of foreigners. "We taught them capitalism, you know," is a statement made by many well-meaning Americans. It makes our way of life seem like a virus deliberately passed on to an unsuspecting people. The idea is made further absurd by the recognition that the Chinese literally invented money—both coins and bank notes—and they have long been famous for their keen mercantile sense.

One hundred years ago, sentimentalists made the equally ridiculous claim that the West taught China how to lie. "It is often said," wrote Stanley High in *China's Place in the Sun*, "that there were no dishonest compradors until the foreigners taught them dishonesty."

In the nineteenth century, foreigners repeated the wisdom that "a Chinaman's word is his bond." Meant as the highest compliment, this common saying referred to the fact that Chinese dispensed with written contracts, relying solely on verbal agreements. Although some foreign writers depicted Chinese businessmen as exemplary agents of upright principles, their more practical contemporaries presented a different picture, one that suggested the Chinese were in the habit of misrepresenting themselves.

American missionary and diplomat Chester Holcombe sought to excuse the perception that the Chinese prevaricated by explaining that the culture was not properly understood. "Much of the falsehood to which the Chinese as a nation are said to be addicted is a result of the demands of etiquette," he wrote in his 1895 book, *The Real Chinaman*. For this people, he explained, the word "no" is often considered "the height of discourtesy." In the same year, Reverend Richard H. Graves published *Forty Years in China*, a book in which he included an amusing bit about how misunderstandings sometimes arise over concerns of etiquette: "I was polite enough to ask him to dinner, and he was not polite enough to decline the invitation."

Chinese believe it is impolite to embarrass someone without cause, and this tradition of saving face naturally leads to instances where dissembling is the preferred course of action. Though the principle was well understood, foreigners still had a hard time adapting to it, and even the British—who themselves knew a thing or two about polite fibbing—were maddened by Chinese circumlocution. Herbert A. Giles, the nineteenth-century British diplomat and co-inventor of the Wade–Giles system of transliterating Mandarin was struck by how little it mattered whether words matched deeds or intent. "Lying, under any circumstances, is a very venial offense in China; it is, in fact, no offense at all, for everybody is prepared for lies from all quarters, and takes them as a matter of course."

Writing in the 1920s, Rodney Gilbert suggested that habits of this sort were a sign of high intelligence. "Polite lying is everywhere an accomplishment," he suggested, with L. C. Arlington echoing the sentiment when he wrote in 1931 that for the Chinese, "a good liar is, speaking generally, a clever man." E. C. Werner, a British government official who worked in China in the period, offered that "untruthfulness is not considered by the Chinese a sin, but as a matter of the play of wits." George Wingrove Cooke, special correspondent for *The Times* of London in the nineteenth century remarked that the ways in which a Chinese juggled words might reflect positively on the individual: "It is with him what a smart repartee is with us. The immediate recipient may wince and retort; but the world applauds, and the sayer of the *bon-mot* chuckles."

Westerners have long been frustrated in China due to variances in communication methods. Samuel Wells Williams—American linguist, Christian missionary, and author of the 1848 classic *The Middle*

Kingdom—summarized his own annoyance with the Chinese thusly: "There is nothing which tires one so much when living among them as their disregard for truth." Some foreigners regarded this cultural feature as an indication of a moral failing. "Being detected in a lie does not produce in the Chinese a blush of shame, but merely silence," wrote former US diplomat Ralph Townsend, who also thought that misrepresentation could be considered a kind of verbal gymnastics, the act of being caught in a lie serving only as evidence of a "want of dexterity."

Westerners complain less these days, so one is inclined to conclude that whatever "unparalleled mendacity" characterized China in the past no longer applies to the present. It is a topic that is hard to flesh out, because nowadays few wish to discuss the subject to any extent. Like in a court of law, folks plea to a lesser offense. Rather than admit they are lied to, foreigners will offer that they simply have a hard time catching all of the facts. Arthur Smith mentioned something along these lines in 1890. In China, he said, "one never feels sure that he has been told the whole of anything."

In my China-based work, I have been misled more times than I care to admit, but I do my best to put these instances out of mind—not merely because obsession is unproductive but also because the pain of betrayal stings. Every once in a while though, some episode comes along that is so absurd that it sticks in the mind.

Looking to fill a sales position, I dropped a note to a young Shanghainese who had the right background. We agreed that he would call me that evening at 8:00 PM to talk about the position. It was a minor formality. My plan was to get him on the phone and then set a date for a face-to-face interview.

When the time came and there was no phone call, I didn't think much of it. Folks in Shanghai can be unreliable, and I figured there was also the possibility that he had changed his mind about the job. I awoke in the morning to find an e-mail from the guy in which he politely explained that he had been unable to call the previous night due to "a storm with thunders nearby," and did I not know it was "dangerous to talk via phones" during such a meteorological event?

There had been no storm, of course, and the best part of the note was the cheekiness of his line, the way in which the candidate turned it around by implying that I was a boor for not understanding the dangers of using a telephone when it is raining.

CHAPTER 4

Beating the System

Chinese humor is varied, and one type of joke in particular—a depiction of local yokels who are too clever by half—is a perennial favorite. A well-known tale within the subgenre describes a man working out where to stash his life savings of three hundred silver pieces. In the end, he puts them in a bag, which he buries near his home. So that no one should suspect what he has done, he places a sign over the spot that reads: *No three hundred taels buried here!*

The nineteenth-century Baptist missionary Adele Fielde recounted a similar folktale involving a man who drills a hole in the wall of his home so that he might "steal" some of his neighbor's light. Stories of this nature tickle the funny bone of China's *laobaixing*—the common folk—because everyone in this land seems to be looking for some way to beat the system.

My wife and I made a trip back to the States that included a few days of road travel around California. Looking to rest one afternoon, we stopped at an outlet mall near Silicon Valley and took a table at one of the only restaurants there, a fast-food joint. Within earshot sat a small group of tourists from China.

"*Meiguo ren hen ben,*" one of them declared. "Americans are stupid. You know how you can tell? Just look at the cup sizes. Every place offers free refills, but they still sell medium and large drinks!"

My wife, who is Taiwanese, suppressed the urge to laugh at their banter, and I found myself looking over my shoulder. The four of them were surrounded by shopping bags, and on the table between them was just one small-sized cup.

American fast-food chains are doing well in China, but they have had to modify their business models for the local market—not because of different tastes necessarily, but because of different consumer behavior patterns. Pizza Hut learned quickly not to offer mainlanders the same all-you-can-eat salad bar option that it does in other markets. Instead, the restaurant chain decided to give customers a chance at only one trip, a limitation that was viewed as a dare by many locals.

I saw firsthand this challenge, taken up by a young woman in Chengdu. After gingerly approaching the salad bar, she looked first to widen the circumference of her ceramic bowl with thick green pepper slices. Careful to be sure that the heaviest items were placed at the bottom, she laid down potato salad to serve as a foundation. Carrot sticks might be for snacking, but here they acted as girders to support what ought to have been considered an architectural project. Walking slowly back to her table while the leaning tower of produce appeared to nearly topple, she grinned at her boyfriend, who beamed back at her sharp display of skill. Naturally, after a few years of losing their shirt on this offering, the chain raised a white flag and scrapped the salad bar concept altogether.

Rather than combating this instinct that Chinese have for beating the system, some companies are smart and play into it. Mainland restaurant chains have initiated reward systems that are needlessly complex by mimicking airline frequent flier programs. Customers collect points for each yuan they spend, and once a number of points has accrued, discounts are unlocked. Gifts may be purchased with points but the value of the points fluctuates, and customers are encouraged to watch for specials available to VIP customers on certain days only.

Americans are turned off by an overly complex consumer experience, but Chinese are titillated by such elaboration. One theory holds that they prefer such an experience because they are bored and involved programs give customers something additional to talk about at the table. Another explanation is that Chinese are naturally drawn to a set of fixed rules because it gives the appearance of a puzzle that can be worked to maximum advantage.

Chinese see society as a game, and learning how to play it well preoccupies them. Those who understand this to be the case were not surprised to hear Beijing recently announce plans to create a *social credit system* with multiple layers of complexity that take into consideration not only such things as whether a Chinese national is paying his bills on time, but also whether he is a good communist by following public policies, obeying traffic rules, and maintaining academic integrity.

Whatever system is ultimately created, we can expect it to be deliberately convoluted so as to present a challenge for average folks who will inevitably seek ways to manipulate it. Chinese lawmakers are, of course, aware of this predilection, so they in turn will also make the rules vague enough to allow authorities to interpret them as they see fit, in hopes of reducing such manipulation. While the government is seeking to create formal systems, given the nature of the populace, it is eternally obliged to retain a certain degree of informalism in all its systems.

―――――――――

Even casual tourists understand that China is a nation with trust issues. If you are planning to travel afield in this country, you have to bring your own toilet paper because many restaurants, hotels, and airports refuse to supply the product for fear it will be stolen. And when you check out of your hotel, it pays to budget an extra fifteen minutes because the front desk will likely quarantine you while housekeeping runs to make sure the paint is still on the walls of your room.

Low trust is an annoyance felt nearly everywhere. Rushing into a department store in Shanghai to buy an umbrella once, I was surprised to learn that I could not pay the shop clerk directly. Handing me an invoice, she instructed me to find a kiosk marked *cashier* at the far end of the floor. Once payment was made and the chit was stamped, I then had to walk back to the shop to get my umbrella. This multistage process reduces employee theft, and the setup has the added advantage of ensuring that the consignee passes along the agreed-upon commission to the department store.

"Distrust saps the foundations of things," wrote Reverend R. H. Graves at the close of the nineteenth century. Around this time,

Reverend Hardy lamented that "cat and mouse games" in China typically required those in a supervisory role to expend no small amount of energy.

We sometimes forget the extent to which civilization rests upon a foundation of trust. The Pony Express would not likely have popped up first in China, a nation where the sender traditionally did not dare hand over a letter for which the postage was already paid in full. How to know that a courier would be sent to make the delivery? Where one can pocket the fee and spare the cost of sending a man, surely some delivery companies would take advantage. A cash-on-delivery arrangement might have solved that problem but then the courier would have to contend with the possibility that after going to the trouble of delivery, it might get stiffed at the other end.

China's solution to the problem, as reported by Herbert Giles, was to establish a hybrid payment formula. Writing in the 1870s, he detailed the setup that balanced the risks held by each party: "About thirty percent of the postage is always paid by the sender to secure the office against imposition and loss," he explained. "The balance is recoverable from the person to whom the letter is addressed."

The thirty-seventy split is a ratio immediately recognizable to those working in China manufacturing because thirty percent reflects the precise amount most factories require as a down payment to start production.

Giles may have believed that he had uncovered some kind of golden ratio because he also pointed out that locals did not eat to satiety, but instead filled themselves only seventy percent. I have heard martial artists explain that certain forms of *gongfu* call for only seventy percent of force to be applied in any given move in order to increase flexibility in combat. Sitting down to tea with Chinese friends, one is also reminded that a teapot is traditionally filled to seventy percent. And of course, China watchers will remember that Chairman Mao was famously described by Deng Xiaoping as having been "seventy percent right and thirty percent wrong."

Mainland Chinese do not appear bothered in the least by the lack of trust that permeates society, but rather take it as a given. When traveling in groups, they willingly hand over their passports to their tour leader ostensibly for safekeeping, though the real reason is to indemnify the operator against loss or embarrassment by any of the tourists. Should one among the group break the law or violate policy, the tour operator need not worry about the perpetrator taking off and leaving the company with a liability.

Many industries in China are stuck in a low-trust trap. China's used car market, for example, has failed to take off because of the widely held presumption that private sellers are motivated to unload a lemon. As a result of this belief, buyers offer less on average than they should, which in turn discourages honest vehicle owners from selling into the market. In a related article, the *Financial Times* noted that in most developed nations, "sales of second-hand cars outnumber those of new vehicles by about two to one, but the opposite is true in China."

China is now a major player in online commerce, but the industry would not have taken off had the low-trust problem not first been solved. In the United States, a simple five-star rating system suffices to keep buyers and sellers honest; in this market, more needed to be done. In China, if you want to buy an item online, you must first send funds to an escrow agency such as Alipay, a kind of electronic middleman. Alipay holds the funds until you confirm that you have received the goods and that they are more or less what you expected. Only then is the money released from escrow to the seller.

When I first began working in manufacturing, I worried that I might offend a factory owner by revealing that his buyer was comparing prices among competing suppliers. Chinese factory bosses promise their eternal friendship to buyers to make the business seem personal. Americans buyers are therefore dissuaded from upsetting the personal link with any suggestion of disloyalty, especially at the beginning of these relationships. But this thinking is wrongheaded; Chinese owners in fact have more respect for their clients who shop the deal.

"*Huobi san jia*," the idiom goes: Compare the goods at three places. Chinese factory bosses, who are in the habit of charging as much as possible, actually find relief in knowing that a buyer is doing his homework. It means they can dispense with games and instead deal with the buyer in a straightforward fashion.

American importers will occasionally whisper: "Don't tell the factory we're looking at another supplier." But such warnings are a waste of time, because the average industrialist is perceptive and will pick up such a vibration. And he believes the opposite of what you tell him anyway. In this low-trust environment, if you suggest that you are not looking, the factory boss will presume you are. And if you tell him that you have a backup supplier, he figures you are bluffing.

"Anything that is direct," said the Belgian poet Henri Michaux, "makes the Chinese ill at ease and gives him the painful impression of being false." No truer words have been spoken. I recall years ago telling a stainless steel supplier that his buyer was about to leave him if prices were not cut to reflect market rates. He figured his customer was bluffing, ignored the entreaty, and continued to hold prices high. Letting him think that we had accepted his terms, we quietly began searching for an alternate producer. I do not know how he found out—a rumor most likely reached his ear—but one afternoon out of the blue, I got a phone call from the man, entirely uncharacteristic, telling me that he had given our earlier conversation some thought and was willing to honor a small reduction.

In China, relationship costs are high and typically involve a lot of time spent drinking and carousing with those in one's network. After a full day of regular work, the average entrepreneur puts in a long night of boozing with customers, colleagues, business partners, key suppliers, and those with links to cash. Those who are currently useful—as well as those who might possibly be a resource one day—are put into the rotation. A stronger emotional bond is no guarantee against betrayal, but to the extent that it helps increase trust by some small measure, this deleterious form of socialization is seen as a worthwhile investment.

Chinese homeowners also know the problem of monitoring costs. In this market, new homes are presented as empty canvasses, and it is up to the homebuyer to take care of refurbishment. Full-time supervision of subcontractors during construction is essential, so many homeowners will stand on top of the workers as they go about their business. If they do not closely supervise their work, the laborers will likely claim to have installed fifteen boxes of laminated flooring planks when the job required only nine. Or they may skimp on a necessary input like adhesives, the evidence of which will not be revealed until one or two years later when ceramic tiles start to drop from the kitchen wall.

Ralph Townsend was of the opinion that Chinese gambled away their savings because there were few channels for investment. Chinese did not trust the banks, and placing money with anyone other than a close relative was considered extremely risky. Under these circumstances, it made sense to take a small nest egg and attempt an increase through a more direct flirtation with luck.

Arthur Smith mentioned that capital was loaned in his day at twenty-four to thirty-six percent per annum, an exorbitant rate for the nineteenth century. The reasoning for such usurious interest rates was that those who lent out money wanted it back as quickly as possible, typically within a year. While short-term loans were good for certain immediate uses, such as purchasing agricultural tools prior to the season in which they might be used, such a limited time horizon did not accommodate grander ambitions. China's low-trust trap effectively stalled economic development because capital could not easily be sourced for infrastructure projects, which often carried a return horizon more on the scale of thirty years and offered a yield of only four or five percent per annum.

At the end of the nineteenth century, China wished to build railroads but could not gain access to capital. Historians have pointed out that though China appeared poor at this time, quite a few prominent families around the nation had accumulated vast sums. Low trust kept these families from putting funds to work on long-term projects such as infrastructure, however. As a result, the Qing government turned to foreign nations for assistance, and so most railroads through the early twentieth century were built with foreign capital.

Although the Americans and the Russians had their projects, the Japanese were the leaders in railroad development. China was initially glad to receive their investment, but eventually it came to envy the Japanese for the ease with which they laid down tracks and made a success of their ventures. When the Japanese invaded Manchuria in the 1930s, it was partly because their railroads there had suffered sabotage for years. The Chinese who lashed out at Japan-owned assets may have claimed to be responding to past transgressions. But much of the vandalism was actually an expression of frustration on the part of the Chinese over not having been able to organize themselves as easily as the Japanese, who did not have the same issues with social trust.

CHAPTER 5

Intermediaries

In ancient times, one did not do business with strangers; low trust kept Chinese from dealing with anyone but intimates and family. This self-imposed limitation was an obvious impediment, and one way around the handicap was to enlist the assistance of third parties.

Two individuals unknown to each other who wished to enter into a business transaction would not attempt to make a direct link, but rather would call upon a third party known to them both. The middleman in such a case was not there merely to provide a character reference. He was also an active participant in what was ultimately a three-way transaction.

The intermediary is such an archetypal figure in the culture that Chinese will often slip unconsciously into the role, even when they have been assigned a different part to play. On a flight to Guangzhou, I watched as a squabble broke out between two men, one seated in front of the other. The passenger in front had moved his seat into a full recline position, which caused the fellow behind him to complain. The flight attendant who turned up to handle the matter did not offer her opinion even though she was likely trained to do so. Instead, she bounced between the two belligerent passengers, listening as each made his case.

When mediating between two parties, Chinese are careful not to show bias—even when it is deserved—because the appearance of favoritism in a matter may lead the disadvantaged party to claim the judgment illegitimate due to prejudice. Chinese are convinced, wrote American sinologist Lucian Pye, "that people as a rule are highly partisan, have hidden agendas, and will in the end, in forthright and devious ways, always act in accordance with their biases or preferences." This set of beliefs adds an obvious degree of complexity to the goal of seeking justice.

In China, mediators may delay a decision in an effort to further the impression that it has been difficult to make the final call. In the United States, you hear the judge slam his gavel and declare that he has ruled entirely in favor of the plaintiff or the defendant. In China, there is more of a tendency for judges to say that both parties in a civil matter are at least partially to blame, even if it is not at all the case.

On its surface, such a feature of the culture would appear to be an attempt to achieve social harmony in all situations. Another way to look at it is as a risk-reducing strategy. "The Chinese, official or otherwise, from the highest to the lowest and from the millionaire to the beggar, lives always in fear of reprisals," wrote L. C. Arlington. In the 1930s retribution often meant physical violence. Today it takes the form of inflicting intentional face loss.

Chinese are lovers of face, we are told, without being offered the other half of the equation: Face as a cultural value weighs most heavily in the threat of its negation. Chinese who feel cornered will commonly respond with attacks that are meant to embarrass, and in their attempt to cause related face loss, things can often get quite nasty. "No other political culture places as much stress upon the emotion of hate as does the Chinese," wrote Pye, a notion that rings true with anyone who has ever run into serious trouble while doing business in China.

I have always found it curious that Christianity's Golden Rule focuses on the positive—*Do unto others as you would have them do unto you*—while the Chinese version of this notion, promulgated by Confucius, concentrates on the negative—*Whatever you don't want done to you, don't do to another.*

Chinese are quick to put others on notice. In a business meeting populated with fresh faces, you sometimes catch vague intimations. They may take the form of a barely audible, well-timed grunt combined with a certain look, the meaning of which is to convey a specific warning: *Harm my interests and suffer the consequences.* The threat is explicit but elliptically delivered. A dropped hint about an individual's mistresses, or knowledge of an illegal involvement, or some other such sensitive detail usually suffices.

Western companies mistakenly imagine that the locals they hire will be ardently loyal to them because money has changed hands. This is another misperception. An American firm that I once worked with paid a significant retainer to an attorney in Guangzhou on an intellectual property matter and were disappointed by what they got in return for the professional fee.

"We should try to understand the factory's position," the local lawyer said at one point.

"I'm not paying *you* to tell *me* to be sympathetic to the factory!" came the response from the owner of the American company.

The Americans were incensed and suspected that their attorney might be taking money from the opposition in return for helping its cause. Chinese intermediaries will sometimes willingly assume a weaker role—*play the soft middle*—for economic considerations, it is true. By serving as an inadequate advocate to both parties, the intermediary may extend the life of the dispute, which may be its own incentive. Ultimately, by deliberately limiting effectiveness, the intermediary may be able to elicit appeals and gifts from either side as each seeks to promote its own specific cause.

An American firm that hires a foreigner to manage its affairs in China will expect that individual to be loyal to the company above all. Chinese factory owners tend to view these representatives in a slightly different way. The Westerner who is hired in New York and sent to China is not seen as representing the American firm alone. Rather, he is viewed as a go-between, and as such he is automatically considered an intermediary. Though paid by only one side, his role, as the Chinese see it, is to bridge the gap and to find common ground between competing interests.

Western firms typically have no idea that such pressures are exerted. An American firm with a buying office in China will hardly notice that its local hires have taken a middle-ground position until there is a crisis. When a product fails, the locally-hired office manager may refuse to join her foreign bosses in expressing extreme disappointment toward the supplier responsible for the error. Instead, she presents herself as a Solomon, suggesting that both sides share in the liability. American managers who hear talk of compromise coming from their own staff may be incensed and suspect that the employee is on the take. In actuality, the local hire is more likely worried about potential reprisals from the factory for not playing the middle role in such a way that it also benefits.

Chinese factory owners show special contempt for the foreign representative who takes his job too seriously, and from the very beginning they will assess the rep's willingness to play ball. Factories that hope to engage in margin-widening games are loath to have a diligent watchman around. If the foreigner appears to be a good sport and have the capacity to "see things from both sides," he will be allowed to remain in his position. If he appears an especially loyal agent of his employer, however, the factory will conspire to have the individual removed.

Steve Dickinson, an attorney who represents foreign firms in China, told me that he has seen local firms use every despicable excuse in the world to get him ejected from a deal. "They will tell my client that I have been rude, or they will say that my Chinese isn't good enough, or if they get desperate, they will concoct a story about an attempt to solicit a bribe. They are so predictable that I tell my clients what to expect in advance, and in many cases, they say to me, 'My gooodness, they did *exactly* what you said they would!'"

Chinese firms that plan to engage in shenanigans cannot afford to have a vigilant watchdog in the mix. The more the local firm is interested in behaving in an unscrupulous manner, the greater its need to remove the would-be intermediary. Western companies—especially larger corporates—tend to get nervous when a Chinese partner starts making noise about a representative they have sent to China though, and as the volume of the complaints grows, so too does the pressure to have that individual recalled. Chinese firms that demand a representative be removed will often link their complaints to a timely sweetener—like an offer of a major concession—in order to facilitate having that pain-in-the-ass individual replaced.

When asked by an American company to assess its operations in China, I will take special care to observe the relationship between any foreign manager and the local business he has been hired to oversee.

If the relationship between him and the locals is utterly contentious—if the Chinese hate his guts—my advice to the Americans is always the same: *You need to keep that guy right where he is.* In more cases than not, though, the opposite is true, with the Chinese firm expressing extreme fondness and devotion for the nonnative manager. In such instances, it is obvious that the foreign firm needs to call the individual home.

Chinese are successful at managing foreigners—very successful— and they are especially adept at handling changes of the guard. They warmly welcome the newcomer and take care to blame all problems on his predecessor.

"He was terrible!" says the factory boss. "He didn't know his job. He made many mistakes. He was a bad man. But you—*Oh, you!*—you are so much nicer, smarter, and more handsome. We will have an excellent relationship, of this we are certain."

Of course, the newbie has a problem in that he is not prepared for the job. Knowing this, the factory promises to get the guy up to speed. This gesture comes as a great relief to the tenderfoot, who had initially been apprehensive about his new role, especially given the history of troubles in the preceding relationship.

The new arrival rings his boss back in the States the evening of his initiation and happily passes along the good news that after only one meeting, he has the factory people eating out of his hand. They like him, and they are already paving the way by helping him learn the ropes. "Great," says his boss, who wants to hear only that there is no longer any friction.

Chinese factory bosses not only understand the new arrival's naiveté, but they even know precisely how long it will take for him to wise up and become a sharper-witted agent. Not every foreigner becomes hard-boiled though, and more often than not the Chinese firm is successful in turning the representative into someone who supports its maneuverings, either tacitly or explicitly. There is a certain breed of long-term foreign resident—and I count myself among them—who has rejected the acculturation process, who recognizes certain failings of the local culture, and who therefore sees less benefit in taking the accommodating route. But most foreigners are irredeemably transformed by the in-country experience and therefore become ultimately useless to those who would rely on them back home.

Chinese dogs bark only at foreigners, Abbé Huc observed in the nineteenth century. This notion was echoed decades later by Rodney Gilbert: "The street dogs in China will tell a man when he ought to get out. They slumber peacefully on the doorsteps while a thousand Chinese go by, but bark and snarl at the newcomer though he may be wearing Chinese clothes, eating Chinese food and be saturated with the aroma of China. They will continue to bristle and snarl when he goes by for five years or ten years, and then, some day, he will discover that they pay no heed to him, that they recognize no difference between his emanations, whether material or psychic, and those of the Chinese mass. And it is then fairly certain that his employer's books register almost as little difference in worth."

China watching is difficult in part because the outsider is often changed in the process of understanding the subject. The fonder one becomes of the place and its people, the greater the risk of losing objectivity. At the same time, however, one must also be careful not to be burdened with too much of one's own cultural baggage and personal policy notions.

Western sentimentalists are notorious for their heartfelt conviction that conflict can be eliminated by imagining that there are no material differences among peoples. While a noble idea, it leads to errors in judgment. Chinese are not a unified people, we are told, but are divided, as we are, into factions. Just as we have our Democrats and Republicans, so China must similarly be polarized into a dichotomy that splits its population in half.

Writing in 1846, Reverend George Smith attempted to promote this exact picture of China when he misleadingly claimed that the Chinese people were divided on the issue of opium. In his *Narrative of an Exploratory Visit to Each of the Consular Cities of China*, he wrote that there were "two grand national factions." One side was "rigidly attached to an exclusive conservatism of national isolation and customs," while the other was "inclined to more liberal views, and more especially advocating the legalized importation of opium at a high duty." In retrospect, it turns out that this imagined bifurcation was more a projection of a Western political fantasy and less a reflection of Chinese political reality.

Chinese are not as easily divided as outsiders imagine, perhaps because they are less apt to see the world in terms of right and wrong, of black and white. While Chinese undeniably enjoy the rigors of discourse, they will eventually cede their positions with reasoned judgment once a particular strategy or decision is recognized by general consensus to be more advantageous. At this point, dissenting opinions are moderated, and much of the tension that remains is the mere grumblings of those who have suffered some measure of face loss.

Just as they succeed in achieving economic optimization individually, Chinese groups are adept at finding maximum efficiency through the decision-making process. Continued stubborn adherence to a differing opinion long after the matter has been settled is counterproductive. So the Chinese tend not to understand those who hold an opinion "on a matter of principle" beyond the point at which it makes pragmatic sense to do so. In the United States, you find opposition supporters calling for a president to be impeached even into the eighth year of a two-term presidency, which, regardless of who is in office, calls into question our capacity for decision-making.

Westerners misinterpret what takes place in Chinese groups because we take too much at face value. Informed by someone in China that a matter is "quite complicated," we ought to presume that the situation is rather easily understood and that the people we are dealing with simply do not wish for us to dig below the surface. At the same time, whenever we are told that a matter is straightforward or when a scenario is laid out for us on a silver platter, we can be sure there are hidden complexities. In China, relationships described as harmonious are often quietly contentious. Likewise, any overt display of discord may in fact be a ruse, especially when it is precisely what the audience in question expects to hear.

An American sporting goods company was ripped off to the tune of around one million dollars. A local hire in its Shanghai office had arranged the fraud by creating fake invoices for a customer that did not exist. Thinking he would easily get away with the scheme, the scoundrel instead found himself running from the police, and from a host of colleagues who had it in their best interest to convey the impression that they were not in any way complicit. He was then made into a pariah within the office setting, with everyone expressing public indignation at his nerve. That's what it looked like on the surface anyway. In reality, several within the office—including the locally-hired general manager—were quietly leaking information to the scamp, letting him know through backchannels when and where he could expect the company's next move. Those in the office who helped him did so not because they liked him, but because they were interested in a hedge. In the back of their minds, they were thinking:

What if the company has been damaged beyond recovery by the fraud?
What if the company fails and I lose my job?
What if the rogue ends up on his feet and in a position to help me?

Chinese have a saying: *Qiang tou cao, liang bian dao.* The grass on the wall leans in both directions. An ardent loyalty is rarely an optimizing strategy. While it pays to appear faithful to the primary group, there are typically further benefits to be had from supporting the other side as well.

Ralph Townsend pointed out that while this sort of behavior was well understood by him and his contemporaries, others abroad missed the point: "The notion of contending factions of differing aspirations, as it is phrased, is found as an opinion only outside of China."

————————

China's culture is heavy, and it has a way of influencing those who spend time in contact with it. Although it is expected that long-term foreign residents will be affected by time spent in China, what may be more surprising is the extent to which Chinese culture is leaving its mark in far-flung lands.

Jeff is a friend who brokers commercial real estate in the United States, specializing in restaurant properties, and his work puts him in touch with restaurateurs of every ethnicity imaginable. Over coffee one day, he mentioned to me that a new wave of buyers from China was approaching him and that he was being offered what he called "lucky money."

In his capacity as a real estate agent representing sellers, Jeff explained, he was not allowed to take cash payments from prospective buyers. He found the phenomenon curious though, and—wishing to learn more myself—I asked him to provide details.

Jeff had a restaurant listed for $900,000, and a Chinese buyer approached him wanting to bid only $650,000. "I told him the offer was too low and that I wouldn't take it to the seller."

"How much to get the building?" asked the Chinese buyer, while promising $20,000 stuffed into an envelope.

"You have to understand, it's totally illegal," Jeff explained.

"Of course," I said, "but why was he offering the money?"

What the buyer was hoping to learn was how low he could go on the bid. In this case, based on information the broker had, $800,000 was likely enough to close the seller. The buyer needed only to put in the offer and wait for the seller to cave in and accept the bid.

For a presumed savings of $100,000, the buyer was glad to pay twenty percent, or $20,000. The motivation for the broker was also obvious, since his five percent commission would have netted him only $5,000 more had he sold the property at the full listing price.

Hearing the story, I still could not figure out how the buyer and the broker could pull off such a caper.

"Assuming the broker takes the payment..."

"Assuming..."

"What happens if while they are waiting for the seller to agree to $800,000, another buyer calls and says he will pay the full $900,000?"

"Oh, that's easy," Jeff said. "I just say we're already under contract and hang up."

CHAPTER 6

Dulled Senses

Expatriates in China have a tendency to wax nostalgic. "All these were fields when I was a lad, Charlie," says the interloper of his dear Pudong, or of his cherished Hangzhou. While we may forgive the tender transplant his mawkishness, we should be careful not to overlook a far more interesting counterpoint—namely, that the Chinese harbor no such sentimentality.

The international press has done an excellent job reporting on the economy's meteoric rise: Construction cranes as far as the eye can see, container ships fully loaded and ready to set sail, a new generation of nouveau riche participating in extraordinary displays of conspicuous consumption. These are the symbols of the new China and its breakneck growth rate. The subtext of each article written and every photograph reproduced is the same: China is transforming so fast that we foreigners can barely comprehend it.

We suffer from *China shock*, the local equivalent of *future shock*, an idea coined by Alvin Toffler, who detailed how advances in technology (and the future promise of it) were driving us batty. "Too much change in too short a period of time," he explained.

The foreigner's inability to process all of the rapid progress was its own story, but not nearly as interesting as the other angle—always missed—that showed the Chinese taking the adjustments totally in stride. There is no discounting the achievement. China has grown bigger and faster than any economy in the history of the world. It is an unprecedented economic expansion. Yet no matter where they stood in the economy, and no matter how much they personally benefitted, the Chinese themselves seemed inured to all of the attendant excitement.

Anyone interested in calculating the perception gap need only consider attitudes toward historic preservation. Shanghai was home to some beautiful old buildings, many done in the art deco style and dating back to a truly golden era. When these buildings were torn down, it was mostly the foreigners who cried. Locals themselves mourned little, if at all.

Westerners do not wish for China to slow, nor do we begrudge the Chinese their success. Quite the opposite—we have cheered them on.

Xiao Yu, a young woman who worked for me briefly and who remained a friend afterward graduated from university at the beginning of China's boom in export manufacturing. Within a span of five years, Xiao Yu's income had increased ten-fold, enabling her to buy her parents a small villa in their hometown in eastern Guangdong. It was quite an accomplishment for a local woman only in her twenties who had started with nothing.

She had always been smart and capable of self-reflection, so I always presumed that some part of her was looking back on all this as it was taking place, saying to herself, "What a strange trip it's been."

What did she think of the changes that had transformed her homeland? I wondered.

Was she satisfied? Did she feel lucky?

I asked her what she thought of China's rapid ascent. "Not growing fast enough," was her clipped response.

What, if anything, does this say of the Chinese? Americans who grow up impoverished have a hard time breaking out of the cycle of poverty. The concept of such a "poverty trap" is virtually unknown to modern Chinese, who have slipped easily out of poverty and into higher levels of wealth, as if their time at the bottom had been nothing more than hibernation.

In the United States, people who move too swiftly out of destitution actually suffer mental distress. The National Endowment for Financial Education suggests that as many as seventy percent of those who come into money quickly wind up broke. Psychologists have a name for the phenomenon: *sudden wealth syndrome*. The lottery winner serves as its poster child, and you can read about these folks in the papers. There they were one day, holding an oversized bank check, and within a few quick years, they managed to lose it all—the money, their connections to family and friends, and occasionally their sanity.

China has generated millions upon millions of sweepstake-champion equivalents. Where were the similar tales of woe? China's money was pancake fresh, and there was so much of it. How could such a dramatic change have had only minimal negative impact?

In southern China, buildings are rarely heated, and one is often forced to wear a jacket indoors during winter. Arriving at the Regency Hotel in Shantou, I found my room so unbearably cold that I called the front desk to ask if there wasn't something they could do about it.

"I suppose we can send up a heater," said the clerk.

The appliance made no impact, so I called back.

"Would you like a second heater?" the clerk asked.

In the morning, heading out of the hotel, I passed the bellman who appeared half-asleep but who gave me a crooked smile all the same.

"Good morning," I told him.

"Two heaters," he chuckled softly.

As it turned out, the hotel only had three. Chinese in this city rarely made use of heaters, so my gossip-worthy request had apparently been humorous to some of the hotel staff.

Mainlanders like their stereotypes, particularly those involving foreigners, whom they perceive as fragile. *Laowai* who complain of secondhand smoke in China—a country that has a high smoking rate—are rarely met with contempt, but instead sympathy. As a foreigner, you never have to feel guilty asking someone to close a drafty window or turn down a radio, because everyone understands that you have a weaker disposition.

The native's character has been tested in the refiner's dual-fire of economic hardship and political repression, so naturally he cuts a more durable figure. Chinese actually pity the foreigner, who is seen as a vulnerable creature, like a conch that has wandered away from its shell. Talk of environmental discomfort is fully expected—and to some extent even welcome—because it affirms the native belief that the Chinese are ultimately indestructible.

Chinese are convinced that their physical disposition is fundamentally and materially different, a point that many foreigners have agreed with in the past. China hands of the 1920s and 1930s noted that Chinese were indifferent to noise, for example. "Nothing is sold in China," wrote William Martin, "be it shoes or silk, rice or fans, without a roar of wireless that drowns the voice of the buyers. The people are so intoxicated with noise that they no longer hear it and must continually have more of it."

Today's cultural explainer attributes this phenomenon to the native concept of *renao*, a notion that loosely translates to "hustle and bustle." But as much as the Chinese like the sound of action, this phrase does not explain a key accompanying concept, namely, the corresponding ability of Chinese to tune out unwanted stimuli.

Stanley High suggested in the 1920s that while "China's vast army of wheelbarrows" screeched endlessly no one seemed at all bothered. "A few drops of oil, applied with some degree of regularity, might eliminate the nerve-wracking noise, but, among the Chinese, nerves are cheaper than oil and the squeak, therefore, goes on in its strident glory."

Martin wrote that, "The Chinese is a man without nerves," a phrase that was echoed by numerous other foreign writers of the era. Rarely mentioned in a disparaging way, foreign residents were rather impressed by this national feature, or at least they found it curious. The Chinese, wrote Alexis Krausse, are able to "endure suffering which to a European will entail the utmost torture with an unruffled countenance." Reverend E. J. Hardy remarked that locals appeared to "combine the active industry of the most civilized people with the passive patience of the North American Indian."

Mainland Chinese have a singular ability to concentrate on any given task. Once I entered a shop and walked in on a clerk who was busy counting a fistful of cash. Worried that I might disturb her concentration, I stood several feet away and waited for her to complete her tally. While still in the process of thumbing her notes, she suddenly shouted at me—"*Shenme shi?* What do you need?"—without missing a beat.

China's export manufacturing juggernaut was made possible through the aid of such cultural advantages, as many who work in manufacturing can attest. It was not merely a cheap labor rate that made China competitive, but also workers' willingness to tolerate long hours in poor conditions. That they could put out of mind such undesirable stimuli as noxious smells and ear-shattering noises also helped. More than a century before academics like Daniel Goleman would expound on theories of *emotional intelligence*, old China hands had developed a similar theory of temperament.

"How can they stand it?" an American buyer asked me while touring a factory that stamped sheet metal. The noise from dozens of forty-ton hydraulic presses was deafening. Seeing that the workers did not wear earplugs, the buyer announced to the factory owner that his company was going to help remedy the situation by insisting on ear protection. Not to worry, though, he said; his company would cover the expense of supplying thousands of pairs of plugs each month.

The news about the earplugs didn't go over well. The following day, the plant owner explained that his workers did not mind the noise as much as they objected to the sensation of having synthetic material in their ears. They also complained that the stoppers would interfere with their work since it was already hard enough to hear a colleague shouting instructions above the great clanging of the machines. They would wear the earplugs if the buyer insisted, the boss explained, but because productivity was expected to go down, the laborers wanted an increase in compensation.

Modern authors have occasionally written on *chiku*, the act of eating bitterness. This word describes only an ability to suffer general hardship and does not capture the full depth of the Chinese ability to endure. Arthur Smith suggested that there was something more to this national characteristic when he observed that Chinese seemed to lack nerves entirely: "In this age of steam and electricity, Western civilization has developed a conspicuous nervous system. The twirling pencil, the twitching fingers, and anxious face are daily reminders of taut nerves. The Occidental composure is easily shattered by delay and disappointment, while to the Chinese it matters not how long he is required to remain in one position; and he will stick steadily to his work from morning till night, plodding faithfully at the most monotonous task. Even the children display a capacity for keeping quiet that would drive a Western child insane."

Western doctors who practiced in the Far East at the time were convinced that the Chinese were more physically robust. "Physicians who have practiced in China," wrote Stanley High, "are almost universal in the assertion that the Chinese physique, in recovering from severe operations and in ability to throw off disease, is superior to that of westerners." As evidence, foreign physicians noted that Chinese were less likely to contract smallpox, polio, and a host of other illnesses. Missionary physicians were often astounded to see patients pull through from illness that would have surely led to a terminal diagnosis for one of their own countryman. "Don't give up a Chinaman till he's dead," was a common saying among physicians of the day, according to Edward Alsworth Ross.

One of the unfortunate byproducts of this belief in physical durability was that it was used to excuse the opium trade. Chinese were said to have a "predisposition for opium," and the sentiment was supported by anecdotal evidence. In describing the sedan chair bearer, nineteenth-century adventurers and missionaries would occasionally wonder aloud how remarkable it was that coolie laborers could smoke opium and go right back to their heavy lifting.

Western physicians of the era were of the opinion that Chinese were better at handling pain. Operations were then conducted without the benefit of anesthetics, and according to medical professionals, this did not seem to bother locals who went under the knife. Methodist missionary Mary Gamewell, in her 1919 book, *New Life Currents in China*, described a patient at a mission-funded hospital who, upon hearing that she was accepted for cataract surgery, assured her doctors that they should feel completely free to remove her eyes, just so long as they put them back after the surgery was completed.

At a trade show in the Bellagio Casino in Las Vegas, I found myself wandering toward a craps table in the late afternoon. It was a space for high rollers, but thinking it might be fun to join for a while, I took a spot along the rail and began placing minimum bets.

The table was populated by an assortment of characters who were laying down chips worth thousands of dollars. The table had begun to cool around the time the dealer pushed the dice in my direction. Picking them up, I noticed that a man at the far end of the table had jumped onto his cellphone. He spoke in English, but his accent gave him away as mainland Chinese.

He spoke loudly and quickly, and the apparent purpose of his call was to confirm a commission owed to him. He referenced a specific figure—$135,000—within earshot of everyone at the table. He offered no hint of what he actually did for a living, but he did want everyone to know that however bad this particular run of bad luck appeared, it would do him no real harm.

In that instant, I was reminded of something I had once seen in Guangzhou. In an upscale mall, a boy, perhaps ten or eleven years old, stood in front of a woman—possibly his mother, or maybe it was an aunt—who had grabbed hold of his ear and proceeded to give it a good twist. While she did this, the boy stared her dead in the eye and declared that he felt no pain.

"*Bu tong*," he said coolly.

The man at the craps table had done something similar. He was losing his ass and wanted everyone at the table to know that, however much it looked like he was in distress, he actually felt nothing.

Chinese factory owners are customarily tough to work with, precisely because of their willingness to play chicken with their customers. Whenever a foreign buyer suggested to his supplier that the factory man's egregious behavior was going to ruin the business opportunity that they shared—and even in cases where the factory had almost no other business to count on—the factory boss would appear unmoved and insist that he could take whatever pain might be coming his way.

CHAPTER 7

Emotional Negotiators

No one is sure when it began, but the phrase "I'm having a bad China day" has become synonymous with the expatriate experience. Long-term foreign residents insist that their moodiness is the result of impersonal factors, such as air pollution. In truth, what gets them down is more social in nature. "Chinese are extremely likable," wrote Edward Alsworth Ross, "and those who have known them longest like them best." It is an accurate statement, yet it belies a great frustration experienced by many foreigners who are vexed by cultural differences.

"The peculiarities of the Chinese character cause occasional difficulties," was the way British adventurer Thomas Thornville Cooper put it in 1871. Speaking somewhat less diplomatically, Reverend Arthur Smith noted simply that the Chinese have "a talent for exasperating you."

Seated in a café in Shanghai and catching the day's news, I read an article in the international press that described an Australian couple, Alesha Bradford and Jarryd Salem, who gave up their careers to travel the world. They spent seven years backpacking through numerous countries when they found their travels—and their relationship—reaching an impasse in the Middle Kingdom. They blamed it on their experience in China, which they said included too much pushing, shoving, and spitting. "China turned us into bad people," Salem said, "and we started taking it out on each other."

Canada's *Globe and Mail* sent a pair on a tour of China. As journalist Mark MacKinnon described it, he and his companion were targeted by dim-witted officials who questioned their intentions. When they were eventually accused of being spies, they admitted to having a "volcano moment."

Living in Guangzhou, I saw a few magma-inspired blowouts. Once, passing through the lobby of the Garden Hotel on my way to the bar, I caught sight of a puce-faced foreigner shouting at a local man. I presumed they were doing business together, but who knew? What struck me about the exchange was that, though the foreigner was going ballistic, the other fellow was completely impassive. The local was being subjected to verbal abuse, yet he appeared Zen-like and calm, pleased even, as if he were listening to the weather report from Bora Bora.

Several years ago, before online travel services became popular, airline tickets had to be purchased the old-fashioned way—through a travel agent. I was hosting a small delegation from Pittsburgh one spring and agreed to do them the favor of arranging their travel out of Guangzhou. Two days before they were scheduled to arrive, I rang the travel agency to confirm their travel arrangements and was told that there had been a mistake. Although the tickets had been paid for, the company had failed to book the seats and now there was no availability.

I jumped into a taxi and went to the travel agency myself. Finding the branch manager and hearing him claim no prior knowledge of the matter, I summarized how we arrived at the current situation and, in short order, read him the riot act. I described the various ways in which heads were going to roll if he did not figure out a way to get my people to their destination on the appointed day. Thinking that I might have overdone it—I had been speaking breathlessly for some time—I paused and gave the manager a chance to explain himself, and perhaps make some suggestions on how we might proceed.

Picking up his cue, he suddenly brightened and, instead of acknowledging anything I had just said, he simply offered, in the most patronizing tone possible, "*Wah, ni hui shuo zhongwen!* My word, you can speak Chinese!"

There are a million reasons to feel bummed out in China, not the least of which is the feeling that you are never quite heard. The sense that you are continually taken for a fool is another. A friend who buys furniture described how he lost it after hearing a potential supplier make what he thought were wild claims about the safety of its products.

"This rep tells me that her factory uses food-grade paint. So I ask her, 'What in the hell is food-grade paint?' She says, 'The paint is so safe you can *drink* it!' I told her if she brought me a cup of that paint and drank it in front of me, I would place a $500,000 order on the spot."

He was flustered in recounting the story.

"Did she drink it?" I asked.

"Are you joking? No one's drinking any damn *paint!*"

Those who become testy in this country are not limited to the cholerically predisposed. China has a way of also taking easygoing milquetoasts and turning them into hotheads. The phenomenon is so common that long-term expatriates have coined various terms: *The Laowai Wigout*, *The Expat Snap*, and *Angry Foreigner Syndrome* are three such expressions floating around the bigger metropolitan areas.

If you live outside of China and are a careful reader of the news, you can catch glimpses of the malady. One story that made headlines involved a New Zealander who taught at Guizhou University. Deciding that he was fed up with the way locals drove, he stood one day in the middle of a busy intersection in Guiyang and began directing traffic. No uniform, no whistle. He just stood there in the street, shouting and waving at drivers, banging on the occasional car hood to emphasize his point. In another well-publicized case, the former CEO of Daimler Trucks and Buses for China, Rainer Gärtner, lost his job after launching into a racist tirade over what he claimed was a stolen parking space.

China gets on the nerves of foreigners, and anger is not their only response. In Guangzhou, a shopkeeper who kept a pet dog tied to a post had neglected the animal to the point where its fur was so long and matted that it could not see. The situation bothered one nonnative so much that he decided to kidnap the poor thing. Heading out early one morning, he stole the mutt and brought it to a pet groomer for what was likely its first bath and trim. After the dog had been smartened up, the rascally *laowai* took the dog and deposited it right back where he had found it. Like others who heard the story, I only wished that I could have seen the look on the pet owner's face when he saw the animal transmogrified.

Rodney Gilbert worked as correspondent for the *North China Daily News*, the leading English-language newspaper in the Orient throughout the 1920s. Gilbert recounted a similar tale of altruism inspired by culture-specific frustration, this one borne by a disdain for the face tradition. Hearing that the noted journalist was planning to take a certain train, a government official rushed to have a special car added so that the newspaperman could write his articles in privacy. Gilbert bristled at the special attention and seeing that numerous Chinese were unable to catch a seat on the train, he invited as many as would fit into his private car. The move naturally infuriated the official, whose gesture was turned upside-down and caused him to lose face. In return for his altruism, Gilbert was rewarded with a ride that was less comfortable than a simple coach fare.

———————

After a meeting with a Guangdong manufacturer one summer afternoon, an American buyer made the mistake of mentioning to me—within sight of his supplier—that he had done much better than expected. The factory boss picked up on his customer's smile and ebullient mood and followed up the next morning by informing us that a mistake had been made and that an updated price sheet was being prepared.

Chinese factory owners hate to see their customers happy, because it means that money has been left on the table. In any given ongoing venture, each time the buyer has settled into a new reality, renewed attempts are made to ratchet up prices or to make other tweaks to the deal that are advantageous to the seller. The buyer's response is continually gauged with facial expressions, tone and body language all monitored for meaningful clues. At the mention of a price hike, a buyer might squirm, but that is rarely enough of a response to get the seller to back off. These industrialists are unmoved by such subtle signs of discomfort, just as they are unsympathetic to logical appeals. The only signal that properly registers with them is an expression of writhing pain, and many are accustomed to laying off only just short of the customer blowing a gasket.

"The Chinese is an expert in the psychological observation of others," commented historian Helmut Callis in 1959. "Nothing escapes him which is advantageous to know." Western business travelers often complain that their trips to China take longer than necessary, but rarely does it occur to them that their supplier has intentionally arranged it that way. Long car rides and even longer meetings, elaborate evening celebrations, and late-night chats in a hotel lobby over drinks—these activities are designed to tire the foreigner. Chinese factory bosses understand all too well that a worn-out buyer is more likely to say something or agree to a proposition that he should not.

A factory boss who can transport a buyer to his plant via high-speed train will opt instead to take him on a three-hour car ride (in both directions). And if the industrialist is not fluent, he will be sure to bring along an assistant who understands English. Boredom alone causes tongues to wag. If his buyer mentions fear of a particular competitor, this information will be tucked away for possible future use. I saw this happen once. The factory learned during a visit that its buyer had a feared competitor. It waited months and then dropped the name of that other company as part of an unconvincing promise: "Of course we would never dream of working with them." The frozen look on the buyer's face revealed his anxiety that the wheels of such a possibility were already in motion. And so it was no surprise to see a few hours later the buyer quickly agreeing to revised contract terms. Chinese are subtle and timely in their use of the leverage they hold over their clients.

Frustration is employed as a strategy to maximize utility not only against small- and medium-sized buyers. Larger foreign firms also complain that they find the Chinese hard to deal with. An American friend who works as a supply chain executive for one of the world's largest athletic shoe companies told me that her company goes through the same song and dance. At the beginning of each season, their suppliers will insist they cannot start production unless they get an upward price adjustment. The American company is then forced to choose between accepting the hike and missing delivery target dates. "The problem is that we have no recourse," she told me. Contracts are in place, but the factory can create any number of purportedly objective excuses, such as a supposed increase in raw material costs, to avoid keeping promises made.

Multinationals are more conservative and, as a result, are more discreet about the difficulties they face. Large conglomerates also have their backs against the wall though, and every once in a while we are treated to a glimpse of their own frustrations. General Electric's Jeffrey Immelt once uncharacteristically shared his feelings about the Chinese to a roomful of executives in Rome. "I am not sure that in the end they want any of us to win, or any of us to be successful," he said. Many smaller players on the ground today know the sort of experience to which he was alluding.

Western companies are scrambling to find alternatives to China and not just because of rising prices. What motivates them to seek partners elsewhere is the hope of a less problematic business experience. Importers are looking at different markets, including Vietnam, Thailand, Indonesia, Cambodia, Bangladesh, and India—even Eastern Europe seems viable. Buyers do not mind paying a little extra if it means better quality and less aggravation.

It must be clearly stated that the issue here is not with ethnicity but rather with the preponderance of unsavory industrialists who operate with impunity on the mainland. All else being equal, American importers prefer to work with Chinese industrialists from Hong Kong or Taiwan rather than with those from the mainland, because the experience with these groups tends to be more rewarding. The factory may be physically located in China; so long as the operators are from one of these other places within Greater China, the chances of success—and happiness—are often higher.

———

In an interview with CNN's Fareed Zakaria, Henry Kissinger once mentioned that "the Chinese have a very unemotional view of international relations." *Harvard Business Review* published an article entitled "Getting to Si, Ja, Oui, Hai and Da," in which the author, an academic, suggested along similar lines that Chinese are "unemotionally expressive." I don't know who these folks have been working with, but it is hard to describe the average businessperson in China as lacking emotionality.

Exiting baggage claim at some small airport in China, a foreign buyer is likely to find himself met by the most effusive factory owner imaginable. The industrialist laughs in an exaggerated manner, slaps his customer on the back, and then physically wrestles him to the ground for the privilege of carrying his bags. If during negotiations things are not going his way, the factory boss will portray himself as an especially piteous individual. "You are so wealthy," he says to the American, "and we are so poor!"—all of which is done in order to motivate the buyer into accepting a higher price.

Abbé Huc wrote in his memoirs that he found the Chinese to be "skilled in the art of shedding tears," an observation that others also made during that bygone era. Gilbert went into some detail on the subject of emotionalism and suggested that the cultural emphasis on face turned everyone in the country into natural-born actors. The important thing to acknowledge is not that the Chinese make use of emotionality—of course they do—but rather to understand that the emotions on display are largely fake. And the reason for the strategy in business is obvious: It increases the chances of success in any deal.

Ralph Townsend thought that this emotionality represented a strategic advantage for the Chinese. Having worked as a US State Department official, he noted that his counterparts in diplomacy employed such tactics "to induce sympathy, to mollify anger, to inspire generosity, or to flatter conceit." Confronted by this talent of the Chinese, he noted, "many a sturdy diplomat has given way against the accusations of his rational self in the manner that Samson melted in the arms of the cooing Delilah."

Westerners doing business in the country eventually realize they are being played in an emotional way, and while in principle they do not mind playing the same game, they find that their emotional toolkit is sorely lacking. Americans are uncomfortable shedding crocodile tears in an effort to catch a price break, just as they find it difficult to sweet-talk someone who is in the process of actively screwing them. The two most common response from foreigners—especially Americans—when facing emotional manipulation is to either put up a big brick wall, or turn to anger.

The foreigner has an advantage when it comes to expressing emotion, because his frustration is usually genuine and therefore it often produces a favorable result. "Please don't be angry," says the factory man upon seeing that he has finally upset his buyer. "I am sure we can work this out."

It doesn't take long for a foreign buyer to realize that displays of annoyance can indeed turn a deal in his favor and that higher levels of expressed dissatisfaction have the effect of motivating local partners even more. Chinese factory owners do not want their buyers to be happy, but at the same time they do not want them to be excessively upset either. Outward signs that the seller has gone too far are an automatic trigger to pull back—which can serve the buyer well.

Also figuring into the equation is the fact that there is almost no downside to a buyer blowing his lid. No matter what you do, you cannot offend these factory people. In the United States, upsetting the person you are doing business with can result in the cancellation of a deal. In China, so long as there is money to be made, all abuses are easily forgiven.

Naturally, this contradicts every book on Chinese business etiquette ever written, but it is nonetheless true: Chinese are never shocked by bad manners, especially not when they come from foreigners. Quite the opposite, they anticipate such behavior. The foreigner as barbarian is an archetype. Chinese consider their civilization to be the epitome of sophistication. Displays of rudeness from foreigners elicit feelings of pity more than anything, since they affirm the view that the Chinese are indeed a more cultured people.

An American friend from New York who works in the lighting industry and has an office in Dongguan relayed to me a story about a fellow importer from Los Angeles who went berserk at a lighting manufacturer. The factory owner had begun producing a lamp similar to the design that the buyer had commissioned him to make. Seeing the presumed knockoffs in the warehouse, he began to express his displeasure by picking up several units and throwing them across the warehouse floor. I didn't have to hear the rest of the story to know how it ended. The factory boss responded by placating his customer.

"*Hao le, hao le,*" he said. "All right, all right."

The industrialist did not complain about the damaged fixtures, which were likely worth thousands of dollars, nor did he banish the irate buyer from his plant. The factory man merely acquiesced by admitting that, given the buyer's extreme response, he may have been somewhat out of line in producing the copycat merchandise.

In many countries, this sort of violence might lead to a police intervention, or perhaps a court case. It was an act of vandalism, offensive in the extreme. In other markets, such behavior would irrevocably damage a business relationship; in China, it merely clarifies it.

Chinese factory bosses lack a moral compass. And without an internal mechanism to guide their behavior, they look to external stimuli. Expressions of displeasure, genuine or otherwise, tend to have an effect on them, in part because the Chinese are nonviolent, but also because ultimately they seek harmony in social relationships. Chinese are group-oriented, and as such, they are troubled by signs that their actions have taken them too far from the accepted mean of social behavior.

These industrialists try to get away with whatever they can and stop only when they receive some piece of external negative feedback as a sign that they have been pressing their luck. Perhaps the factory would stop selling the competitor's products for the time being or maybe it would do a better job of ensuring the goods did not find their way into the market of the original customer. In any event, an outburst of this sort serves as an important signal to the factory boss, that he has crossed the line.

———————

Chinese are fond of using emotionality in propaganda. Beijing has made provocative moves in the South China Sea, building manmade islands in places far from their shores and then claiming sovereignty over them. Rather than make claims based on maritime law, Chinese political leaders have focused on emotional appeals that suggest these contested territories are historic and therefore "engraved in the hearts" of the Chinese.

Whenever a foreign government announces that its head of state will soon be meeting with His Holiness the Dalai Lama, Beijing issues a statement suggesting that the encounter "hurts the feelings of the Chinese people." Journalist Fang Kecheng did research on the emotional tactic and uncovered more than one hundred instances in which Beijing has claimed that, for one reason or another, a foreign group or government has caused the Chinese such "hurt feelings." Japan scored the greatest number of mentions with Beijing claiming its people were affronted in such a way forty-seven times since 1980.

Following that analysis, Amy King at Princeton's Woodrow Wilson Center researched the use of "feelings" in the Chinese press and discovered that a China Foreign Ministry spokesperson offered up the line in a meeting with Japanese officials in September 1959.

My own reading suggests that the origin of this emotional ploy predates any use by the Chinese Communist Party. Foreign Minister of the Qing government Wu Ting-fang published a book in 1901, *The Causes of the Unpopularity of the Foreigner in China*, in which he went to great lengths to defend his government against bad press from abroad. Wu was likely the mastermind behind the rhetorical device as he implored foreign critics to make more "gentle arguments" and to "respect the feelings of the Chinese."

In China, pretending to have thin skin is a common gambit. It does not require great thought or energy, and it often has the effect of emasculating a counterparty, paving the way for manipulation. Westerners are easily convinced that they need to handle their local partners with kid gloves, a shortcoming that ultimately hampers their success in China.

In a joint venture I was involved with, the American investors requested financial documents that they had every right to review and were told in a near whisper by their Chinese partners that the request came at an inconvenient time. When after an interval they began to press harder for the information, the foreigners were told that their insistence on sharing financial information was going to damage the relationship. Chinese are fond of such *quicksand proposals*: If you do not move, you are promised nothing bad will happen to you. But if you act in any way at all, you are guaranteed to sink fast. Under such pressure, Westerners are often paralyzed.

Chinese factory owners are great about pitching bad news in a positive light. If the factory boss comes bouncing into the conference room, smiling and announcing that his people have found a way to improve the product they have been contracted to manufacture, you can be sure that the plant is attempting to introduce a regrettable change. Whatever kind of "improvement" the factory proposes is more than likely something that will make the product worse, and in exchange for allowing the factory a chance to reduce its cost, the buyer will pick up only an increase in product liability in return.

China's Communist Party has a similar talent for wrapping up troubling news in such a way as to make it more palatable. When China announced that it was removing crosses from Christian churches around the country—as many as 1,200 in just one campaign—it did not reveal the true motivation for the move, but instead suggested that it was taking down the T-shaped structures because they might fall and hurt someone.

China has redefined authoritarianism through *smile diplomacy*. As you pass through immigration at the Pudong International Airport, you are greeted these days by *Nihao*, a cartoon mascot shaped like the sun. Cuteness is a veneer plastered all over the place to soften public perceptions of a draconian government.

Air pollution in major cities around China has gotten so bad that pollution level predictions are now part of the daily weather forecast. The public is told to be wary when the ambient level of particulate matter smaller than 2.5 microns in diameter reaches above a certain threshold, and these days locals discuss PM2.5 readings as Americans in some regions might speak of the wind chill factor.

Around the time PM2.5 began showing up in headlines, toady marketers at Starbucks launched a China-specific campaign to let the public know there was nothing to fear, because PM actually stands for *Perfect Monday*, and customers could now enjoy a special discount on that first workday of the week.

Further looking on the bright side of pollution, Chinese news reporters occasionally suggest to their viewers that a pall of smog is not necessarily a bad thing as it provides protection against harmful ultraviolet radiation. The People's Liberation Army took a similarly optimistic approach by declaring in the press that mainland pollution serves as an excellent natural defense against enemy missiles.

Beijing wishes to be taken seriously as a global player, which is why it initiated an ambitious space program that was able to land a remote-controlled vehicle on the Moon. Just in case rival superpowers might feel threatened though, China anthropomorphized *Yutu* (Jade Rabbit) the Chinese moon rover, giving it a social media persona. When the rover's batteries failed, authorities covered up the embarrassment by ratcheting up the cloying cuteness of the stranded bunny. But then, as it became clear the rover was a goner, its online voice grew maudlin: "My masters are trying to save me, but I might not make it through this moon night!"

Shakespearean actor Patrick Stewart went on Comedy Central to make fun of the robot. Dressing up as the Jade Rabbit himself, he recited dialogue that the Xinhua News Agency insisted had been sent by the rover, giving the display of state-sanctioned cuddliness the response it deserved: mocking parody.

I once had the displeasure of informing the owner of a toy factory in Guangdong that his merchandise had failed inspection. He protested, insisting that there was nothing wrong and that I must have made a mistake. He implored me to look again: *"Zai kan yixia ba!"*

As we were standing in the warehouse near the completed production run, I casually picked up a sample, only to have it fall apart in my hands, the pieces of plastic making a terrible racket as they dropped to the concrete floor.

"You did that on purpose!" he cried.

Though it had not been my intention to cause embarrassment, it did no good to launch into a denial. To confirm that I had only accidentally broken the toy would be to accept at least partial responsibility for the problem, in which case the factory man's next move would have been to suggest that my "sincerity" be proven by some gesture such as, say, accepting his shoddy goods for export.

Chinese factory bosses are better at guilt tripping than Jewish grandmothers. They are especially skilled at eliciting unnecessary apologies, and they enjoy capturing the moral high ground, even though (or especially when) it was not theirs in the first place.

I learned from experience to keep my mouth shut whenever someone in China accused me of damaging their personal interests in some form or other. And it is worth noting that whereas the Japanese—who some claim understand the Chinese better than we Americans do—have apologized to Korea for bad behavior in wartime, they have consistently refrained from making a similar overture to China.

American buyers who are put in a corner by a Chinese supplier will often unwittingly take the guilt bait and issue an apology.

What downside could there possibly be to apologizing, the artless foreigner figures, especially if it's done in private? The problem is that the apology will be turned down as a matter of course, with the Chinese party insisting that it had not been genuine. The buyer in such a case, rather than telling his supplier to forget it, typically decides to double down. He does not know what is meant by a sincere apology, but he takes a deep breath, slows his speech, and strings together a few words that sound a bit more heartfelt.

"Not enough!" the factory owner cries.

During the Mao years, self-criticisms were used to great effect as a means of manipulating others through intimidation. The *ziwo piping*, as it was called, typically began as a simple admission of personal flaws or incorrect thoughts. The cadre would take this initial statement and use it to press for a deeper revelation. Locked in a room and figuring that acquiescence remained the easiest way out, the poor fellow would end up signing a confession that was essentially his death warrant, after which he was shot in the head.

CHAPTER 8

Oliver Wendell Holmes

American children all know that if you dig a hole deep enough, you will eventually wind up in China. The funny thing about this myth is not that it is geologically inaccurate—New York's polar opposite is closer to Perth than Peking—but that the story is repeated by youths around the globe. In China, I once met a woman from South Africa who told me she had heard the tale as a child and believed it.

China occupies an antipodal place in the Western psyche, often represented as a bizarro world where everything is topsy-turvy. Taking the otherness of places as an inspiration, we came to see China as Ultima Thule, the extreme limit of travel, or "The World's Most Exotic Place."

Abbé Huc emphasized the otherness of China by claiming, "All that you see there is opposite of what you see anywhere else." In his 1900 book *The People of China*, J. W. Robertson-Scott described the country as "more foreign to us than any other nation." In this mysterious place, he wrote, "Everything is upside down. Their first name is last. The men were in gowns, and the women often in trousers." The sardonic Reverend E. J. Hardy noted that the best real estate in China went to the dead and that the Chinese, who preferred hard pillows, liked to sleep on wood and stone. George Wingrove Cooke offered his own catalog of invertedness: "In a country where the roses have no fragrance, and the women no petticoats; where the laborer has no Sabbath, and the magistrate no sense of honor; where the roads bear no vehicles, and the ships no keels; where old men fly kites; where the needle points to the south, and the sign of being puzzled is to scratch the antipodes of the head; where the place of honor is on the left hand, and the seat of intellect is in the stomach; where to take off your hat is an insolent gesture, and to wear white garments is to put yourself in mourning—we ought not to be astonished to find a literature without an alphabet and a language without a grammar."

China as an inside-out empire was only one portrayal, however. Westerners were also in the habit of viewing China through another lens, one that depicted the Middle Kingdom as some sort of parallel universe. "China is just like the United States" may sound like a ridiculous statement to many long-term foreign residents, yet the notion is widely promoted, especially among sentimentalists. No matter what problem we discuss related to China, foreign apologists jump in to remind that, "We have those problems too."

China is either portrayed as exotic in the extreme, or else a mirror of our own society—and such a narrative is at times promoted even when it contradicts casual observation. The People's Liberation Army will march tens of thousands of soldiers in goose step, and the response of our liberals is to dare insist that the nation is not a monolith. China is a diverse place—it must be—these folks insist. How diverse? Well, to the precise extent that we are, naturally.

Of course, Beijing wishes for us to believe that China is just like any other advanced economy. That way, they measure up. Erecting carbon copies of iconic landmarks of the world proves you are a modern nation. China now has several versions of France's Eiffel Tower, as well as a London Bridge, and real estate developers have even replicated entire European villages.

Stranger than the fake landmarks is that few Western writers mock China for these corny imitations and comparisons. Quite the opposite, we encourage such behaviors by reporting seriously on companies as "China's Twitter" (Weibo), "China's Google" (Baidu), and "China's YouTube" (YouKu). With a straight face, we speak of "China's Warren Buffett" and "China's Carl Icahn." The implication of these mirrored reflections is that the Chinese have finally caught up to the West, which isn't helpful because it isn't true. Trumpeting such strained metaphors may give China face, but it obscures the image we have of the companies and business leaders that are being compared. And it hinders our ability to better understand their unique qualities.

If this business of mirror imagery seems old hat, that's because it is. In the 1930s, Carl Crow referred to Sun Yat-sen as "China's George Washington." In the 1920s, Arthur Ransome described "Hangkow's Trafalgar Square." In what may be among the earliest such mention, in 1856, Thomas Taylor Meadows in his *The Chinese and Their Rebellions* referred to the historian Sima Qian as "the Herodotus of China."

Most can see no harm in mirror portrayals and are inclined to let the habit pass. What possible harm could come from such a silly indulgence?

In the nineteenth century, after hearing so much Bible talk from missionaries, an enterprising Chinese, Hong Xiuquan, figured that China ought to have its own messiah, ultimately determining that he was indeed "China's Jesus" or, in the words of Jonathan Spence, *God's Chinese Son*. Hong created a movement founded on this notion of a mirror-image savior. The end result was the Taiping Rebellion, a decade-long civil war, which led to the deaths of an estimated twenty to thirty million.

Christian missionaries were not exactly perfect guests and they were occasionally known for expressing insensitive opinions. English missionary Walter Henry Medhurst suggested in 1838, for example, that the Chinese deceived their gods in religious offerings. They did not burn actual money but fake bank notes. Sweetmeats ceremoniously laid out were allowed to be eaten after a brief interval and so could hardly be considered genuinely sacrificial.

Westerners who wish to highlight mainland hypocrisy these days look less at religion and turn a cynical eye to politics instead. Beijing has issued warnings to Party members that they should "not indulge in empty talk," but then you see televised parliamentary sessions in which officials take turns droning on for hours in indecipherable speeches. China's Communist Party announces that it is prohibiting official "pomp and circumstance" and then puts on a massive military parade for the seventieth anniversary of its founding. In Shenzhen, I walked past a notice decrying "empty slogans," leading me to wonder why this exhortation did not also apply to posters plastered onto brick walls.

The Chinese Dream is a concept that has been promoted by the government as a rallying cry. I'm not sure how Thomas Friedman of *The New York Times* came to take credit (only partial credit, he says) for the broad, vacuous concept in 2013, but I remember reading in a *China Daily* article published in 2006 that Chinese scholars were assembling for a colloquium entitled "The Chinese Dream and a Harmonious World."

For some time since, academics and pundits have been trying to work out a definition of this supposed dream. The government has been no help as it has issued conflicting interpretations, including the idea that it should be about political rejuvenation. In Beijing more recently, another symposium was held, this one called the "International Dialogue on the Chinese Dream," with numerous foreign speakers brought in to assist with the navel-gazing. China watchers embarrass themselves when they mimic the Politburo, which thinks it the height of sophistication to spout nonsense on make-believe subjects from a rostrum.

One of the advantages of a China-watching career is that you never run out of things to say. No one in the world knows what "socialism with Chinese characteristics" actually means, which gives young academics something on which to cut their teeth. Expounding on this single topic at great length in a speech or in a long essay is but a foretaste of the ultimate pointlessness of such careers that involve cir-cumlocution. China's Communist Party recently awarded its president the additional honorary title of *core leader*, which led many to scratch their heads. You would think that academics and pundits whose careers are dependent on their ability to elucidate would be annoyed by such an inexplicable development. But no, quite the opposite, they take to it like a dog to a juicy bone—something to gnaw on for a good long while.

From time to time, I get suckered into a conversation with someone who asks me to explain the difference between communism and socialism. *Which one is China? How are they both?* Americans who ask such questions tend to be hung up on the Cold War, which emphasized competing ideologies. It was not that long ago that our newspapers referred to the People's Republic of China as *Red China* and the Republic of China as *Free China*—a reflection of our salt-and-pepper, good-guy-versus-bad-guy worldview. In China, nothing is black and white, however, and while ideological ideas are bandied about, ideology does not play nearly as significant a role as outsiders suspect. In the 1930s, Mao Zedong spoke frequently about democratic ideals and even published a book entitled, *On New Democracy*. Sun Yat-sen himself, who as the father of modern China is revered by the communists, spoke in the 1920s of a China that would be "of the people, by the people, for the people."

William Martin wrote, "The Chinese do not believe in the incompatibility of opposites," in 1934, some time before George Orwell coined the term *doublethink*. "They are perfectly capable of accepting at one and the same time two contradictory ideas—a thing, by the way, that makes Westerners imagine them to be disingenuous. It is not disingenuousness; it is intellectual eclecticism."

In cases where the Chinese appear to be grasping at frameworks—and especially when contradictory elements are involved—I am led to wonder whether it is because they have a fundamental aversion to mutual exclusivity. Mainland Chinese airlines that provide a selection of movies will sometimes place the same film under three different categories—comedy, drama, and new releases, for example—because it lends the appearance of greater choice. Chinese do not like limitations, which is why when you ask one of them whether he will be dropping by your office in the morning or in the afternoon, he will respond by saying "yes."

Twenty years ago, I wandered into a tiny shop in Beijing's Haidian District and set a small shoulder bag on a glass shelf. Although the bag was not heavy, the shelf broke cleanly into two pieces. Before I had the chance to apologize or even look up, the shopkeeper flew into a false rage. He cackled and cried out, acting as if I had burned the place down. At once he demanded a king's ransom, asking for more than ten times what the shelf must have been worth.

You learn fast to defend yourself against folks like this who go gunning for your wallet. Making a generous offer, which was promptly turned down, I set a higher amount on the counter and walked out.

The vendor followed me into the street.

"Someone call the police! I've been cheated!"

He was so loud and insistent that he was universally ignored.

"Holy fuck," I muttered to myself.

At this, the shopkeeper became even more animated.

"*Fah-kuh! Fah-kuh!*" he shouted. "Have you not heard the foreigner curse? It is forbidden, and he has cursed a Chinese no less!"

At this point, a *chengguan* officer approached us to have a look. The shopkeeper said nothing now about his precious glass shelf but focused instead on language. It was an ingenious strategy because the matter of cursing someone (*ma ren*) would be seen as a more serious crime than the accidental breaking of a shelf, and the vendor was going to use this to pressure me into settling for more.

The guard looked at me. "Is this true?" he asked.

I thought of defending myself by offering a quick language lesson—such a word used in exasperation is not necessarily a curse—but then I had another thought: *What do these people care about some word in a foreign tongue?* I could understand the outrage that might have followed a few choice words uttered in Mandarin, but this was nothing local. What if instead of English I had muttered something similar in Dutch or Swahili?

In the end, I forked over more than I should have and quickly excused myself from the situation. But I do occasionally reflect back on that day, especially whenever I catch myself issuing an automatic "Thank you" after saying *"Xie xie"* to someone who clearly does not speak English.

––––––––––––

In the nineteenth century, Christian missionaries were on the lookout for any phrases in the Chinese language that might help open doors and make conversion more likely. In an effort to convey that they came in peace, foreign clergy quoted Confucius: "In the four seas, all men are brothers."

Missionaries also borrowed heavily from local wardrobes, thinking that dressing like locals sent the right message. They ditched their tall boots and stiff hats and went in for flowing silk robes and soft caps instead. The more dedicated foreigners lengthened their fingernails and grew out their hair, which they fashioned into a queue.

Though well meaning, missionaries eventually realized that it didn't pay to ape the Chinese. Although their localized appearance allowed them to walk down the street without being gawked at, these outsiders missed the curiosity factor. Chinese, as it turned out, wished to see the foreigner in the style of dress to which he was accustomed.

By the early twentieth century, Westerners who dressed in the native style did so only ironically, because Chinese were racing to drop their traditional outfits in favor of what was popular in the West. In his personal archives, Rodney Gilbert is found in one photo, dated 1918, wearing silk and sporting cloth shoes. Brandishing a water pipe, a common accoutrement of the age, he gives the camera a wry grin. Meanwhile, standing next to him, a Chinese friend is seen decked out in a three-button suit, bow tie and lace-ups, symbols of the new imported fashion.

Gilbert points out that while Chinese occasionally violated Western fashion standards by, for example, mismatching certain wardrobe components or by improperly buttoning a jacket, the effort was nonetheless well received by the average foreigner, who was flattered by the "emulation of his ways."

Westerners are like this today. The businessman from New York who hears his Guangdong business associates struggling to string together a few words in English is likely to believe that his partners get it. Americans are sometimes shocked to learn that the Chinese speak not only English, but are also busy learning all of the world's major languages.

The China Global Television Network broadcasts the nightly news now in multiple tongues, including Spanish, Arabic, and Russian. One suspects that native speakers of these languages are flattered by a perceived acknowledgment of their cultural heritage. In actuality, these efforts are propaganda-driven. In order to get a message across, you naturally want the listener to understand what you are saying, and it helps to drop the right cultural references to each target audience.

In the *China Daily*, I once caught an editorial that made a strong political argument, borrowing a few words from Oliver Wendell Holmes for rhetorical support. It threw me off to see a quote by the late Supreme Court Justice in a state-run newspaper. Who was this man to the Chinese? I wondered. But then the brilliance of the device struck me: Of course you want to appropriate ideas from the reader's own culture to make your point. Under this method, it is difficult to make a counterargument.

Old-time vacuum salesmen would take this approach when pitching a homemaker: "But Mrs. Jones, you just told me that you are looking to save time, and you admitted yourself that this is the best cleaner on the market, and you have also said that saving money is important to you."

Chinese factories did this to their customers, as well. Making some unauthorized change to a product without informing us, they would eventually be caught and subsequently defend their behavior using a similar line:

"But you said yourself that you liked that color..."

"But you yourself said that you needed a lower price..."

"But you insisted that you needed faster delivery..."

Whatever tweaks the factory wished to introduce for its own benefit were always pitched as having been directly motivated by something the buyer once said.

Factory managers are careful listeners, because it aids their mirroring strategy. In Xiamen, I once attended a meeting between an American importer and his Chinese supplier, and along the way, the buyer made an offhand comment about how while in principle his company would always seek the lowest price, he would not leave a proven supplier for savings of only five percent.

Fast-forward nine months later: We were in a follow-up meeting and pricing had become a sticking point. As a part of his pitch, the factory boss spit back the encapsulated philosophy almost verbatim: "You can always save some small amount at another supplier, but you won't want to leave us to save only five percent."

"That's true," said the buyer, nodding in agreement, unaware that he had been spoon-fed his very own line.

Around the same time, I was working with an American group that had run into trouble when its supplier delivered a shipment of products that were unsalable. The seller acknowledged that he was at fault, but naturally, he did not want to cover the loss. "Let's split the difference," he offered.

It was the second time that year that I had heard a factory invoke this exact phrase, which had apparently become a new rhetorical tool for clever industrialists. Chinese do not normally apportion expenses this way but were happy to adopt the quintessentially American model in order to divert costs. It sounds so reasonable, so natural, and so politically correct: "Let's split the difference." Any factory boss who employs it against an American buyer is showing only how much he understands his buyer's culture.

In the belief in the superiority of their ideas, Americans have a habit of forcing homegrown notions onto others. "Here's what I think—surely you agree?" A more powerful approach is to stitch together an argument based on the belief system of those whom you are trying to persuade.

Diplomats typically ingratiate themselves while abroad in the interest of smoothing ties, but none lay it on thicker than those traveling from the People's Republic of China. On a visit to London, Beijing's top man will reference in a single speech such key British icons as William Shakespeare, Jane Austen, Charles Dickens, Charles Darwin, and Adam Smith, plus a few fictional references are thrown in for good measure, including Sherlock Holmes, James Bond, and Harry Potter.

Beijing seeks to tailor its message to whichever audience it is addressing, so when it speaks of its ties to the United Kingdom, it will suggest that the two countries work out a way to remain "best friends." When traveling to Africa, officials will drop the chum talk and opt instead to speak of their "brothers" on the continent. For the United States, familiar jargon includes "win-win cooperation" and the hope that relations will be guided by "positive energy."

The mirroring habit is not merely verbal. Look closely at the news, and you will find even physical examples. Chinese diplomats will observe a counterpart's hand gesture or posture and mimic it with near perfection. At times, this mirroring business can appear so staged as to be humorous. In worldwide press photos, you will sometimes see two admirals, one from the Chinese Navy and one from the US Navy, dressed identically in white uniforms, the only difference between them being that the Chinese officer has taken care to display a slightly larger ribbon rack.

The language that Chinese military officers use is a direct mirror of our own. Beijing will accuse the United States of "engaging in provocations" in the South China Sea, which "threaten regional stability." It claims that we are the ones "escalating tensions," then breathes a sigh of relief when we do not scoff at the suggestion, as we rightly should, but instead go on the defensive to explain ourselves. Chinese leaders must be tickled to learn that we are so easily manipulated by our very own buzzwords.

Much of the diplomatic talk that we think of as being quintessentially communist is in fact of foreign origin. An example of this is Beijing's frequent cry that foreign powers should not "interfere in the internal affairs" of China. Put in such a way, it sounds as if we are encroaching on a traditional concept and that in addressing certain political issues we are somehow offending the Chinese in an ancient manner.

In the 1860s, J. Ross Browne, American minister to China, wondered aloud whether it was good policy to "not interfere in the internal affairs of the Empire, when our very presence is an interference." In the 1850s, Meadows wrote that he had offered assurances to Qing officials—as if they had never heard the concept—that "it was an established rule of the British Government not to interfere with the internal struggles of foreign states."

In his *Mind of Empire*, Christopher Ford highlights an episode from 1864. Having learned of a foreign book entitled *Laws and Precedents of All Nations*, a Chinese prince suggested to the emperor that it would be wonderful to get hold of a copy. Thinking that the book might hold "foreign secrets," the prince assumed that the foreigners would want to keep the book out of Chinese hands and in the end was surprised to discover that the outsiders were willing to make the volume freely available. In other words, while Westerners held that the law is something universal, the Chinese saw it as nothing more than a set of cultural precepts that could be used for the manipulation of the foreigner.

In his 1930s book *Tortured China*, Hallett Abend wrote that he believed Chinese were successful rhetoricians because the culture prepared them for it. "Because considerations of 'face' have for hundreds of years played an important part in Chinese life," he said, "it is only natural that the Chinese should prove adept at political propaganda, both at home and abroad."

Chinese are successful rhetoricians also, ultimately, because of their proclivity for avoiding confrontation. If your opinion differs dramatically from others and you insist on pushing it, you should not be surprised to find others are resistant. The smart move really is to have no opinion whatsoever. Instead, hear out the other fellow, appear to agree with his views, and then use everything he has said as an argument for why he should move in the direction that you desire.

China's efforts at linguistic pilfering are laughable when scrutinized against their own cultural values. From time to time, Beijing will accuse Washington of "displaying a double standard," which is ironic given that there is no such concept in the Chinese culture. "What's good for the goose is good for the gander" is not something we hear in China, a hierarchical place that allows different standards to be applied to separate groups.

In business and in politics, Chinese like to invoke the principle of mutual respect. The notion is most commonly promoted by a disadvantaged party in the hopes of equalizing the relationship. Of course, once the tables are turned and that party is on top, the phrase is then cited to convince the oppressed party that it is being treated on equitable terms.

Chinese do not commonly believe in universal values, and the smarter ones come to the table believing in nothing at all. As Bruce Lee would say: "Empty your mind, be formless, shapeless, like water." Ideologies are inconvenient because they limit options. The strategically advantageous position is that which is most adaptable.

American policy analysts must be at least a touch worried to hear Beijing proclaim that it will "never seek hegemony," if only because this is language borrowed directly from international relations theorists in the West. Beijing's claim that expansionism is "not in the DNA" of the Chinese people is equally troubling for the same reason. Such terminology is not native to the Chinese, but rather is another case of linguistic lifting. "Hegemony" is considered a bad thing, so of course the Chinese would never connect themselves to the term in any way. The same goes for "expansionism," though we obviously see the Chinese implementing precisely this policy. Beijing has been aggressive not only in the South China Sea, but also in such faraway places as Latin America and Africa.

Beijing is so fond of purportedly ideological expressions that we presume it must have a concept to match every political aspiration. For the Chinese, language is more about obfuscation than elucidation though, and true intentions are often difficult to discern. As unsatisfying or frightening as it may sound, Beijing has no actual terminology for much of what it hopes for or plans.

CHAPTER 9

Chemicals, Guns, and Gimcracks

Beijing has poured untold billions into infrastructure in recent years, with much public criticism focused on the nation's sleek high-speed rail network. The network, it has been said, was built so far in advance of any actual need that many cars run empty, ticket prices are prohibitively high for the average Chinese, and in many instances the stations are located in the middle of nowhere.

From one perspective, the investment has been smart. China's labor rate is rising fast and the project is labor-intensive. Every yuan spent now could conceivably return a significant dividend on that basis alone. More importantly, Beijing has the political clout for such a project today. Train lines have required the seizure of land, and in some cases populations have had to be relocated—actions that may not be feasible in the future.

No, the problem with the high-speed rail network is not that it has been built, nor that it has been set up too fast. The issue is that the technology has come to serve as a symbol for the new economy. China's cheerleaders point to the high-speed rail network and claim that it represents a high-water mark of technological achievement. China is no longer an unsophisticated place, they say; the swift trains represent a mindset that has been updated, a reflection of national transcendence.

In the nineteenth century, China similarly busied itself with infrastructure development in an effort to prove that it was no longer a sleepy, backward empire. Writing critically of such motives in 1856, Thomas Taylor Meadows reminded us that "good roads, railways, carriages, hotels, canals, passenger vessels, and postal establishments, together with large expensive private dwellings . . . are not themselves civilization."

In the Republican era, China showed a similar interest in the symbols of progress but not in the Western culture that had made such advances possible. Japan had jumped right into westernization around this time, but China somehow convinced itself that it was too civilized to require fundamental change, and so it sought only to add a few bells and whistles to its economy. This, of course, was a misguided policy. "The secret of Western strength does not lie in machines, chemicals, guns and gimcracks," wrote Rodney Gilbert, but in its culture, which the Chinese had deemed inferior.

"Science and technology are not things, like automobiles and power plants, but are the knowledge and computational power that allow us to create such things," as the modern political scientist Herbert A. Simon put it. Throughout a wide range of industries in China today, the end result is emphasized almost to the exclusion of the processes by which it is achieved.

Chinese factory bosses will often express an interest in copying some newfangled product from the United States, but they never take a moment to reflect on how the original was created. In all the time I have spent working with Chinese industrialists, I have never once been asked, seriously or jokingly, "What is it that causes you Americans to have so many ideas?" Given what is at stake, the lack of curiosity is remarkable.

It is somewhat ironic that China should be thought of today as a leader in high-speed rail not only because the primary technology was stolen from Japan, but because China's first foray into rail transport resulted in a classic example of state-orchestrated Luddism.

In 1876, British investors received permission to build a narrow-gauge track running between Shanghai and the nearby port of Woosung, a distance of only nine miles. When more senior officials learned of the project, they sought to shut it down. They used the excuse that the locomotive disturbed the area's *fengshui*, and to prove their point, officials arranged to have a man throw himself under the wheels of the train, presumably in exchange for a sum paid to the victim's family. Popular riots broke out, which led officials at the national level to force the removal of the train line. The Qing government bought up the rails cheaply from the British and sold them to a company in Formosa.

For nearly thirty-five years, my Uncle Jack ran a junkyard in Flint, Michigan. When technology came to the industry and other yards began making use of industry-specific software, my uncle was convinced that he could not be helped by it, but he bought the computers and software anyway, because he wished to appear up-to-date.

The equipment was installed but it was never put into use. His business thrived, but only because he kept a full inventory and because he charged less than his competitors. He was a good salesman, and he also dealt only in cash.

Many of Jack's customers who saw the new computers concluded that his business thrived because of the new technology. In fact, he operated a technically unsophisticated cash cow, and on the success of that business model he was able to purchase technology that could serve as a showcase.

China has done something similar with its high-speed rail network. The railways are financed by the government, which in turn has been propped up by export manufacturing. Chinese factories made money the old-fashioned way: They produced in large volume using slave labor and stolen designs. China's high-speed rail network is not so much a reflection of modernization as it is the fruit of an outmoded yet still successful way of doing business.

The American Chamber of Commerce in China asks its membership annually what, if anything, might be done to improve the business environment. For years, member companies have claimed that their biggest challenge has been finding educated workers. This is odd since China produces millions of university graduates each year, and local papers are filled with stories of candidates who cannot find employment. China's problem is not a lack of educated or trained workers, but rather a difficulty in identifying candidates who can think critically.

"Chinese were said to have their own 'system of reasoning,'" wrote Alexis Krausse in 1900, "and it was observed that sending Chinese to Europe for tertiary education yielded no special results, and that they tend to 'retrograde' to the 'Celestial philosophy.'" Such a line sounds undeservedly harsh until one considers the hundreds of thousands of "sea turtles"—recent graduates from overseas—who return home only to wonder what impact, if any, they will have on the nation.

Returnees are tragic figures in China. Employers are not keen to pay them much more than the standard local salary, and there is even less interest in capitalizing on whatever knowledge foreign-educated individuals may have acquired abroad.

Feeling they are of no use to their own country, returning grads perform a brain flush. They forget whatever knowledge they gained overseas and instead look to plug themselves into whichever old-boy *guanxi* network might have them.

———————

Part of the issue is an inferior approach to problem-solving. In China, the focus is typically on symptoms and manifestations, and only later, if at all, on root causes. This principle is embodied in the critical path of every factory project: You first figure out the housing, and only then do you focus on the internal mechanism, the part that provides actual intrinsic value.

Beijing central planners understand that an economy can be considered "advanced" once a certain percentage of its population resides in an urban environment, and so it has chosen to forcibly move people from the countryside into the cities. While this plan will likely work in the end, in the meantime we can appreciate that the effort is mostly about adjusting outward appearances. Rather than allowing migration to happen organically, central planners are forcing the situation with the expectation that they will manage a way to the new reality.

Beijing similarly understands that advanced economies have fewer workers in agriculture and manufacturing, and that a larger proportion will be employed in the service sector. Wishing to appear up-to-date, Beijing now claims to have rebalanced the economy in favor of services. But no matter how the government goes about convincing us that this shift has already taken place, it is particularly hard to think of China as a services-oriented economy when expertise is still so little valued.

An American acquaintance based in Shanghai who sells technical know-how to Chinese companies in the renewable energy sector told me over a beer, "You have to sell them a box." Information alone is not enough, so his company makes sure to pair its value-added service contract with equipment. Shaun Rein, principal of a boutique marketing firm in Shanghai, echoed this sentiment: "It's hard to sell a service to a Chinese company without including something tangible. They either want something physical to change hands, or they want a guaranteed result."

Service providers, including architects and industrial designers, complain that prospective clients try to steal information through the pitch process. Told that they nearly have the job, a bidding team will be asked to produce details on what it hopes to accomplish. After finagling a few key ideas, the client will announce that it is no longer interested in moving forward; it will instead take the information gleaned through bidding and half-ass the project on its own. The more unscrupulous clients will invite several such service providers to make a pitch and use the appearance of competition as an additional pressure to induce higher levels of disclosure.

A German firm that develops solutions for the transportation industry recently signed a deal with a Chinese train company that wishes to build a public transportation system from the bottom up. Though the deal is serious and though a great sum of money changed hands at the outset of the project, the Germans, who have seen the move before, predict that the Chinese will pull out of the deal after maybe sixty or seventy percent of the payments have been made. Chinese companies that purchase technology outright in this fashion are in the habit of agreeing to a service provider's higher fee and then bailing out of the contract once they think they have nailed down the key technologies. Chinese firms who pursue such a strategy are generally comfortable with the fact that the final product might fall short.

Shanghai's magnetic levitation line, which runs between the city and the airport in Pudong, reaches a maximum speed of 267 miles per hour. Although the train's key technology may be something of an engineering marvel, the interior is a disaster. Paying a bit extra so that I could sit just behind the driver, I was surprised to see that not only was he separated from me by no more than a simple piece of glass, but he appeared to lack central air conditioning as well. An old fan was placed on the floor with an electric cord that stretched out to a power strip. The driver had a comfortable seat, but next to him was positioned a rusted two-dollar chair. The carpeting was made up of cheap tiles and was missing a large square. When I showed the photo to the owner of the German train company, he admitted that he was not surprised because he had seen such examples of perfunctory design on other transportation projects around China.

In China, one tends to have the same conversation over and again.

"You are a foreigner," the taxi driver says.

"Yes, I am," I say.

"You speak Chinese," he says.

"We are speaking it now," I say.

"That's good," he says.

Drivers from the provinces are notoriously thick, and one that I met, a recent transplant from Henan, appeared to have been waiting for the encounter his entire life. "China has the four great inventions," he informed me as we pulled away from the curb near my home in Guangzhou. Staring into the middle distance, he recited them: "Gunpowder, the compass, the printing press, and paper."

"That's three things," I said. "The paper and the printing kind of go together." He glanced sideways at me and repeated, as if in school: "Four great inventions. *Si ge da faming.*"

The hectoring didn't bother me; I knew all about these grand achievements. China had discovered gunpowder—an admixture of charcoal, sulfur, and saltpeter—but while the discovery was harnessed by the Chinese for pyrotechnics primarily, the West took these same ingredients and developed formidable firepower. China had also invented the compass—a magnetized needle that always pointed in the same direction—but whereas the Chinese most commonly applied it to superstitious geomancy, Westerners adopted the technology for long-distance travel.

Chinese did not use compass technology at sea, noted John Barrow in 1804. They "keep no reckoning at sea, nor possess the least idea of drawing imaginary lines upon the surface of the globe, by the help of which the position of any particular spot may be assigned; in other words, they have no means whatsoever of ascertaining the latitude or longitude of any place, either by estimation from the distance sailed, or by observation of the heavenly bodies, with instruments for that purpose."

The greater irony of the four great inventions is that they come to us not from the Chinese but from Francis Bacon, who compiled the list for his book *The New Instruments*. Another foreigner, Joseph Needham, did even more to raise awareness of Chinese technology by cataloging the empire's many inventions in a serialized work he published in the 1950s. His compendium, *Science and Civilisation in China,* runs to seven multibook volumes and fills the better part of a bookshelf.

China may be home to a number of antique inventions, but its populace does not hold inventors in the same high esteem that they are held in the West. "No Chinese boy was taught hero worship for Marconi, Edison, or the Wright Brothers," noted Vaughan White in the 1940s.

In China, technologies were quickly adopted, but few, if anyone, knew of their origin. Key inventions have either come unattributed from antiquity itself, or else they have been ascribed to an ancient emperor. The popular game of Go, or *weiqi*, is said to have been invented by the legendary Emperor Yao some 4,300 years ago, and the Chinese calendar was credited to the illustrious Yellow Emperor who reigned 4,600 years ago. The Yellow Emperor's wife, Leizu, was presumed to have discovered silk, while inventing the loom that made its production possible. Music—as in music itself—was said to have been the invention of Emperor Fu Hsi, who similarly reigned five millennia ago.

The more important its link to Chinese tradition, it seems, the more likely an invention was to be attributed to the Son of Heaven. In hindsight, foot binding may be seen as a backward custom, but for centuries it was the height of propriety, so naturally the origin of its practice is traced to the tenth-century emperor Li Yu.

The most unlikely emperor-related discovery involves tea. One popular myth suggests that the leaf was discovered when the ancient ruler Shennong fell backward into a tea shrub. Another version of the same story has Shennong accidentally dropping a few tea leaves into water that had just been boiled. My personal vote is for a hybrid of the tales in which the mythical leader stumbles, Mr. Bean–like, through a slapstick sequence to create the ultimate happiness.

———

The Chinese language used to have hundreds of dialects and, along with it, a matching variety of cultural traditions. "Customs change every ten *li*," was a common expression in ancient China. The *li* is a measure of distance that approximates to one-third of a mile, though the measurement differed over time and by region. In 1905, Reverend E. J. Hardy lamented another quirk. Distances were never fixed but would "vary according as the ways to them are rough or smooth, hilly or level." On flat ground, he noted, "One mile is called two *li*, on a hilly road five *li*; when the way is very steep it may be as much as fifteen *li*." In 1916, James Bashford clarified further by pointing out that uphill distance was never the same as downhill.

"Everything is possible in that country except obvious consistency," wrote Arthur Ransome in his 1920s book, *The Chinese Puzzle*, and though the average foreigner was frustrated by the hodgepodge of standards, the Chinese hardly seemed to mind. In fact, they preferred the confusion, because it afforded opportunities to take advantage. The coolie who offered to deliver goods an estimated distance of 200 *li* might collect a fee on that basis and subsequently farm out the work to someone else, insisting the distance was only 160 *li*.

Early foreign travelers complained of different weight standards, and many remarked on the absurdity of currency exchanges. Arthur Smith pointed out that whereas a "string of cash" was supposed to be made up of one hundred coins, in some places it was acceptable to include only ninety-nine or ninety-eight, "or it could be as low as 83."

———

We tend to think of manufacturing as an objective process, but there can also be a great deal of informalism involved. Chinese workers prove this to us with their almost neurotic compulsion to play around with intended specifications. There is a subconscious abhorrence for consistency in the Middle Kingdom, so we find workers automatically injecting small amounts of variability. Factories dare not allow their workers to operate unsupervised or to make subjective decisions. Instead management lays down overly detailed rules about the production process. If this is not done, workers tinker and experiment, tweaking details until the end result is something very different from what was ordered or had been intended.

There is no platonic ideal in China. The first time I realized this was not in the factories but in local restaurants. Each eatery has its own twist on Kung Pao Chicken, for example, and then at any given spot one finds the dish varying one day to the next. For a while, I thought that place-specific variability was the result of different chefs each introducing his own interpretation. I was disabused of this notion only after encountering wild variations at a quaint "fly restaurant" where the only person authorized to work the kitchen was the business owner himself.

China Daily tackled the issue in a 2012 article, noting that domestic franchises have had difficulty expanding precisely because "making sure every dish at every restaurant is exactly the same is problematic" in this country. Sichuan cuisine is famous, yet there is debate over how it is defined. In the capital city of Chengdu, the flywheel of culture has failed to provide consistent, definable traditions, so authorities have felt compelled to nominate old-timers to standardize some of the region's better-known dishes.

As traditionalists, Chinese prefer to stay close to the mean. The culture rewards this behavior and conversely punishes those who veer far away from accepted norms. But China as a civilization could never have survived, however, if no one ever did anything differently. So there developed in the culture a natural tendency to fiddle ever so slightly with norms, and that instinct has somehow become hard-wired.

CHAPTER 10

Sinocentric Thinking

Mainland Chinese tourists have acquired a bad reputation recently, and the problem has gotten so out of hand that tourism boards in both Thailand and Japan have decided to issue handbooks in Mandarin that highlight dos and don'ts. Even Beijing has felt the need to get involved by creating a blacklist of the nation's worst international offenders.

One incident that made headlines involved an elderly airline passenger who figured she was welcome to take the life jacket under her seat as a souvenir. Other passengers have made the news after opening the door of an aircraft while it was taxiing on the tarmac. "I wanted fresh air," one reportedly explained. Another, who launched the emergency slide attached to the door in a separate incident, offered that she merely wanted to exit the plane quicker.

In business, Chinese are monomaniacal about increasing economic returns. When they travel, their focus somehow becomes the maximization of personal convenience. In my own travels, I have happened across numerous squabbles that erupted between members of a tour group and the flight staff. Although everyone understands that seating is prearranged, you get these air travelers who insist on changing their seats upon boarding so that they can sit next to their

latest chat partner. When such tourists are loud and insistent, Chinese
flight attendants tend to let them have their way.

A couple of years ago at San Francisco International Airport,
I went to pick up a vehicle at the car rental desk and noticed a fair
number of mainland tourists standing behind me in line. I asked the
rental agent if he was seeing more such tourists.

"Oh!" he said, revealing an Indian accent. "I had twenty-six of
them here last week. They wanted to rent seven cars, and each of them
wanted to be listed as an alternate driver for *each car*."

Not understanding the issue, I asked him why that was a problem.

"I'm not writing a contract with twenty-six names on it," he said.
"And I'm certainly not doing that seven separate times."

"So what did they say?" I asked.

"Oh, they complained to me very loudly."

"And then?"

"I told them four drivers per car maximum. They fought me, so
I said they can either do it my way or they can walk out from SFO."

"You told them that?"

"Oh, absolutely. You must be firm with the Chinese. Very firm,
or else they will walk all over you."

Mainland Chinese are audacious when abroad, but they can also
be just as brazen at home—especially when it comes to exchanges with
foreigners. Abbé Huc wrote in the nineteenth century about fending
off locals who had broken into the lodge where he was staying just
so they could get a careful look at the stranger. When I first arrived
in China, reports of this sort of behavior were still fairly common.
Foreigner travelers looking to spend a quiet evening might find the
door of their room unlocked by a hotel worker, who would escort
just about anyone who wanted a quick look-see.

George Wingrove Cooke, who had blue eyes, mentioned that
locals would stare at him for sometimes up to a half hour. An American acquaintance who lives in Shanghai with his wife and their two
blonde-haired, blue-eyed children told me his three-year-old son had
been so traumatized by such unwanted attention that he threw a fit
whenever it was time to leave their apartment. On one occasion, the

family had been out for a stroll when the boy suddenly vanished. A few heart-pounding moments later, the father found his kid in a nearby shop. A local woman had seen the boy, thought he looked adorable and simply carried him off, as if he were an objet d'art, to show a friend.

Chinese who engage in presumptuous behavior—"I just wanted fresh air"—will insist that no harm was meant, and any attempt to highlight their offense is typically met with a response along the lines of: "Oh, c'mon!" The self-regard and lack of empathy are reminiscent of classic narcissism.

When former Prime Minister of Israel Shimon Peres died, the mainland press announced that his passing had "caused the Chinese people to lose an old friend," as if the point were China's need for sympathy.

When Steve Jobs lost his battle with pancreatic cancer, the world sank into an immediate funk. Having inspired millions, Jobs led global cultural change through technology products, many of which were manufactured in China. This might have given the Chinese special reason to mourn, but instead they focused inwards: *Why don't we have our own beloved technology icon?* they wondered. Chinese officials in Ningbo then made an awkward announcement: They vowed to "create 1,400 Steve Jobs." No one knew what it meant or why they were shooting for this precise number of Steves. Perhaps the point had been merely to shift some of the attention away from Silicon Valley and back towards China.

This instinct of the Chinese, to make absolutely everything about themselves might hint at an inferiority complex, but as a matter of fact, an opposing factor is at work. Chinese consider theirs the crème de la crème of civilizations, and they are convinced not only of their greater intellectual acuity, but also of their superior practices and methods.

An American company that was having difficulty in a joint venture asked me to talk sense into the local partner, who insisted on running their business the old-fashioned way. The mainland company worked hard to show no profits in order to avoid taxation, for example. While this benefited the Chinese partner, it made the business unattractive to strategic investors and potential acquirers.

The factory boss was a short, tubby man who just happened to be enamored with Warren Buffet. "So very rich!" he had said to me one day. Thinking that it might help, I pointed out that the Oracle of Omaha was famous for playing things straight. Buffett had not made his fortune by cutting corners. He did not hide financial information from his partners, nor did he do backdoor deals. Buffet was one of the world's wealthiest individuals, and he followed generally accepted accounting principles. His businesses were not opaque, but models of transparency.

At the time, Buffett was worth roughly fifty billion dollars, and I named the figure as a way to drive home my point that doing things the right way usually pays.

"Fifty billion?" the factory man asked, as if he could not believe the number. "If he were Chinese, he would be *twice* as rich!"

The exchange was reminiscent of one that Reverend E. J. Hardy relayed in 1905: "An inhabitant of Canton being told that the King of Great Britain was, on certain occasions, drawn in a carriage by eight cream-colored horses, answered without a moment's hesitation, 'China Emperor twenty-four!'"

China's belief that it is better than other nations has caused some to drum up a buzzword: *exceptionalism.* A far more accurate label might actually be *collective narcissism,* which involves an inflated sense of superiority felt by an entire group. One of the key features of narcissism is an inability to accept fault or failure combined with a tendency to project one's own flaws and mistakes onto others. Lucian Pye did not reference narcissism specifically, but he did unwittingly make a link with antiforeignism: "Nothing can be wrong with the Chinese spirit and their inward identity. All problems must lie outside and therefore be the work of 'foreigners.'"

Chinese superstition involves a similar projection. Chinese traditionally did not name their own babies but relied on fortune tellers, thereby absolving themselves of any metaphysical responsibility. Should some boy grow up unlucky, the fault would lay not with the parents but with their spiritual guide. *Fengshui* practitioners are often brought in by businessmen to determine the most auspicious date for a grand opening, just as they are also consulted to locate a suitable burial spot for an aging relative. If things take a bad turn in business or in the afterlife, they have someone convenient to blame.

Mainland Chinese are notoriously bad marketers, and I think part of the problem is that they are constrained by an endemic narcissism that prevents them from seeing things from another perspective. On a train out of Shanghai, I once purchased a bag of pistachios and glanced at the packaging. Printed on the back was an overly detailed chart of how to distinguish various grades of nuts. This was no consumer guide; it was a specifications sheet, the sort that might aid a purchasing manager or sorters on an assembly line. Because they cannot imagine what things look like from the perspective of others, manufacturers simply presume that consumers have the very same concerns they do.

Communist nations are not known as hothouses of creativity. The very notion of competition holds little or no meaning in a place where everyone is working ultimately for the same stakeholder—the State. The make-believe entity that we call "the corporation" must have seemed an unwieldy concept to those who started businesses in the post-1949 era, and so why not give the government-linked enterprises cardboard-inspired monikers like "Shanghai Number Three Silk Weaving Mill" and "Number Two Grain Depot of Jinan"?

The Chinese were never able to make the leap to a customer-driven outlook. When an entrepreneur chooses to give his business a name that includes the characters for *luck* and *wealth*, it is not the customer who he is intimating will become lucky or rich, but rather these are the owner's own ambitions.

China's leading electric-car company, BYD, is run by a boisterous pitchman, Wang Chuanfu, who is fond of telling the press that the initials of his brand stand for Build Your Dreams. The average car consumer is, of course, not looking to build anything, so the only dream being fulfilled here is the one held by the founder and his business partners.

China Inc.'s lack of success in marketing is bewildering when you consider that the Chinese have mastered the art of face and impression management. China's recent solution to the deficit in marketing capabilities has been to purchase foreign companies that have already done the legwork of building a brand and reputation. The acquisitions themselves are quite often face-creating moments meant to compensate for related failings, and given the motivation behind such investments it seems doubtful they will be successful in the long term.

In the factories, the inability to see things from the customer's perspective at times appears to be a mere tactic. Wishing to highlight a production error, I would go to the factory owner and point to a problem only to hear him say that he "couldn't see it." For the longest time, I thought these industrialists were playing thick, but then I came to understand that they had willed themselves into this state, and that this ability to tune out that other perspective afforded them advantage. A problem that was invisible did not need to be resolved. One of the easiest ways to win an argument is to feign ignorance of the very premise presented. While the approach has occasional benefits, it has the unfortunate downside of causing blindness.

In Guangzhou, a trader from Australia relayed to me an unusual encounter involving backpacks. Having placed a large order, he went to the factory to inspect the finished goods and found that they had been produced in dark blue instead of black, as had been ordered.

"What's this?" he asked the factory boss.

"What do you mean?" the boss responded.

"These bags are supposed to be black."

"They *are* black."

"That's not black," said the Australian.

The industrialist appeared confused.

"It's not?"

The buyer retrieved his computer bag.

"*This* is black," he said. "And *this* is navy blue."

The factory man inspected both bags as if he was observing the most curious thing and then announced that the problem was due to a misunderstanding.

"'In China', he says to me, 'navy blue can be also called black.' Can you imagine it?"

"What did you tell him?" I asked.

"I told him my customer is in Sydney, and that unfortunately I was going to need the bags in *Australian* black."

Working in China, one may observe many instances of *sinocentric thinking*, this notion that things are wholly different in China. Assisting a US-based private equity firm out of Chengdu, I was once sent to meet a pair of chemical engineers who had, they claimed, discovered a unique compound for improving the steel manufacturing process.

On my visit, I was taken to a warehouse where heavy bags filled with rocks were stacked onto pallets. I asked them what sort of minerals we were talking about and was told only: "Something secret." Western companies do not typically invest millions, I explained, without having at least some idea what they were getting into, but the company owners held firm. Not wishing to go back empty-handed, I asked if they could at least hint at the chemical properties.

In their office, I found a copy of the periodic table of elements and pointed to atoms like carbon and magnesium, thinking it might help prompt at least a half-response. "Here," I said. "Point to some of the elements we're talking about."

"Our chemicals are not on that chart," he said.

"What do you mean?" I asked.

"That's a *foreign* chart," said the engineer. "Our chemicals are found *only* in China."

Chinese are convinced that they live in a world apart, and this has led many in marketing to convince foreign clients and employers alike that their corporate message needs to be dramatically altered for the Chinese. As a result of this misconception, Western companies have engaged in some of the most egregious examples of pandering.

Boeing, having been told that the number *eight* is lucky—because it sounds like *wealth* in Cantonese—designated its new 747 model as the 747-8, or "dash eight." The same instinct led other marketers to recommend United Airlines list its new San Francisco to Beijing route as Flight UA888.

No one is quite sure when the number eight became so popular in this country. Equally unclear is when its inverse, the number four, became so unpopular. Though they have been presented as ancient superstitions, these beliefs are of modern origin. Western writers of the nineteenth and early twentieth centuries detailed many Chinese superstitions and remarked on the matter of auspicious dates, yet there is no mention whatsoever about an "inauspicious four" or a "lucky eight" in the books from that era.

Another great, more recent myth has to do with the color red. Though it just so happens to be the color most commonly associated with communism, red is also claimed to have deep meaning in the Chinese culture and is associated with good fortune. In the 1920s and 1930s, the most common reference to the color red had to do with the vermillion pencil, a euphemism for feared edicts handed down by the emperor. Beyond that reference, the subject almost never came up.

Samsonite, the luggage company, was somehow convinced that it should produce a new line of bags playing off this cultural feature.

"You mean we should make all our bags red?" an executive asked.

"No," a local marketer replied. "Let's just *call* them red."

In what has to be one of the strangest marketing campaigns of a major company in this region, Samsonite has produced a new line of luggage in shades of brown and blue and green. Yet stamped onto each piece is a chrome-plated logo that reads: *Samsonite Red*.

If such a brand were offered in the United States, one might presume it was meant as an intentional conversation starter. The problem here is that East Asians are not particularly receptive to messages that make use of cognitive dissonance or irony. Because the line is available only in Asia, the company has been spared any criticism in this regard. And in fact, sales for Samsonite Red appear brisk despite the nonsensical pitch.

China is disadvantaged by what might be termed a surfeit of sincerity. The code of face dictates that when someone is nice to you, the favor is to be returned. Clinical narcissists operate similarly by rewarding those who treat them well, while ignoring anything that takes place outside of that beneficial relationship. "Cutting a person's acquaintance," wrote Ralph Townsend, "because of what he did to some unknown third party would rarely enter the head of a Chinese."

Americans like to think twice before befriending a person with a bad reputation, or with someone whose values are materially different. In China, thanks to bilateral compartmentalization, it matters little whether an acquaintance has defrauded his business partner, cheated on his wife, or even committed murder. All that matters is what takes place within the confines of that one-on-one relationship.

Beijing works closely with many undesirables—North Korea and Iran are two examples—and Americans cannot understand why. We imagine the world as a playground made up of various cliques, and our instinct has long been to call out to China and suggest that it come hang out with the other cool kids. Beijing is unable to see the world in terms of broad alliances and instead insists upon viewing each of its political relationships as residing within a bilateral bubble.

Clinical narcissists have another psychological tick, which involves magical thinking, evidence of which we see in China. Chinese factories commonly seek to convince buyers that they are able to pull off some difficult project, even when the chance of success is zero. For years, I thought this was an issue with judgment, but I came to understand that these operators were merely being hopeful in the extreme. The probability might be only one in ten thousand that a fly-by-night operator might succeed in building, say, an electric garden tool with dozens of moving parts. But they convince themselves that through hard application—and a lot of luck—they can somehow pull it off.

Reverend Hardy was a critic of the civil service examination, which in his day was on the verge of abolition. His main issue with the test, which called for candidates to produce turgid essays in the style of Confucius, was that it did not also test for math or science. This archaic system, he pointed out, had led to a class of officials that spoke seriously of "growing coal" and of building sailing ships that could reach the Moon.

In the nineteenth century, before the Opium Wars, Chinese officials came up with a serious plan to chase off the British by withholding tea and rhubarb. In an anonymous memorial to the emperor, an official wrote, "Inquiries have served to show that the foreigners, if deprived for several days of the tea and rhubarb of China, are afflicted with dimness of sight and constipation of the bowels, to such a degree that life is endangered." It was an instance of magical thinking as much as it was a projection by officials who themselves likely suffered from opioid-induced constipation.

China's many secret societies throughout history were often emboldened through the belief that they were able to make use of magic. The Boxers—also known as the Society of Righteous and Harmonious Fists—were a nineteenth-century antiforeign group founded in part on fantastical beliefs. Convinced they could conjure spiritual strength that was proof against metal, they believed that they could stop bullets with the power of their minds.

Even today, we find plenty of evidence in magical thinking. Chinese economists are claiming that they have solved the *impossible trinity*, a mathematical precept subscribed to by the world's leading economists, which holds that an economy can succeed in controlling only two of three policy positions—a fixed foreign exchange, free capital movement, and an independent monetary policy.

China considers itself so special that even the most fundamental laws of nature do not necessarily apply to it. When the whole ball of twine comes undone, we will look back in hindsight and realize that with so much clear evidence of magical notions, something was bound to go wrong.

CHAPTER 11

"That's My Hand"

After Deng Shuchao leapt from a bridge in the middle of winter, drowning himself in Sichuan's Jinsha River, it took three days for his body to be discovered. Over the course of another three days, his parents sat on the bank of the river, pleading with area fishermen to retrieve their son from the water.

The fishermen were more than glad to help fetch the body (which the family would not touch for superstitious reasons), but they insisted on first being paid eighteen thousand yuan for the job. Family members wailed and begged for mercy, but the fishermen were unmoved. When police arrived, they did nothing more than act as mediators, politely suggesting that the fisherman discount their rate. It is the sort of story that touches a nerve with Chinese, because it reminds them of where they live.

China has no real tradition of philanthropy due to the expectation that families will take care of themselves. As a result of this cultural precept, Chinese tend to look suspiciously on those who offer a helping hand.

The Charity Aid Foundation publishes a survey called the World Giving Index, which reveals China to have one of the worst rates of volunteerism in the world, as well as one of the lowest rates of charitable giving. Warren Buffett and Bill Gates have gone to great lengths to convince the world's billionaires to commit their accumulated wealth to posterity. Although they had luck in other parts of the world, and despite their wide popularity on the mainland, the pair got nowhere with the Chinese.

Chinese are too cynical to believe in aid, and they are of the opinion that those who offer it have ulterior motives. The first thing Chinese of the nineteenth century thought when they saw Western missionaries arriving from distant lands was, "*Why would these strangers help us? What do they* really *want?*"

In the nineteenth century, British and American clergy who built orphanages were suspected of secretly boiling children to create potent elixirs. Many of the foreigners who came during this era were physicians, and the eye clinics they established were also presumed to be a ruse. Instead of treating eyes, the Chinese figured, foreigners were scheming to steal them—either in order to sell the eyeballs on the black market or to make glass mirrors, a novelty import. As the numbers of missionaries grew, Chinese became convinced that it was part of a nefarious plot. They were spies, it was presumed, "maneuvering for the invasion of the empire."

A century earlier, foreigners had not been allowed into the country at all but had to stay in Canton, and even then they were allowed to reside there only a few weeks out of the year. There was one exception to the travel ban: a boat excursion to nearby gardens. Group size was restricted to ten people, and an assigned escort led the tour. "No asylum full of dangerous lunatics," wrote Rodney Gilbert, "was ever sequestered from the general public with greater vigilance than the foreign community in Canton was from the Chinese commercial public."

Chinese themselves were accustomed to paranoid treatment. Bureaucrats were rarely, if ever, posted to a place where they spoke the local dialect for fear that they might gather grassroots support. Scholar-officials were not given much information about the roles they were meant to play, and many didn't learn of their next assignment until the day they were removed. China's population was stuck at three hundred thirty million for many decades, suggested Arthur Smith, not because of a lack of actual growth, but because authorities did not dare conduct a census out of concern that such an intrusion might incite widespread panic.

Chinese are private to a fault. Yet, ironically enough, this prevailing caution has had the effect of encouraging secret sharing. "There must be treasons, stratagems and spoils, in anything which is not accessible to everyone," wrote Smith, who, to illustrate his point, described a pair of merchants in a market taking great pains to conceal a negotiation from others through hand signals hidden within the sleeves of their silk robes. Although the two might enjoy a momentary privacy, he offered, "it will go hard" if they do not eventually share the results of their bargaining with fellow merchants.

It is amazing to see today how much information is shared among factory bosses. Competition is intense, so one expects these industrialists to do as much as possible to prevent any peer from becoming a future threat, but nonetheless they help one another to an extent that makes them appear like business partners.

The key to the habit is in the kind of information passed along. A factory owner does not help another for no reason at all, but does so in an effort to receive some in-kind reciprocal benefit. It is an arbitrage, and great care is taken to pass along less-than-critical information in exchange for what may be a more material benefit. *Open secrets*—those involving counterfeiting techniques, for example—will spread quickly across an industry sector as a direct result of such efforts at quid pro quo.

———————

Chinese office workers can be annoying in the way they carefully dole out job-related information, and sometimes even the most innocent of questions is treated with great caution. During a holiday period, I asked one woman who worked in an American client's office when the office would return to work.

"Is everyone back on Tuesday?" I asked.

"Is that what you heard?" she responded.

This was common treatment in China. The woman did not wish to contradict something that a coworker might have said.

Years ago, in my own office, I had such issues with communication.

"Do you have the file on that plywood?" I asked a colleague.

"File?" she responded.

"Yes," I said. "The plywood file."

"Plywood?" she asked.

She had been working on nothing else for two weeks, so the reference was clear. Thinking that perhaps I had been mumbling, I clearly enunciated my words this time. "Yes, the file on plywood."

It took me years to work out that this was no more than a delay tactic. While I was asking (and repeating) my benign question, the office worker's head was spinning: *Why is he requesting the file? Why now? Is this a trap? Does he suspect something wrong with my work? Should I buy time and review the data? Maybe the information is good and he will make the faux pas of complimenting me in front of my colleagues, who already despise me for my diligence. He seems the sort who would make that kind of mistake. What if my colleagues become envious? Better to appear reluctant to hand over the file at least, just in case.*

Like Deep Blue working out its next chess move, she was running scenarios and calculating odds.

Around this time, I was working with an American who was purchasing aluminum parts out of China. While on site, he asked the factory to release a sample from production. The goods had already been produced and paid for, they were just sitting in the warehouse waiting to be shipped. Though it was a reasonable and straightforward request, the factory boss refused to provide the item.

The factory man eventually admitted his concern. He worried that his customer would take the sample and show it to a competing factory.

"If that was my intention," said the buyer, "I could just ship the sample from the United States after receiving the full container."

"We know you can do that also," said the industrialist. "We just don't want to make it any easier for you."

Chinese producers understand the indolence of foreign buyers. Not putting a sample in the buyer's hand might make him angry, but it also made him less likely to pursue a competing bid, which more than compensated for the increased friction in the relationship.

At the Shangri-La Hotel in Hong Kong, I sat down with a pair of American engineers who design wooden roller coasters for a living. They wanted to speak with me because they had questions about their China business, and they thought it would be worthwhile to trade notes. One thing they wanted to discuss was a recent project of theirs in the south. It had been challenging in so many ways, and one of the harder-to-understand elements had been a pervasive paranoia expressed by their customer.

The Americans had installed electronic monitors on their roller coaster so that they could see from their office in the States just how smoothly it was performing. There was no after-sales service component to their contractual agreement. They simply wanted to keep an eye on the ride for the benefit of everyone involved. If anything happened, they wanted to be able to alert the operator, in case the operator itself did not notice.

A month or so after the wooden coaster was put into operation, and with no warning, the electronic link to the ride was cut. The Americans had not been consulted, so they had no opportunity to make a further case for why it was a good idea to keep the censors in place. "Thank you very much, we'll take it from here," was the message from the Chinese.

One of the engineers was mystified by the move, because it went against the park's best interest. "Do you know why they would do that?" he asked.

I did not, I told him.

Chinese have been actively stealing corporate secrets from foreign firms for years, so it should come as no surprise that they worry about the same thing happening to them. I worked with a Guangdong manufacturer producing construction components for high-rise buildings, many of them for export. As we prepared to leave the factory one balmy afternoon, a security guard approached the car we were in and asked that the driver open his trunk. I didn't know what he was looking for, but any construction blueprints that might have left the building would not have been printed on paper and rolled up in a tube. They would have been saved to an electronic drive and slipped into a pocket. Chinese companies understand this, but to make themselves feel better they go through the motions anyway.

Chinese engineers have an unusual habit: They like to leave key information off of their technical drawings, so that others cannot steal their work. One expects engineering blueprints to be complete and not presented enigmatically like some treasure map. Yet this is what is done here in the name of secrecy. China is planning to put a man on the Moon and we can only imagine what the schematics look like, fretting as the Chinese do about who might get hold of such plans. No one ever talks about the drag coefficient that paranoia creates in this economy, but when I think of China's manufacturing landscape, I see tens of thousands of factories, all operating with self-created points of resistance.

Photojournalists working the China beat seem to have a favorite shot; you see it often in the news. It is an image of a security guard's open palm thrust out in a half-hearted attempt to block the camera lens. I have a small collection of these images myself, having attempted to take numerous photos and been told that I was doing something forbidden. No one wishes to have their secrets revealed in this country, and that goes for retail shops and even retail bakeries, whose operators worry what might happen if images of their cakes and rolls are made public.

At the Canton Fair a few years ago, walking around with a newly purchased digital camera, I snapped a photo of a product that an exhibitor had on display.

"No photographs!" a sales representative shouted.

"I just want to show a buyer in the United States," I explained.

"Photography of our products is strictly forbidden," he said.

"I know, but how are you planning to sell anything if buyers can't see what you're offering?"

"I'm sorry," he said.

"No problem," I said.

He stepped in front of me, preventing me from leaving.

"You need to delete the picture."

After taking my one and only shot, I had already glanced at the camera and seen that I had not been successful, because the rep had blocked the camera lens with his hand. But because it seemed like a fun thing to do, I let him think that I had the crown jewels.

"This is a public space," I said.

"Delete," he said.

"I will not," I said.

He called for his colleague to alert a security guard.

"You must delete the photo," the guard said.

"On what principle?" I asked.

"I'm sorry," the guard said. "You must do it."

The entire absurdity—that a company would spend tens of thousands of dollars to display products for export that could not be shown to overseas buyers—was lost on these people. Thinking that the farce had gone on long enough, I decided to deliver the punch line. All of this bickering, I would let them know, had been for nothing, because in the end I had not even managed to get a clear image.

I opened my digital camera to show the one photo I had managed to take, an out-of-focus half of a palm.

"You see? Nothing," I said.

"You must delete the photo," the company rep said.

"What? You can't see anything here but a bit of a hand."

"Yes," he said, "but that's *my* hand."

CHAPTER 12

Lack of Conscience

O f all the reasons to do a deep dive into old historical writings on China, the primary one is to disprove once and for all this notion that responsibility for the country's pervasive ills lies exclusively with the current regime. China apologists are fond of blaming the communists, suggesting in effect that everything was great "until *these* guys showed up." But that is not even close to the truth. As we have been discovering, many of the nation's problems were present before the communist revolution.

Mainland Chinese have a sense that something is wrong in the world, and this feeling has shadowed them for thousands of years. In the third century BCE, the classic poet Qu Yuan composed his famous poem *Li Sao*, in which he lamented the same kind of societal rot that many complain of today:

> *Truly, this generation are cunning artificers!*
> *From square and compass they turn their eyes and change the*
> *true measurement,*
> *They disregard the ruled line to follow their own crooked fancies:*
> *To emulate in flattery is their only rule.*
> *But I am sick and sad at heart and stand irresolute.*
> *I alone am at a loss in this generation.*

Mao Zedong was said to have suffered from borderline personality disorder. Lucian Pye suggested this was why the chairman had a tendency to see things in black and white, and why he could be found changing his mind about a subject or a person in the blink of an eye.

Although not a fan of psychopathography, I did once hear an interesting hypothesis, that the average factory owner is a sociopath in the clinical sense, which made me curious enough to investigate.

Checklists for sociopathy—referred to also as antisocial personality disorder—read like a description of every factory boss I ever met.

"Intelligent with a superficial charm?" Usually, yes.

"Tendency to make hollow promises?" Check.

"Engages in shameless maneuvers." Double check.

"Refuses to take responsibility for his actions?" Ditto.

Superficial charm as a criterion is an especially interesting one, not only because we see it in factories, but also because it characterizes just about every politician that ever rose to the top in this country. Leading politicians—from Mao Zedong to Deng Xiaoping to Zhou Enlai— have universally been described by outsiders as jovial and charismatic. This includes even those condemned by historians as monsters.

Western journalists have long linked the charisma of communists to their ability to play the part of a good host. Felix Greene, a journalist who worked for the BBC and who went to China soon after World War Two, was wooed by this charm and testified that the Chinese have "a rare sensitivity about a traveler's needs. They seem to know exactly when he's had enough, when he wants to be alone, when he needs a nap, when he needs a beer."

Factory owners are great at throwing parties, and they also happen to have a knack for spontaneity. Chinese factory bosses will rarely tell us where we will be going for dinner, and if the location is known in advance, chances are they will announce a change while we are en route. In her book, *The Sociopath Next Door*, psychologist Martha Stout explains that improvisation is one of the hallmarks of these personality types and that sociopaths tend to convey a sense of spontaneity "in an attempt to increase their apparent charm."

Mainland Chinese who are in business will often turn up late to meetings—if they show up at all—hoping to cultivate the appearance that their lives are so exciting and entertaining that they can hardly commit to even a simple appointment.

For the longest time, I presumed this habit of projecting mayhem was a byproduct of the full-tilt economy and all of its attendant exhilaration. How strange to learn that Chinese have traditionally had related issues. "When a Chinaman intends to give an entertainment," wrote Charles Eden in 1877, "he issues his invitations thrice. A few days before, or perhaps only on the previous evening, he sends out a crimson card inscribed with the day and hour at which he desires 'the illumination of his friend's presence.' He renews this invitation on the morning of the day fixed, and repeats it for the third time when the feast is ready."

Coined in the 1930s, *sociopathy* is a modern term. Prior to then, the antisocial personality was described merely as an individual who "lacked conscience." We should be at least a little curious to note the frequency with which foreign writers highlighted the issue of a missing conscience in the nineteenth and early twentieth centuries. Abbé Huc once remarked that while the Manchu rulers were a standup people, the average Chinese subject did not "heed conscience." In 1834, a missionary tract issued by the Methodist Church referred to China as "a nation of traders with very little conscience." In 1905, the writer Alexis Krausse made the claim that "conscience is an unknown attribute" of many in the land.

Mainland Chinese today who have an inkling that something is wrong focus on this cultural aspect, as do many foreign writers. In his article titled "Driven to Kill," American lawyer Geoffrey Sant wrote about the phenomenon of *double-hit cases*, where drivers who accidentally run over a pedestrian subsequently back up and crush the victim multiple times, believing that it is "better to hit and kill than to hit and injure." Victims who are merely crippled, Sant explains, are compensated over a lifetime, whereas the dead are paid out only once. Mainland Chinese react strongly to such macabre news, not so much because it is a common occurrence, but because it is representative of certain attitudes.

Reverend Arthur Smith believed that the Chinese were callous in the extreme and that their indifference to suffering was "probably not to be matched in any other civilized country." Years ago in Chengdu, a similar thought crossed my mind when I happened upon three sidewalk beggars crawling on the pavement, each suffering from nearly the same unlikely deformity. Their legs—one or both—were emaciated from atrophy and were contorted into an awkward position just behind the head.

American poet Eunice Tietjens spent time in China just after the collapse of the Qing dynasty. In a poem titled "The Beggar," published in 1917, she described something eerily similar.

> *Christ! What is that—that—Thing?*
> *Only a beggar, professionally maimed, I think.*

The poem reminded me of a story told to me by an importer from Canada. While he was visiting a supplier, a shop floor worker had lost a finger in a piece of machinery. Holding his injured hand, which was wrapped in a towel and bleeding profusely, the laborer sat on the floor while colleagues went to find the missing digit. The factory boss then rushed over and, after pausing to assess the situation, began hitting the injured employee over the head. "How many times," he said, while beating the poor worker, "have I told you to keep your damned fingers out of that machine!"

British officers who fought in the Opium Wars remarked on the cruelty that Chinese soldiers suffered at the hands of their commanders. Reverend Richard Hastings Graves, writing in 1895, described one such British officer who bristled at the treatment given Chinese recruits. "What do I want with wounded men?" a Chinese general was quoted by Graves. "The sooner they die the better. China has plenty of men."

In China, callousness and ruthlessness tend to go hand in hand. Chinese are "highly alert to the importance of being skilled at manipulation," wrote Pye, and they "tend to see the manipulation of human relationships as the natural and normal approach for accomplishing most things in life." It sounds like a condemnation yet is not seen as an outrageous claim to a population that understands the extent to which "ploys, stratagems, and game-playing tactics" constitute the normal run of events.

———————

Western literature's first sociopath is arguably Iago from Shakespeare's *Othello*. In the play, Iago is seen stealing a handkerchief, using it to convince Othello that Cassio and Desdemona are having an affair.

Iago is an instigator, a troublemaker, and his primary motivation is to prove to himself (and the audience) that he can pull off this deception. Manipulation may be the hallmark of sociopathy, but trickery without a bottom-line cause makes almost no sense to the Chinese. For this play to work with a Chinese audience, there ought to be a profit motive, and it would also help if the play were rewritten as a comedy.

Placing a deposit on a new pair of eyeglass frames one morning in Guangzhou, I returned to the shop a few days later realizing that I had lost the deposit slip that showed how much I had left with the shopkeeper. "How much do you think you left?" she asked with a devilish grin. Chinese find humor in this sort of awkward situation. Made to report the amount myself, the implication in this game was that if my memory failed me and I named a figure that was too low, I would end up paying a larger balance. If instead I named an amount too high, then the woman behind the counter would suddenly remember that she kept a ledger under the counter in which all such deposits were recorded.

Running low on business cards one week, I placed an order for four small boxes. Two days later, the printer arrived carrying ten boxes of cards instead. Southern Chinese pronounce "four" and "ten" similarly in Mandarin because of an issue with accents. Although quite certain I had been clear on the phone, the printer insisted she heard "*shi*" instead of "*si*," so I accepted the larger order. The Chinese are skilled at taking advantage of misunderstandings, wrote Reverend Arthur Smith: "They find them as a January north wind finds a crack in a door, as the water finds a leak in a ship, instantly and without apparent effort."

In their willingness to manipulate for advantage, some sociopaths go so far as to make a person think he is going crazy. Psychologists refer to this behavior as *gaslighting*, a term derived from a 1940 suspense thriller in which a woman is manipulated into believing she is insane.

China hands commonly get such treatment, as when they are told in the middle of a business deal: "You don't understand China." It took me years to realize that such a comment is never meant as an actual critique of a foreigner's ability to grasp the culture, but is simply an act of desperation. It is the card played against the outsider when a local feels cornered. Chinese truck in opposites, flattering the neophyte by telling him he is an expert and by insisting to a twenty-years-in-the-country-and-speaks-the-language foreigner that he knows little.

Talk of sociopathy may appear unkind or unproductive, but to the extent that there are lessons to be extracted, we must pursue the line of inquiry, if only out of curiosity. British psychologist Kevin Dutton has suggested that sociopaths are extreme pragmatists, a feature that is shared with the average factory boss in China. Paradoxical as it may seem for a character who will stop at nothing to achieve his aims, sociopaths exhibit a "greater willingness to accept unfair offers, favoring simple economic utility over the exigencies of punishment and ego preservation." Furthermore, these characters are also "less bothered by inequity." Confucian culture is practically built on the acceptance of inequities, so it is easy to make a connection.

Sociopaths fight hard for what they want and are inclined to employ devious tactics. In their effort to win at all costs, they may appear to become unhinged when, for example, they try and fail to wiggle out of a contractual obligation. In his effort to evade responsibility and increase his portion, a factory owner may become emotional. He may appear to us on the verge of tears, or he may raise his voice in anger. Threats that started off as veiled will become more lucid, and as the heat level of the conflict builds, the foreign team will become increasingly nervous about tensions reaching a crescendo.

Seeing that the factory man is ambitious in the extreme, we presume he will explode if he does not get his way, yet this does not happen. After a point, understanding that the pressure to honor his obligations are significant and satisfied that he gave wiggling out of them a good shot, he simply shrugs his shoulders, cedes the round, and begins planning for the next transactional challenge.

CHAPTER 13

Tacit Collusion

A woman from Jiangsu surprised me once with some of the most unusual information about Serbia, which made it sound as if she had lived there. She had never even been to Europe, she told me, but had a friend whose brother-in-law ran a business in Novi Sad, a town north of Belgrade, and it was from this tenuous link that she had come to know so much about the tiny country.

Chinese take gossip seriously. In the nineteenth century, George Wingrove Cooke commented on the habit. "Nothing is secret for more than a quarter of an hour," he said of the Chinese in Hong Kong. "One of the main enjoyments of the Chinese," noted Stanley High, "seems to be chatting with one another, and whether they are old friends or perfect strangers makes little difference."

The rate at which information spreads throughout the country has always been impressively fast. In the 1920s, foreigners thought the speed of information flow had everything to do with the newly free press, just as today we are inclined to believe that social media is responsible for a robust national grapevine.

In the nineteenth century, before the telegraph, the fastest mode of transportation was the coolie-powered sedan chair. Candidates of the civil-service examination—who wasted no time getting home after the three-day exam—commonly found that news of their passing or failing had somehow preceded their arrival.

Chinese gossip networks are not only distinguished by the speed with which information flows but also with the breadth. Chinese tend to natter with a great number of individuals and on a broad range of topics, a habit that was likely developed long ago as a tool for survival. Imagine millions of peasants living in villages loosely connected with one another. No sooner was an improvement in agriculture discovered than it was shared with the neighbors. The advantage went to those who were nosy and talkative, while those who kept to themselves were often the first to hit on hard times.

Dangers were also of a social and political nature. In order to avoid a violent mob or a rapacious militia, it often helped to have advance warning. In a world where scholar-officials held great power—and were capricious in their exercise of it—it paid to know where and when an official might be traveling and what was on his mind. Authoritarian rule is countered by a strategy of hanging tight, and it is in this spirit that the country's *laobaixing* have long been incentivized to keep each other informed.

Beijing views the national grapevine as so robust that it sometimes finds it necessary to attack *rumormongering*. When Shanghai's over-heated stock market took a dive in 2015, the government rushed to identify individuals it could blame for inspiring the stampede. Though we may be disinclined to accept the notion that a few individuals are able to manipulate a liquid, open market in this fashion, there actually have been instances when the rumor mill has been harnessed for expressly that purpose. In Shanghai, police arrested a group of real estate agents for causing a buying frenzy after they started a rumor suggesting that the government would soon raise mortgage down payment requirements.

In 1858, Cooke noted that the Chinese were "constantly putting false reports in circulation." Timothy Richard, an early twentieth-century Welsh Baptist missionary, suggested that such reports often had to do with superstition. In his book, *Forty-Five Years in China*, Richard mentions a rumor about a scholar-official who was said to have risen from the dead, prophesying that one-third of the population would fall ill and die. Such a detail was taken as real news, so naturally everyone did their best to ensure that friends and neighbors were sufficiently forewarned.

———————

Not long after we pulled out of the airport in Shantou, my taxi driver began grumbling. The factory was farther than he expected, and for the distance covered, he wanted more. This sort of thing did not happen often, but I had been in this spot before. Thinking that ignoring him might do the trick, I put on my headphones and pretended to listen to music.

The factory boss who had invited me to his plant was coming out of his office just as we pulled into the property. The smile on his welcoming face waned as he saw through the windshield that I appeared to be having trouble with my driver.

Bracing for a scene, I was surprised when the factory man leaned into my open car door and said in a low voice to the driver: "*Zheshi wo de kehu.* This is my customer."

What happened next was like a scene from *Invasion of the Body Snatchers*. A signal had passed between them, as if through a shared morphogenetic field, and the driver said not another word but put his car into drive and floated toward the road that led back to town.

This is my customer?

Something like this could not happen in a city like Philadelphia, not with a cabbie who was convinced he was owed something extra. "That's your customer? So what? What's that gotta do with me?"

There is a *hierarchy of values* in China. People are now allowed to earn as much as they can and if that means taking advantage of hapless foreigners, so be it. But if that ambition should conflict with the greater good of propping up the export-manufacturing juggernaut, well, now that's a different story. The individual's selfish motive would have to take a back seat. Foreign cash is seen as a necessary step toward national rejuvenation, so any move that gets in the way of that goal is *ipso facto* a despicable, treasonous act.

At a different supplier, I was once drinking tea with the factory owner, discussing the falling price of aluminum, when someone walked into the room.

"Hey, this foreigner says aluminum is at eleven thousand."

"Eleven thousand!" said the visitor. "Ha! Impossible! Too low!"

"You see?" said the factory boss. "It's not just me who says so."

The boss was acting as if he had picked some random fellow, forgetting that he had introduced me to this other guy months earlier. His name was Xu, and he was a sponge, the factory owner's drinking buddy.

In his book, *The Presentation of Self in Everyday Life*, the sociologist Erving Goffman talked about life being a performance, a dramaturgical stage on which the *actors* within any given social setting may share a *backstage* with others. Kitchen workers, for example, tend to have a private language. Or a husband and wife might share a meaningful glance between them at a cocktail party. Mainland Chinese live for backstage operations, and in the presence of any foreigner, they instinctively break into their respective public roles while coordinating behind the curtain.

When a New York recycling company asked me to find out why its Chinese partners were having difficulty securing a line of credit, I traveled to Jiangmen, the city where the sorting facility was located, only to discover that the operating partner had already set an appointment at the Bank of China for us later that afternoon.

Four of us were in the meeting at the local branch office: me, the local partner, and two Bank of China representatives, including the vice general manager. Seated at a rectangular glass table in a glass-walled conference room, I listened as the bank executive explained the situation.

"Perhaps you have read in the newspaper," he said, "that credit in China is very tight at the moment." I had indeed read the reports, I told the bank officer, but I was unaware of just how serious the matter was.

"It's *very* serious," he said. "Chinese authorities have instructed all banks to not issue *any* letters of credit."

"None?"

"I'm afraid not."

The manager was apologetic but offered that he had hope things would change for the better within the next few months.

I was acquainted around this time with an Australian who lived in Guangzhou and who imported wastepaper from abroad. Thinking that he might add some dimension, I rang him and told him what I had just heard.

"Ha! The Bank of China no longer issuing letters of credit? That's the funniest thing I've heard all week!"

"I don't understand. Why's that funny?"

"Are you kidding? The entire economy would shut down without credit. Someone's pulling your leg, mate."

Instead of informing the Americans that they were unable to back a line of credit, the local partners created this wonderful charade, knowing that I would dutifully report my observed findings back to New York. There was nothing illegal in the setup; in fact, bank officials involved likely believed they were doing the honorable thing in helping a client.

Of course, you could hardly explain this to someone in the United States. Why would someone go to such lengths?

If you want to know the extent to which culture weighs heavily, just look at how a mental illness like schizophrenia expresses itself in different parts of the world. In the United States, that homeless individual you see wandering the streets, who has both visual and auditory hallucinations, is still so very American. Pushing a shopping cart into which he has crammed as much as possible, he is an emblem of consumerism. Or we may find him reflecting another side of our national character when he takes to the corner and preaches the gospel, or at least his version of it.

In Sapporo, Japan, I once saw a poor waif of a woman pulling a dilapidated piece of luggage down a sidewalk. Somewhat disheveled, she was otherwise neatly presented, and as she passed by, I heard her mumbling to herself. She looked mad, yet was intent on hiding it. As sick as she must have been, her comportment was impressive. Though facing demons, she was the epitome of Japaneseness, and if you opened that carry-on of hers, I bet you would have found a neatly folded towel, a small toothbrush, and a set of chopsticks to round out her kit.

I was once walking with a factory owner down a busy street in Dongguan when we approached a homeless beggar similarly afflicted, though this one was holding a worn and dirty paper cup with spare change in it. The bum was in a bad way. He was barefoot, his clothes torn, and it appeared as if he had not bathed in months. As we drew near, my host raised his hand, indicating that he was to leave us alone. In response, the vagrant politely withdrew his cup and slightly bowed his head in our direction. Although clearly sick and obviously in need, he was still somehow able to grasp that he had an important role to play in supporting the national effort: *Chinese businessman making impression on foreigner—do not disturb.* China's mentally ill are rarely so out of it that they forget what it means to be Chinese.

The international press has run numerous articles on "nail-house" holdouts, individuals who refuse to leave their homes when asked to do so by the government in order to make way for new dams, roads, and property developments. Beijing has moved millions, and though once in a while someone refuses to go, the vast majority hold their tongues and inconvenience themselves for the benefit of the nation. As valiant a figure as the nail-house victim may be, the real story is the millions on the other side of the equation who do not protest in any way, but who go along with the grand plan.

There is a history to this sort of support. "When it was decided some years ago to erect telegraphs throughout the empire," wrote John Macgowan in 1912, "the question as to how much would be required to meet the expenses of trespassing on people's property never entered into the calculations of the Government. The lines would pass over thousands of miles of country, through densely populated regions, amongst peoples fierce and independent in their manners, and through tracts of country where the authority of the mandarins was of the loosest possible description, and yet the question of the right to plant holes in fields or gardens, or in a man's front yard, was never once seriously raised."

———

Around the time I graduated from Wharton, a pair of classmates had famously lost their startup business to a cash-flow crunch. Their company, which found success selling a patented earmuff that goes behind the head instead of over the top, had grown in sales to fifty million dollars. Following a successful season, a couple of large customers filed for bankruptcy protection, leaving the entrepreneurs in a lurch. They went to their main investor, a venture capitalist, who, instead of helping them out with a short-term loan, turned vulture and swallowed the company whole, booting the founders in the process.

American startups quite often have only one key investor or just a single bank supporting the business. Chinese entrepreneurs know more people with capital, and they usually raise funds from a range of sources. In a time of crisis, not only are they able to reach out to a broad group of active investors, but also they tend to have a number of backups. Chinese companies are in this way more antifragile, to borrow a notion from Nassim Nicholas Taleb, a modern authority on risk theory. Chinese companies create more options for themselves and as a result are more likely to survive a difficult patch.

Western economists have worried about Chinese bank debt for as long as I have been in China. In the 1990s, we were promised that nonperforming loans would sink the banking sector, if not the whole economy. It didn't happen. The cries are now even louder, but again no collapse appears imminent. The alarm has reached a fever pitch because debt levels in China as a percentage of overall economic activity have exceeded those of the United States. So what is going on?

China's financial sector does not boast independent oversight, and it has issues with transparency. All the same, we may wish to consider the extent to which their robust financial networks serve the economy well. Chinese financial networks operate like their grapevine does. The network is characterized by a greater number of nodes and capital flows more rapidly to where it is needed most. While the chickens will come home to roost on excessive lending at some point, in the meantime we can appreciate how debt ratios have been able to climb without risking immediate damage to the economy.

More than twenty years ago in Taipei, I lived in a newly established neighborhood where most of the apartments went unrented. Looking out my window and seeing dozens of For Rent signs, I wondered why these landlords did not lower their asking price and let out their apartments, rather than let them collect dust.

You would never see such a vast expanse of empty apartments in the United States, partly because landlords there must bear the expense of property tax. In Asia, property taxes are usually minimal. Another motivating factor for the American landlord is the mortgage that needs to be paid. Chinese who purchase property often do so with cash, so they can afford to keep the homes empty. When they finally agree to rent, they typically do so only at the benchmark that brings a sufficient level of face. They want to be able to brag about how much they are receiving each month. As a result of this proclivity, the landlords tend to get an unrealistic figure in their heads, or a number that often has little to do with property yields anyway. "Everyone knows that apartments around here rent for X," they will say, fully aware that the price is ridiculously high.

Not saddled with such burdens as property taxes or even mortgage payments, Chinese landlords in any given neighborhood are better situated to hold out for a premium. The benchmark that they choose is a tacitly agreed-upon figure, and their rule of thumb typically defies logic, because it all but guarantees that the district remains a ghost town. Eventually though, some prospective renter visits the neighborhood and determines that for one reason or another he has to be there; and though there is plenty of supply, no one will give him a price break. When this first sucker moves into his new place, he sets a precedent that emboldens the other householders: "You see? X truly is the going rate around here."

Chinese appreciate a good monopoly, and as a part of that instinct, we find players in various markets engaging in *tacit collusion*. We have seen commodity prices spike in a way that is inexplicable, and foreign analysts have presumed that either the government itself must be taking a long position, or else it has instructed third-party holders to hoard. When the price of aluminum spiked recently, many presumed it was because China's largest supplier was warehousing excessive stock. Yet as big as that company's volume may be, it still accounts for a mere fraction of market activity within the sector.

In the nineteenth century, Cooke mentioned that the British were greatly frustrated by silk wholesalers: "Chinese have a tremendous silk crop and are holding out for the most extortionate prices." In so many industries today, we hear similar reports of excess supply and weak demand, yet prices remain high because sellers can and do collude.

Westerners have no trouble making sense of a simple oligopoly. Where three or four companies get together to fix prices, we understand how such coordination might take place, and we can even comprehend a group as large as a couple dozen players. But when the number of complicit parties stretches into the hundreds, we have to wonder by what mechanism such tacit collusion operates.

Importers of China-made goods occasionally have the sense that all suppliers within a fragmented sector are colluding to offer the same heinous deal to buyers: poor quality at high prices. Adam Smith's promise that some will wish to offer more for less, thereby capturing market share, seems not to apply in China. Chinese recognize that some competition is principally necessary, but at the same time their baser instincts remind them that economic returns are greater when market participants cooperate and no one breaks rank.

In the 1800s, China lost its lead in both tea manufacturing and silk production because of widespread quality problems. The tea industry collapsed in part because growers were sending leaves to market without first drying them. This was not a time-saving maneuver. It was done because wet leaves weigh more, and the additional weight brought in more revenue. The problem with moisture is that it leads to mold, which affects taste. British soldiers who were stationed in Singapore at the end of the nineteenth century were among the first to notice the difference and began avoiding Chinese varietals, preferring instead to drink tea from India and Ceylon.

The same thing effectively happened to the silk industry. Chinese quality began to falter as operators engaged in the sly manipulation of quality. China's reputation for silk products tanked internationally, and Japan picked up the slack. This philosophy—*if we all hold out for more, we can all benefit*—works when all of the players reside within the hermetically sealed empire economy. Once competition is introduced from without, the model effectively collapses.

CHAPTER 14

Networked Behaviors

On the way to visit a factory in Vietnam, my driver was pulled over by a pair of cops standing at the side of the freeway. From the passenger's seat, I watched as he prepared his license and registration, along with a small amount of cash. Shakedowns of this sort are common across Southeast Asia, and on motorcycle trips in places such as Cambodia, Thailand and Vietnam, I have occasionally been forced to cut a deal with a uniformed officer.

The amounts are never all that much, but they serve to remind a person that such things do not commonly occur in China. Corruption there takes other forms.

In Shantou, I was once surprised by a driver who avoided a tollbooth by riding along the shoulder of the road. "*Fubai,*" he muttered as he bypassed the gate. "This road should be free."

The local government, he insisted, was in bed with the road company, and together they took advantage of hard-working people like himself. That the tollbooth operator allowed him to pass in such a way without so much as a sneer suggested that she shared the same view.

Chinese feel corruption in their daily lives. New homebuyers have to make use of backdoor connections to find an apartment to purchase, and the bribery continues after closing. An acquaintance who bought an apartment in Shanghai was informed by the management company after finalizing the deal that the previous owner had breached code by modifying the balcony into a living room extension. For a small fee, it explained, the local inspector could be encouraged to ignore the matter. Working to outfit an office in Shanghai, a foreign company that I once worked with similarly had to decide whether to pay off fire inspectors or risk a delayed move-in date.

Chinese hospitals post notices that red-packet payments to doctors and staff are unnecessary, but the signs are merely taken as confirmation that such practices are customary. Chinese parents wishing to arrange primary education often find it necessary to make a donation to the school administrator or to a local official. Once the child is placed, parents may then want to make supplemental installments to the teacher to ensure their child receives a fair amount of attention in the classroom.

Chinese who support the campaign against *official corruption* do so not because they necessarily care that high officials are on the take. Chinese all but expect that a person in power will enjoy certain privileges. What bothers them is the sort of corruption that affects the average citizen, and feeling that they are powerless to stop corruption at the grassroots level—a truly corrosive cultural element—they have latched on to the campaign against corruption in government as a kind of proxy steam valve.

Grassroots corruption was everywhere in China in the nineteenth and early twentieth centuries. "Throughout China," wrote Alexis Krausse, "there is a custom known as squeeze, a word which signifies an unearned profit or commission wrung out of another without his knowledge or consent, and this he obtains in well-nigh every transaction recorded. Your servant who does your shopping receives a percentage of the purchase money back from the shopkeepers. That is his squeeze. He annexes a portion of well-nigh every commodity you buy for yourself. He receives a commission from your landlord on your rent, an interest from your banker on your account, and a blackmail from your tailor on the cost of the clothes you wear."

Chinese would complain of squeeze right up through the communist revolution. In her 1941 book, *China Shall Rise Again,* May-ling Soong Chiang—wife of Generalissimo Chiang Kai-shek, leader of the Nationalist army—listed it as one of her "seven deadly sins" that had set back modern China.

Westerners had an odd response to squeeze. Helpless to avoid being subjected to it, they often excused it. Harry Hussey was a well-known architect who worked professionally in China in the 1920s and 1930s. Publishing a memoir in his retirement, *My Pleasure and Palaces*, he felt compelled to defend the corrupt commercial practice: "Whenever Chinese servants are discussed the question of 'squeeze' is usually mentioned as one of the problems and objections. Many a foreign family in China has missed that smoothness in running their homes that makes life so pleasant in that country because they misunderstood this custom; they continually felt that they were being robbed in some way. Yes, we paid the squeeze. A better word would be a commission on everything that was purchased for our home, regardless of whether we or the servants made the purchase, and we paid it willingly. It is a custom of China, a good custom, and is part of the wages the Chinese servants receive for their services. In some Chinese homes this commission is all the wages they do receive; in our home we also paid a small additional salary, but I am sure that this additional amount that we did pay them was little enough for the extra trouble we foreigners caused them."

The practice of squeeze persists. Western importers will often hire someone to manage their affairs in China, and that agent may elect to arrange for under-the-table payments. The problem with such a kickback scheme, as it is more commonly referred to today, is never the lost margin but rather the way in which the acceptance of such bribes affects pricing. An individual on the take will want to steer his business to the vendor who pays best and who—more importantly—knows how to keep his mouth shut. The producer, aware that he has the commission-taker in a precarious spot, charges more than he should for his merchandise, comfortable in his knowledge that the business will not be lost anytime soon.

China expatriates who are not confronted with such behaviors prefer to remain in denial that it takes place at all. One Friday evening at The Paddy Field, an Irish-themed bar located behind the Garden Hotel in Guangzhou, I joined a number of clubby expats who were having drinks when one of them, a French trader, launched into what promised to be a juicy tale of unscrupulous behavior. I was looking forward to a good story, but a British woman standing there, sensing the conversation was moving in a certain direction, cut him off unceremoniously. "Come now," she said, before he got started. "There are good and bad people everywhere you go!"

The Frenchman appeared dejected. Though I did not know him well, I joined him away from the others to hear his tale, which turned out to be run-of-the-mill. It had been a long week, he explained, and China had put him through the wringer. He was looking to vent, and he felt bad that he had been shouted down. "You know, it's true what she said," he said, "that there are good and bad people everywhere. The problem with China is that the ratio will kill you."

In his book on evolution, *The Selfish Gene*, Richard Dawkins speaks of equilibrium in nature, and through an example of a make-believe bird population, he shows how two animals—hawks and doves—might arrive at an "evolutionarily stable strategy."

In the fictional example, which is derived from game theory, hawks are violent and doves are pacifists. The birds bump up against one another randomly, having no warning which kind they will meet until contact is established. If a dove runs into another dove, no harm is done. If a hawk enters into a scrap with another hawk, both die. If hawk meets dove, the hawk always wins. Given the strength of the hawks, their numbers tend to increase within the population, but only up to a point because they do not do well in high concentrations.

Dawkins uses the analogy to show that neither a "pure hawk" nor a "pure dove" population is evolutionarily stable. Doves might do well on their own because they do not fight, but as soon as a single hawk is introduced to the population, the percentage of hawks rises within the group. Eventually, hawks outnumber doves and the chance that two hawks will fight and kill each other becomes so high that their numbers are drawn down. Depending on the "damage points" assigned in these theoretical cases, we can determine a specific point of equilibrium for the two-bird population.

If this analogy is too esoteric, consider the example of a high-tech company that hires only nerds. A group of egghead engineers develops an amazing new product but the company has no revenues to speak of because it forgot to hire a salesperson. A fast-talking sales specialist is added and revenues rapidly climb. The board of directors gets very excited about this development and determines that it should add another salesperson. Again, sales go up. It doesn't take long before the company is directing all available resources to the sales function at the expense of the engineering effort, which sets back product development. The company learns the hard way that a sales-only strategy is not stable. Over time and with experimentation, equilibrium is ultimately established here also.

National economies are like corporations in that they also do better with an ideal mix. A place that is made up exclusively of passive, honest individuals may sound like a paradise, but we can expect that the economy tied to such a population will lack verve. By the same token, an economy made up entirely of mercenary personalities not only sounds unpleasant, we are likely to find here that growth is limited due to internecine competition.

China has always been a competitive place, and many of its inhabitants have responded to excess competition by moving away. If you are a hawk and want to do all right, you go to where there is a greater concentration of doves. Just as New Yorkers are fond of suggesting that "if you can make it there, you'll make it anywhere," Chinese figured out long ago that their pressure-cooker environment is also a good training ground for success in other markets.

In the 1930s, British journalist J. O. P. Bland remarked that all Chinese overseas communities are characterized by one incredible feature, "the economic superiority which they display per the inhabitants of the countries in which they establish themselves." Stanley High noted in the 1920s that while there were only 50,000 or so Chinese in the Philippines—around one percent of the total population—they controlled "90 percent of the retail trade." And this was taking place at a time when China itself was labeled the sick man of Asia.

My father, who immigrated to the United States from Israel in the 1960s, has been fond of pointing out a similar paradox faced by the Jews. Although they did well in countries like the United States and benefited the economy, for some reason Jews had a tough time making a go of it in their own country. He was proud of his Israeli background, but when he left some fifty years ago, it was in near disgust at the general lack of economic opportunity, and the contrast in conditions made a lasting impression on him. "The Jews are like fertilizer," he used to say to me, "Spread them thin in some part of the world, and everything grows. But put them all together in one place, and all you have is a pile of manure."

China's economy has expanded so rapidly that it is hard to imagine anyone complaining, yet excess competition is a reality. No matter what business idea you may have, you will likely find that others have beaten you to the punch in this vast pool of quick, market-savvy folks. And if you are lucky enough to find a toehold in an industry niche, you must be equally fortunate to maintain your position. Chinese are dexterous in business, and one of the reasons they display an exceptional willingness to alter their business plans—or even abandon a business altogether in favor of some other opportunity—is that they know their survival depends on such flexibility.

On the subject of ratios and bad elements, social psychologists claim not only that there are sociopaths in every society, but also that their frequency is fixed across all populations at roughly four percent. In other words, one of out every twenty-five people is said to exhibit antisocial personality traits. Whatever its actual rate of sociopathy, China is widely understood to be a more difficult place in which to do business, and my own experience in the country suggests this is due to a higher-than-average concentration of a certain bad element, but who knows? In any case, we do not need mountains of quantitative data to ask a potentially interesting qualitative question: Would we not see signs of societal strain in a population that has a higher concentration of sociopaths?

Martha Stout's book, *The Sociopath Next Door*, is filled with individual portraits. In one example, a sociopathic woman with no medical training, Doreen, convinces a psychiatric hospital that she is a licensed therapist when the woman in fact has no qualifications. Everyone in the hospital is portrayed as an innocent, and it is only through a series of accidents that they uncover the scheme and then seek to have the sociopath removed. There are other interesting examples in her book, but all cases involve a lone sociopath operating among nonsociopaths and seeking above all to avoid detection. Most books on sociopathic behavior do not cover the ways in which sociopaths coordinate among themselves.

I am particularly fond of movies that portray con artists. In a screenplay where one trickster bumps into another, we may witness an awkward hint of mutual recognition, then we watch as one attempts to chase the other off his turf. In China, where fraudsters are plentiful and boundaries are unclear, it is impractical for individuals (or groups) to make specific territorial claims. What we find instead is a tendency for parties to cooperate with one another, even in cases of great antipathy. Chinese troublemakers easily spot one another, and their first instinct in such encounters is not to chase the other party away but rather to put out a feeler: *Is this someone who might impede my plan? If not a threat, might I enlist his help? Or should I be helping him in his own scheme?*

A while back, I interviewed a candidate for a general manager's position in Shanghai. In our first meeting together, held at a restaurant, it was clearly understood that I was reaching out to him for an opportunity to take over a sizable business operation. Among other things, I wanted to know whether this was someone who could be trusted—*is this an ethical person?*—which is why I was surprised when he said the strangest thing: "Why are we going through this interviewing nonsense? What we *really* ought to do is start our own company, you and me."

In the United States, a comment like this would automatically disqualify a candidate. But in this world, where people suss out one another, a hint of monkey business serves as a kind of secret handshake. It was his way of suggesting that he was management material, because only a qualified applicant for such a senior position would know how to run away with his employer's business.

There is a danger in appearing too honest in China. A woman who receives a marriage proposal from a man might turn him down for no other reason than his artless condition. Life presents only occasional opportunities. Scrupulousness may be an honorable character trait in some places, but in this market it describes an individual incapable of guaranteeing his own survival.

More interesting than the actual incidence rate of sociopathy in the culture is the general familiarity with related kinds of behavior.

Mainlanders are honest for the most part, but this does not mean they are always innocent. Chinese do not speak of a clinical definition of sociopathy, but they know a certain breed by sight, and more importantly they know how to deal with them—by getting the hell out of their way.

When fraud takes place in a Chinese office setting, it tends not to be carried out by a lone operator but rather by a small coterie of individuals within the company. An associate in sales can create fake invoices on his own, but he needs a helping hand from someone in shipping and an assist from accounts payable. Where such a caper is pulled off in an office of eighty persons, we may find only five individuals are directly involved. But this does not mean that everyone else in the place is unaware of what has been taking place.

Like a prison block alert to which individuals may be planning an escape, Chinese workers find little value in ratting out others without cause. For one thing, the possibility of retaliation exists. For another, there are potential rewards for those who are in a position to report but do not.

I have worked with some great people over the years but not by accident. When building a team, I have interviewed as many as fifty individuals for every one hired. The process is more art than science, and sometimes I like to mix things up in order to learn more about the folks who come in for interviews. On one project, where we needed to hire dozens overnight, I asked my assistant, Lily, to bring them in three at a time.

"Isn't that going to be awkward?" she asked.

"That's the point," I told her.

Sitting across from a trio of young women who had come in for a position in merchandising, I asked the one seated in the middle what she would do if she learned that a colleague had received a commission, or a squeeze, from a supplier.

"As long as it wasn't *too* much," she said without hesitation, "I wouldn't do anything." The correct response is to report the fraud, naturally, but in the spirit of "there are no wrong answers," I kept the ball rolling.

"Let's say the kickback was two percent," I said.

"That doesn't sound like too much," she said.

I was about to tell her the margin on this imagined product was only ten percent, but before I had a chance to speak further, I spied the girl to her right rolling her eyes at this exchange about bribery. This was the thing about Shanghai in particular: Four out of five recruits would tell you point blank that it was okay to take an unreported "commission."

I glanced at Lily and could see that not only had she heard the exchange, but she had also noticed the other candidate rolling her eyes. Lily and I had worked together successfully for some time, and she knew this was the sort of thing that I appreciated in a new hire—a visible disgust toward certain practices that passed for business as usual.

Not everyone is a rotten egg, as they say in Mandarin, but the percentage of bad-faith operators is a good deal higher in this country. And they are often so well-coordinated that the average person can do nothing more than keep out of sight. There are many in China who disapprove of bad behavior, but too few are willing to do anything about it. How different this country would be, I have wondered, if only enough of them got together and rolled their eyes all at once.

In the factories, one sometimes sees evidence of coordination, though not over the issues you might expect. Line workers rarely take a break alone, but instead round up a couple of colleagues. Managers are more inclined to reprimand a worker who is on her own, so there is safety in numbers.

In the offices, workers cover for one another and go to great lengths to do so. Managing a pool of merchandisers, you might learn one morning that one of them has made a major mistake, so you ask the employee to step into your office. Just then, a colleague of hers stands up to take the blame, claiming that she is the culprit, not the girl asked to the office.

"Fine," you say to the one who has spoken up, "Let's talk about what went wrong."

Suddenly the one you originally believed was at fault is on her feet, insisting that she alone is to blame. Speaking over each other and with each claiming full responsibility for the muck-up, the manager—like a hawk confused by a flock of pigeons darting about in different directions—throws up his hands and says, "Never mind!" which was the goal of the office workers in the first place.

In a factory where there had been quality issues, I tried to nail down the problem by splitting the plant into two teams—Team One and Team Two. There were only two conveyor belts, so it seemed like a straightforward way to figure out which workers didn't know their job. When the end of the day arrived and it was time to assess performance, the workers happily announced that the scheme had been foiled, because throughout the day they had been going back and forth. They intentionally switched positions in a bid to nullify the attempt to identify incompetent performers.

Descriptions of this sort might lend the impression that Chinese teams are well-coordinated, but these are the exceptions to the rule. In fact, the default is excessive disorder. Chinese workers show a startling lack of initiative, in general, and just about the only time we see a really impressive display of organic coordination is when heads are put together in an effort to pull off some covert mission.

Chinese work environments are like an American high-school classroom: the teacher is strict, the students bored and uninspired. Should a number of them decide to relieve the tedium by engaging in some forbidden activity—note passing, for example—the participants will coordinate while taking precautions to ensure they are not caught. To effectively cover their naughtiness, those involved will feign rapt attention to the teacher's words and strict adherence to the lesson plan. Chinese managers know this all too well: When everything seems to be working *too* smoothly, that's when you need to take a closer look. The biggest frauds occur inside those offices that run like clockwork and without any apparent need for oversight.

With the emphasis Confucianism places on social hierarchy, it is no surprise that Chinese are obsessed with status. Individuals within any given social circle know the precise position each holds relative to the others, and this tiny assessment is just the beginning of mental calculations that take place. Chinese understand who is linked to whom, and if one party is indebted to another, each within the group will know the nature and the extent.

A holistic comprehension of social relationships helps individual members make optimal use of the social web. Psychology researcher Michael Harris Bond points out that within a network, if an individual (X) needs something from someone not well-known to him (Y), he can ask a contact they share in common (Z) to get involved. "He is indebted to Z in this case, who can do his collecting from Y."

"Reciprocity is an exact science," said Arthur Smith, who also pointed out that Chinese make use of a "system of social bookkeeping." Smith was not describing the art of *guanxi,* a practice most often associated with government officials (and which was not referenced in English-language texts prior to around 1980 anyway). Instead, he was commenting on the custom practiced by workaday Chinese who have no connections to power.

China's system of reciprocity is complex and is dependent on that almost unfathomable cultural feature—the ability of Chinese to accurately assess the value of any favor performed. In most instances, the value is at once understood, but at other times there may be differences of opinion. Chinese will sometimes speak of "sitting down to tea," which can be a euphemism for the elliptical chat involving the fine-tuning of an assessment.

Hollywood portrayals of criminal networks highlight cultural differences. Chinese are made curious by American silver-screen gangsters who work out all of the details of a transaction in advance, and who speak of "taking ten percent off the top" or becoming "fifty-fifty partners"—before any of the work has begun.

The bank heist gone bad is a motion picture cliché that further confounds the Chinese. Fade in as a group of five discusses its plan to rob a bank. Listen as they happily agree to split the haul into equal portions. And watch as they express feelings of inequity almost immediately upon having pulled off the job. The haul being not quite what anyone expected, the safe cracker grumbles that he ought to receive a bigger share than the lookout. Or perhaps the getaway driver, who has taken a bullet, thinks he has a case for a bigger cut. The end result in this hackneyed scene is that, incapable of making adjustments that minimize hard feelings, gang members begin shooting one another dead. Chinese teams are more flexible than this.

The inherent problem in the bank heist—in any project, really—is that circumstances change over time. Things look different coming out than they did going in. Chinese partnerships appear to us to be far better coordinated because often they are. Chinese do not so easily constrain themselves to the initial terms of a deal, and they show a willingness to reevaluate at any point along the way. This is not to say that those who are in a position of power do not still take advantage of whatever leverage they hold. But, all else being equal, participants have a higher expectation that their contribution will be rewarded in a more or less accurate way on a flexible scale that is subject to adjustments.

There are sectors in which manufacturing agents can reasonably expect to earn a predictable commission. Factories within a certain sector may, for example, gladly pay a three-percent fee to any sales agent who brings in a customer. It is a mere rule of thumb. An agent may argue that because his client is particularly loyal to him, he has cause for a four-percent commission instead. If in the course of closing the deal the factory boss sees that this is in fact the case, he may easily agree to four percent. If, on the other hand, it is discovered that the buyer dislikes the agent, resents his involvement, and wishes to never see him again—because, perhaps, he prefers to "go direct"—the agent may remove himself from the deal, while quietly collecting two percent.

American lawyers have a preference for detailed partnership agreements. Even when the partnership is between good friends—or especially when the parties are personally close—attorneys will argue for an insane level of detail because in their experience, "even the best partnerships have a way of unraveling."

The problem with working out all issues up front is that one can never account for every eventuality. Something is likely to be left out, and if a relationship sours, the thing that is missing from the contract is likely that which ends up sinking the deal. All things being equal, a person is better off working with trusted individuals and especially with those who have the capacity for constant flexibility. The ability of the Chinese to accurately assess the value of a person's contribution—combined with a confident faith that decision makers will act upon this information—opens up endless opportunities.

Chinese manufacturing representative do not have to go to a factory and get the boss to sign a piece of paper stipulating how much shall be earned if a customer is brought to the business. All of that gets worked out later. Sales agents will spend months developing new business, unsure quite often who will pay them their commission. To the uninitiated, it appears like a huge gamble. But in this world where value is assessed and compensated at unwritten though reliably predictable rates, it represents a very small gamble indeed.

Americans have a hard time wrapping their heads around a culture that can handle such levels of informalism. And because we cannot imagine such a model, we misunderstand reports that suggest, for example, that as many as 500,000 mainland Chinese are actively employed by the Communist Party to generate propaganda on social media. It is unreasonable to believe that such a large number of people would receive a regular stipend from the government. But it *is* believable that large numbers are performing such activities "on spec." Chinese youths with time on their hands especially have no problem sinking untold hours into a project where compensation is not guaranteed but which is based on an assessment of impact in the not-too-distant future.

We know from commercial espionage cases made public that those who sell sensitive information are not often sent on a mission to a specific target. Instead, these operators first go looking for something of value. Then, once they have found it, they shop for a buyer.

In his book *Tiger Trap*, journalist David Wise describes a spying technique he refers to as the "thousand grains of sand." Mainland Chinese in the United States who cooperate with the Communist Party back home are not sent to seek specific information. Rather, they are tasked with going about their business and bringing back the smallest, most insignificant details. Beijing figures that it can put together a meaningful picture with great volumes of minutae, a curious strategy that would seem to make sense. The challenge in such an approach is how to motivate so many thousands to collect such information.

Chinese are not ideological, and by extension they are not necessarily nationalistic. But this one feature of the culture—the ability to accurately assess the value of group participation—provides motivation to the unlikeliest of players. Cash may be received for a tidbit of information or reward may come in the form of clout. Where individuals feel confident that a favor will be reciprocated, they will invest more of their personal time, they will accept a longer-term investment, and they will take greater risks.

CHAPTER 15

Partner on the Deal

Although it has a reputation for being a difficult country in which to do business, China has always given visitors the impression that it is otherwise safe. In the nineteenth century, a time when buildings were not secured, Herbert Giles noted with some fascination that foreigners who went on vacation could expect to return and find everything right where it had been left.

Stanley High, writing in the 1920s, described a long journey from Chongqing to Tibet, in which he employed no fewer than seventy-five coolie laborers. To finance the camel-driven caravan, he secured several hundred dollars in silver and packed it away. Each one of the laborers, he figured, knew precisely where he had stashed the money. And yet this small fortune, an amount "sufficient to provide a lifelong endowment for any half dozen of them," remained untouched.

I have lost two mobile phones in China and was lucky enough in each case to have the handheld brought back to me. All I had to do was ring my number and speak to the kindly fellow who was in possession of it. Of course the person who answered the phone was never the one who had actually found it, but he was nevertheless glad to assist. All we had to do was discuss the small matter of his travel expenses, because *somehow*—within a matter of minutes—the device had wound up in a distant town, and surely I would insist on personal delivery.

Scamps of this variety typically ask for only a fraction of the replacement cost but more than they could get selling it on the black market, and thus it is economically expedient to follow their lead. In such cases, you were inclined to resent the extortion until you had a phone stolen in some other place—as I did in Vietnam—and found that the thief had turned it off and thrown away the module chip, making it impossible to negotiate the device's return at any price.

Because there is greater economic efficiency in returning a lost item to its owner, we are not surprised to learn that this is yet another old tradition. In this country, noted Giles, "Many cases of theft are compromised by the stolen property being restored to its owner on payment of a certain sum, which is fixed and shared in by the native constable who acts as middleman between the two parties."

China is home to a better class of criminal, I believe. Property crime is more humane and less violent. Purse snatchers, for example, often take care to drop the purse in their wake for the original owner to more easily recover—*sans* its monetary contents, of course.

In Guangzhou, I know a man who had his computer stolen while sitting at a Starbucks. He didn't mind the loss of his laptop, he said, but in his computer bag were some irreplaceable business documents. In this city of millions, the police somehow managed to recover his bag, along with the papers, though naturally the computer was still missing.

The dropped purse is a risk-reducing move calculated instinctively by perpetrators. A victim, glad to recover some part of what she has lost, may be made so happy by the seemingly altruistic gesture that she decides to call off any attempt to chase after the thieves. And if the perpetrators are caught, there is always the chance that the police or a judge will interpret the gesture as a sign of good-naturedness and pass down a more lenient punishment. Criminals who give back some meaningful portion are somehow seen as less bad, so it may pay for them to make that small effort.

Chinese in business sometimes make a similar gesture of consolation to those they have managed to outsmart. Rodney Gilbert hints at one point that "a successful looter" is sometimes made to feel "obliged through a consciousness of his own weakness to placate the looted by the restitution of some portion of the spoils." It may be hard for some foreigners to imagine, but quite a number of the banquets held across

China are actually about honoring someone who has just been given the shaft. Some of the greatest efforts to create face in a business context are made by those who have intentionally or accidentally caused another party to lose face.

Foreigners are less often treated to such consolation prizes, though the instinct is still there. An American importer that I worked with had taken a serious drubbing at the hands of his supplier and walked away with a contract that left him with almost no profit. The factory boss himself insisted that he was not earning anything either—though a conciliatory gesture he made suggested otherwise.

As we left the factory, I watched the factory man as he draped an arm around the shoulders of his dejected buyer. Holding an open umbrella high above his head as we crossed the parking lot, he said to him: "You must take care not to get wet." Looking up, I noticed that though it was a bit cloudy, there was no real sign of rain.

In China, there is no finality to any bargaining process, and this particular gesture was a hint, that the buyer should have removed the hand from his shoulder and told the seller that they needed to return to the negotiating table to rehash the terms of the deal.

During the time that I lived in Guangzhou, a story circulated around the foreign community involving a well-liked American who had gone into business with his Chinese girlfriend. Using the excuse that their customers insisted on working with her alone, the woman managed to take the business away from him entirely. Having lost both the business and the girl, he naturally went into a depression, but the part of the story that gave it legs was that she had invited the poor guy—now her ex—on an all-expenses-paid trip to Europe.

The American sporting goods company that had been ripped off by its mainland employee in the amount of one million dollars was able—after applying some pressure—to recoup a small portion of its economic loss. The Americans got fifteen percent of their money back from the con artist and called it a settlement, but the cash recovery was really nothing more than that small amount returned by a thief in an effort to ameliorate hard feelings. The fact that the Americans actually celebrated their "victory" at the end went toward proving that the bandit's token gesture had its intended effect.

At the Elephant & Castle pool-and-darts pub in Guangzhou, an American importer named Jerry told me a story about a plywood deal.

After placing a deposit with a known supplier, he waited the requisite six weeks before ringing the factory to arrange the shipping container. There was a small problem, the factory told him. The goods had been prepared and were sitting in the warehouse when another buyer saw the wood and asked if he could pay cash and take immediate possession.

"You understand, it was my wood," Jerry said. "They sold my wood to this other guy, and I had to wait *another six weeks* to get my order filled."

Jerry said he would not have minded, but his customer was so irate about the delay that he almost lost his business.

"Sounds terrible," I said to him.

"It's all right," he said. "The factory was so happy with how much they were able to get from the other buyer that they offered me a five percent commission."

"A five percent commission? — On your own wood? — That they sold to someone else?"

"That's China for you," he said. "They screw you and then bring you in as a partner on the deal."

CHAPTER 16

Self-Regulating Empire

Not long ago, I saw something in Shanghai I had never seen before in China: a police officer issuing a traffic ticket. The nation's reputation for totalitarianism leads many outsiders to suspect there is a cop on every street corner, but this is hardly the case. China has police, of course, but they are not often visible in an obvious way. Part of the reason for their limited numbers is that the Chinese are a civil people who require little direct supervision.

In the 1920s, a period characterized by political disintegration, Richard Wilhelm noted the irony. "Practically nothing is forbidden," he said. "Here you may do almost anything, and yet everything proceeds quietly and in an orderly fashion."

One of the keys to social harmony in the empire has historically been the *pao-chia* system of shared responsibility, whereby not only criminals were punished, but potentially also the perpetrator's family, neighbors, and associates. The incentive is obvious: If you knew someone considering a felony, you would stop the individual before he had the chance to get you into trouble.

"The *pao-chia* system guaranteed good behavior by making everyone accountable to everyone else," wrote British sinologist Arthur Waley in the 1950s. "It is far from just, and yet at the same time we can admire the system for its great efficiency!"

In the villages, irrigation works required group cooperation, and as a result of so many "relatively self-sufficient contiguous local cells," China became something of an empire on autopilot. Throughout history, villages managed their own affairs, and the imperial government rarely got involved in matters below the county level.

China was a self-governing empire that required little administrative oversight. In the Ming dynasty, according to Lucian Pye, "as few as 100,000 officials managed an empire of 100 million people, and a single magistrate was responsible for a county population of about 50,000." In his 1930s book, *The Tinder Box of Asia*, George Sokolsky suggested that it was the people who demanded such a setup: "Chinese dislike governments and are unaccustomed to them. They prefer a loose system under which family groups police themselves with little more to guide them than a racial and ethical tradition and individual sense of decency." The people's reliance on social networks and intermediaries further made such an informal world possible.

When the Manchu invaded China in the seventeenth century, they had a relatively easy time taking over the country. This should not have been the case because the Manchu were foreigners, few in number, and looked down upon as barbarians. They were a separate people with a different culture and their own language, which made use of an alphabet instead of ideographic characters.

In his 1917 book *The Fight for the Republic in China*, Putnam Weale explained how the Manchu ruled through a dual control system, which "beginning on the Grand Council and in the various great Boards and Departments in the capital, proceeded as far as the provincial chief cities, but stopped short there so completely and absolutely that the huge chains of villages and burgs had their historic autonomy virtually untouched and lived on as they had always lived."

One reason the imperial government did not bother with the burgs was that it was too much trouble. Chinese officials have long preferred arrangements that produce maximum return for minimal effort. Managing the affairs of each village would have proven too much, and as the remote districts were generally quite poor anyway, there was little to be gained in the way of tax receipts.

Scholar-officials sent to administer the poorer corners of the Flowery Kingdom did not receive a stipend from the central government but instead were expected to raise their own means of support. Historians suggest this was most easily done by finding sponsors among the landed wealthy. Revenue was also derived from taxation of the peasantry, but that move came with no small amount of risk. "Officials had to render to Caesar what was Caesar's," suggested history professor Helmut Callis, "but they had to be careful at the same time not to 'squeeze' the people to the point where they would rise in open revolt."

Sun Yat-sen once proposed raising revenue by taxing private property. The challenge was how to assess land values. Training an army of appraisers was not only impractical but also presented an opportunity for corruption as landholders might find it in their best interest to bribe anyone sent to evaluate land holdings. In an interesting twist, Sun proposed that each family assess its own property—and that the government would retain the right to purchase any piece of land at the self-appraised value. How a cash-strapped government was going to exercise such a right was not addressed in his impractical proposal, but in any case, this demonstrates the extent to which the Chinese favor systems that are autonomous and self-regulating.

The concept of self-regulation has a meaningful analogy at the corporate level and has important implications for management. Western companies that open an office in China usually put someone in charge, and in such cases where they do not, the local workers will select a leader from among their number. Whatever hierarchy is established within such an office, the team is not likely to offer too many details about the setup to its foreign managers. In most cases, the foreigners could not care less anyway. This approach is taken at their peril. Cohesion among a workforce can be beneficial but rarely in a leadership vacuum and never in a place where workers put their interests ahead of the company's.

"My staff is great," the foreign buyer says, referring to the twelve-person office that he manages from half a world away. If you buttonhole this man and ask him how he keeps control of an office through only telephone and e-mail, he will tell you it is because of the *relationship* that he has formed with his employees. They barely know him—and he knows them even less—yet he is convinced that his people do right by him because he is well liked.

As happy as he appears to be about his office in China, you would think that it is a major profit center for him. But in actuality these offices do little more than break even, with upside only barely covering costs. No matter the setup, these China-based concerns are almost always a wash.

It does not matter what the on-the-ground staff are specifically tasked with, the results are the same—even when circumstances vary over time. In the case of a buying office, as export volumes rise, the office conspires to find ways of increasing expenditures by corresponding amounts. The local workers will insist that they need a larger office space and more bodies, even though the only thing that has changed is the number of units ordered. The foreign boss is inclined to grow suspicious, seeing that expenses climb in lockstep with increases in business volume, but this is not where we generally find a smoking gun. The more interesting revelations take place during a downturn. When the foreigner announces that he is considering closing down his China office because it no longer seems worth operating, his own staff will suddenly discover numerous cost-saving measures. Some among the team will proactively fire themselves and prices at key suppliers will suddenly soften, as if by magic.

A Chinese office operates like an autonomous village and the foreign boss is viewed as an aloof government official who lives far away and visits only when necessary. The local office goes to great lengths to create the impression that everything is functioning so normally and independently that there is really no need for any central oversight at all. When workers conspire to leech profitability from a company, they will want to keep the home office ignorant and uninterested. The key to doing this is to make sure that the office sits right at break even year after year.

I am often surprised by how little foreigners know about what goes on in their China-based offices. In one case, though every single local worker in a thirty-person buying office was aware that the general manager was romantically linked to the office manager, the Americans remained clueless. Such key alliances among senior staff must be recognized as red flags because such a consolidation of power within a work setting increases opportunities for malfeasance.

Workers who wonder whether they can engage in shady activities tend to be emboldened by lax oversight. As the saying goes, "The hills are high and the emperor is far away." The foreign boss who is not curious about what takes place in his local office has been lulled into a false sense of security, because the place seems to be doing all right without his direct involvement. The trouble is that such aloofness is taken as a tacit green light.

There are a hundred ways to siphon profits from a stable venture, and one of the more common is the kickback. In a joint venture scenario, the local partner can get away with it by inflating raw material costs. Alternatively, he can create phantom employees, make up tax receipts, or falsify utility bills.

Speaking with the local fixer for a high-profile Silicon Valley startup, I was not surprised to hear that the human resources manager in their Shanghai office was suspected of hiring only applicants who would slip her money under the table—easily negotiated because the jobs were high-paying. Meanwhile, the American told me, the manager in charge of procurement made sure that not a stick of furniture or piece of electronic equipment came into the office without his first receiving baksheesh.

American companies rarely care about a business unit in China that merely breaks even. Just as the ancient emperors were content to leave be the empire's thousands of smaller villages, China-based operations that are performing unspectacularly are accepted by foreigners just so long as they appear to run smoothly.

One of the least understood—and most important—aspects of Chinese history is eunuchism. The common understanding is that eunuchs were used primarily to guard the emperor's harem, because a male without genitals was presumed to be no sexual threat. Although this may have been their original purpose early in imperial history, over time the eunuchs became a necessary component of a properly functioning empire.

During the Ming dynasty, eunuchs oversaw key agricultural programs. They supervised tax collection, they were ambassadors, they served as commanders and navy admirals. They were in positions of authority across the empire, and their number exploded during the period. At the dynasty's start in 1368, there were only one hundred eunuchs serving. Over the next century and a half, the figure would swell to ten thousand. By the end of the dynasty in 1644, there were as many as one hundred thousand.

In his excellent history *The Eunuchs in the Ming Dynasty*, Shih-shan Henry Tsai points out that the number of eunuchs grew in lockstep with the size of the royal family, which also started with around one hundred members in the fourteenth century and which expanded to more than eighty thousand by the end of the dynasty. Tsai argues that the eunuchs' primary role during this time was to serve as a check against the royals, who were seen as duplicitous and scheming. Without any hereditary claim to legitimacy, eunuchs had to work harder to prove their loyalty, and they were often counted on for alerting high imperial officials of any plots to undermine the emperor. Yet again, we see an autonomous system at the core of a cultural dynamic.

China's most famous eunuch was Zheng He, the admiral whose naval campaign brought the Middle Kingdom to Africa and the Middle East. Some have suggested that Zheng's successes were the reason behind the dismantling of eunuchism. But Zheng sailed in the early fifteenth century, in the run-up to peak eunuchism. The decision to bring down the eunuch population came only at the beginning of the Qing dynasty, two hundred years after Zheng returned home from his sea voyages.

Qing dynasty officials began reducing the number of eunuchs in the empire from the very beginning of their rule, thereby disrupting an important equilibrium. China thereafter lacked an important check against imperial corruption. More important, with ambitious eunuchs no longer around competing for power, Qing dynasty officials had less need to prove their competence. Absent the threat of competition at home, and with no apparent competition from abroad, leadership in the empire atrophied.

China is a vase teetering on its edge, and maintaining balance has been a goal throughout its history. The communist era has been no exception. At its founding in 1949, the People's Republic of China comprised six administrative regions, each managing its own political and military network. Worried that this setup might lead to independent fiefdoms, Mao Zedong sought to bring power back to the center. By 1954, the new regime had consolidated power with decision-making centralized in Beijing. This new model proved inefficient, however, so power shifted again. In 1956 another campaign for local autonomy began, which was followed by yet another wave of centralization that carried the nation through the Cultural Revolution.

Starting in the 1980s Beijing switched back to decentralization, encouraging the provinces and special administrative regions to find growth, each in its own way. At the local level, officials were granted unprecedented latitude, resulting in breakneck economic expansion. No one complained about disparate growth rates as long as economic activity was up overall.

But two decades later, starting with the economic crisis of 2008, when the economy inevitably showed signs of a slowdown, there was another push toward centralization. This made sense because during this period of lower growth rates, some regional economies actually shrank. Only a centralized approach guarantees that resources from better-off regions will be distributed to troubled areas.

China watchers currently worry that the more recent shift towards centralization portends an increase in draconian control. As much as this appears to be the case, we can rest assured that as the inefficiencies caused by concentrated power increase, pressure will mount for yet another wave of decentralization. China is under normal circumstances a nation striving for balance, and as such, it is always a mistake to see short-term moves as a march in one direction only.

Chinese have a natural distrust of markets. In the early 1700s, the first commercial trades the British made with China went through a single broker known as "the emperor's merchant," an agent who paid the imperial court a significant amount for the right to operate the monopoly. Although this was an effective way to control commerce, the emperor opted a few decades later to create a new model whereby a select handful of Chinese merchants would control trade with the outside world. This small collective known as the Cohong—the setup being also referred to as the Canton System—would run business for the empire through the middle of the 1800s.

There were no more than about ten Cohong members at any given time, and by keeping an eye on one another the emperor was assured to get his percentage of duties collected. The members helped one another with liquidity issues, and together they also prevented piracy and smuggling. Western merchants preferred the Canton System to having a single monopolist because it lent the impression of choice, but in the end they would view it too as overly restrictive.

At the conclusion of the Arrow War—also known as the Second Opium War—England captured Canton and, along with it, the leading statesman of the region, a fat and sallow viceroy by the name of Yeh Mingchen. British journalist George Wingrove Cooke sailed with Yeh to Calcutta and along the way they had many earnest conversations, which Cooke recorded for his readers.

Cooke describes lengthy interviews and even claims to have debated the old viceroy. At one point, Cooke argued that trade with England had benefitted China, pointing out that the Shanghai custom house "pays annually two and a half millions of *taels* to the imperial treasure." In response, Yeh remarked that the emperor was "not wanting in money," but then agreed that there was certainly no harm that he had received such sums. When Cooke made the case that additional ports ought then to be opened, Yeh disagreed, arguing that "the opening of the four ports had increased competition, and competition disarranges all things."

Nineteenth-century foreigners in China who employed domestic workers learned that it was counterproductive to manage a team of local household staff. Almost universally they instead appointed a majordomo or comprador. Although the manager of a household might cheat his employer with abandon, suggested Cooke, he made sure at least that no one else was doing it. Herbert Giles pointed out in 1876 that protection money was occasionally paid to a gang to "abstain from pilfering," while making sure to prevent others from doing the same. Western writers of the 1920s noted the same sort of protection on offer. While chaos reigned in the warlord years, it was common for a single group of armed individuals, paid by a wealthy patron, to rise up and create a semblance of social order within a locality.

Writing in the 1930s, Nathaniel Peffer noted that the granting of monopoly rights was a strategy that had the advantage of limiting counterfeiting, a problem that has plagued China across time. One of the great benefits of concentrating commercial activity is that, in the event of trouble, one knows precisely where to point a finger. Chinese authorities who wished to stamp out counterfeiting often did so by granting monopoly rights to license holders, who would then have both the motivation and the authority to go after offenders.

Today, we may find similar examples in commerce. When the Chinese company Ninebot decided to purchase Segway, few had any idea why it would bother. The proprietary technology that Segway developed had already been hacked, and there were dozens of copycat companies in China producing similar two-wheeled, self-balancing vehicles. The domestic market was flooded with them, and they were being exported abroad in great quantities. In buying the rights to the technology, Ninebot was effectively nominating itself as the mob force that would clean up a market in disarray—"one gang to rule them all." The only difference in this case was that mafia-style pressure was applied not through violence, but rather through lawsuits.

CHAPTER 17

Corps de Ballet

One should never give a clock as a present, it is said, because *song zhong*, the act of gifting a clock, is a memento mori, or a symbol of death. The Chinese superstition is of fairly recent vintage, however, and we know this because it was never referenced as an explanation for the failure of England's first trade mission to the country in 1793.

Lord George Macartney, His Majesty's envoy to the Middle Kingdom, carried with him more than 600 bundles of presents on the maiden voyage, and a great deal has been written about several custom-made clocks that were presented to the emperor. In his famous letter to King George the Third at the conclusion of the diplomatic event, the Qianlong emperor dismissed the British and what they had to offer: "We have never valued ingenious articles, nor do we have the slightest need of your country's manufactures." Many believe the reference here is to the clocks, which were presumably brought as evidence of England's technological advancement.

Although chronometry was not exactly prevalent in eighteenth-century China, it would be wrong to conclude that a modern clock had never before been seen in the Forbidden City. Macartney noted that members of his mission caught sight of several *sing-songs* (as musical clocks were called then) in the emperor's pavilions.

Of all the gifts that Macartney brought, the one that he placed the greatest emphasis on was an automatic planetarium, which Chinese translators at the time incorrectly listed as a musical clock. Used to intricately depict the revolutions of the planets of the solar system and many of its moons, the planetarium—also known as an *orrery*—was a relatively new device in Europe. Although the device would have been unfamiliar to the Chinese emperor, it was not meant as a showy display of British technology per se because the Hahn Weltmaschine (as the great orrery was specifically called) was actually made in Germany. Many of the items that Macartney brought with him were not even procured in Europe. On their way to Peking, Macartney made stops in Macau and Canton, purchasing other astronomical instruments, including a Herschel reflector, a telescope, and another planetarium.

British historian Maxine Berg has pointed out that if the intention had been to make a show of British technological advancement, the Macartney mission might have brought along a steam engine. The industrial revolution was just then moving into high gear, and the newfangled machines were harbingers of economic change. In fact, Macartney considered transporting one to China, but ultimately rejected the plan: "Having conversed with several intelligent persons who have been in China & having considered the size of the machine, the difficulty of showing it & other circumstances attending it, the idea of carrying one aboard with us is now given up & some other articles are to be substituted in its place."

In his book *Chinese Rules*, Tim Clissold suggests that the planetariums were given as gifts in order to demonstrate "Europe's achievements in combining an understanding of the motion of celestial bodies—including the four moons of Jupiter—with the latest in precision engineering." Clissold falls in with many historians in this misunderstanding of the orreries, which were not about technology and technique, but were rather about philosophy.

The Enlightenment was in full swing when Macartney sailed to China, and European thinkers were intoxicated by certain ideas that had been developed in eighteenth-century Europe, one of which was the notion that science and logic ought to supplant blind faith. Along the way, thinkers such as René Descartes, Gottfried Leibniz, Benedict de Spinoza and Immanuel Kant came close to rejecting traditional religion. In his book *The Age of Reason*, published while Macartney was on his mission to China, Thomas Paine argued that Christianity had become for him something like atheism, because it emphasized the part of the redeemer while diminishing the role of the creator. Europe was swept up by Deism, a philosophical precept which held that, while God was responsible for the magnificence of the universe, he had not remained actively involved beyond its creation.

David Wootton, professor of intellectual history at the University of London, has written extensively on the invention of mechanical devices and philosophy. The first machines ever built—in the seventeenth century—had an almost religious aura about them, he explains. "In all the early usages the standard example of a machine or automaton was a clock, and like clocks before them, machines and automata soon became powerful metaphors for thinking of God as a clockmaker and the universe as a giant clock."

When traveling great distances and hoping to encounter important strangers, you take with you the best of what you have. In 1977, when the United States launched Voyager 1 into deep space, we made sure to include a *golden record* filled with mathematical equations and suggestions of scientific advances. The record also included a fair amount of music written by Baroque and Classical composers, including Bach, Beethoven, and Mozart. We even added a sample of rock 'n' roll by Chuck Berry. The message Americans wished to convey was essentially: *Look, this is how far we have come, and we would like to share it with you.* Macartney and his team were doing something similar when they presented their great planetarium.

Enlightenment figures took their way of thinking about machines and ultimately applied it to systems. "A machine is a little system," wrote Adam Smith in one of his essays on astronomy, "created to perform, as well as to connect together, in reality, those different movements and effects which the artist has occasion for. A system is an imaginary machine invented to connect together in the fancy those different movements and effects which are already in reality performed."

Our modern concept of government—the system of checks and balances—is derived from such notions. It came out of the

Enlightenment anyway, and it is quite likely that Macartney had such a system in mind when facing the prospect of meeting a government known to be highly reactionary. Britain had just watched the Americans create their own people-led government and was starting to believe itself that a reliance on monarchs was outmoded. Europe was, during this time, dreaming of ways to automate government so that it resembled a machine of sorts.

"A government is a mere piece of clockwork," wrote John Trenchard, the English writer and politician, "and having such springs and wheels, must act after such a manner." In a republic, the interests of the governed should be aligned with those governing, he wrote, with everything made automatic, so "a rogue will as naturally be hanged as a clock strikes twelve when the hour has come."

China's government had its systems, but what kept the empire in a state of equilibrium was most often of an informal nature. China watchers are fond of addressing the matter of why China failed to develop its own Industrial Revolution—they call this the Needham Question—but a more pointed query might address why China did not experience its own Scientific Revolution, or its own Age of Reason.

The British were not looking down their noses when they showed the emperor their great planetarium. They were simply inspired by ideas and wanted to share them. If they made an error in judgment, it was in presuming that the imperial authorities would be receptive to sharing in these new thoughts and revelations from Europe.

If the above explains Macartney's intentions, then what are we to make of the Qianlong emperor's insulting letter to George the Third? The British did not appear to be bragging about their technological superiority, and the point of philosophy seems to have been missed. The emperor sounded clearly displeased in his letter, and there was maybe even a hint that he was shaken by his encounter with the British. The subtext of his message was in any case clear: *Don't call us, we'll call you.*

A great deal of planning and negotiating had taken place in the run-up to the historic voyage to China, and the British took great pains to bring the planetarium disassembled in several crates. This was a delicate instrument that could be assembled only with the assistance of technical specialists, so Macartney brought numerous craftsmen along on the mission. Professor Berg suggests that the British regarded the skills of these artisans to be particularly unique and that negotiating their inclusion became "an issue of contention with the Chinese officials once they arrived."

While the specialized craftsmen from England busied themselves with the assembly of the great Hahn Weltmaschine, China's Grand Council did something strange: It issued a notification summoning any foreigners with skills in clock repairing who might be residing within the empire. Berg has taken this edict as evidence that there must have been more missionaries in China at the time than previously believed. A more likely interpretation is that the emperor was somehow made desperate to cover a perceived loss of face caused by the spectacle of tradesmen working together so skillfully. China was not accustomed to this sort of group dynamic, which must have appeared like an assembly line, or some corps de ballet.

China as a society was traditionally atomized with social emphasis placed on the family unit. This other social institution—the modern work team marshaled together on the basis of skill and not on family—revealed a national deficiency so raw that the imperial authorities did not even bother trying to suggest that they had any Chinese who could do the job. Instead they concocted a face-recovering story about having the right sort of foreign inhabitants who could handle it.

No one knows where the presumed foreigners came from or how missionaries hanging around China just happened also to have clock-making skills. In any case, in a note to Macartney, written while he was still in China, the emperor rebuked: "Now that the tribute Envoy has seen that there are also people in the Celestial Empire who are versed in astronomy, geography and clock-repairing, and are now helping alongside those who are setting up the articles, he can no longer boast that he alone has got the secret."

China understood that it was lagging behind the West technologically and that it did not produce the kinds of merchandise commonplace in foreign lands. These points did not bother the Chinese. What struck a chord was that they might be missing something far more abstruse and social in nature.

CHAPTER 18

Informal Paradox

One morning many years ago, having just arrived as a student at Beijing Language and Culture University, I decided to catch breakfast off campus. Passing through the gate at the western edge of the school, I turned the corner and almost tripped over an obese woman who was sitting cross-legged on the pavement selling cartons of cigarettes from a dirty burlap sack.

As I passed by, she called out in a flat drawl: "*Ni qu nar?*"

She wanted to know where I was going, and thinking it was none of her business, I ignored her.

The next morning, when she asked me the same question, I was somewhat less surprised and figured that she must be either mad or mentally handicapped. On the third morning, I felt this had gone on long enough.

"*Ni qu narrrrr?*" she droned, placing emphasis on the retroflex common to Beijingers.

"I'm going to buy a steamed bun," I told her.

Surprised that I had responded perhaps, she stared at me in a vacant way, blinked, and then asked when I would be coming back.

"*Ni shenme shi hou hui lai?*"

In Beijing the following summer, this time as a tourist, I stopped by the university and discovered that sweeping changes had been made to the area around the school. The shops just off campus had been torn down, the vendors forced to take up space along a narrow commercial strip set up on university property. I passed the spot where the woman on the pavement had been, and seeing that she was gone, I felt a small pang of sadness. She must have been removed in the effort to clean up the neighborhood, I thought.

I glanced over at the line of new kiosks, and from one of the tables emerged a familiar face—it was the same woman. Someone had given her retail space! She was still hawking cigarettes, but her goods were set up on a table, and she was now seated in a chair. She did not call out to me this time, but only raised her hand in an awkward gesture. Thinking that she might have actually recognized me, I waved back.

It was fascinating to see this woman made whole, and I wondered whether some local official had done this because it was easier than chasing her off. If she had not been given the role of cigarette vendor, someone else surely would have taken the position. Had she been placed there because she was a known quantity?

Chinese factory bosses quite often come from similar origins. Once operating informally in some corner of the economy, they were invited to go legitimate by someone in government. There weren't too many of them, but every once in a while I have found myself working with this sort. The way they spoke, their mannerisms, their drinking habits, and hints of tattoo work all combined to reveal former lives as gangsters.

Living in China, I was curious about other signs of informalism in the economy. On my way to the airport, I stopped at a hotel to pick up a copy of the *South China Morning Post*. On this particular afternoon, for some reason, the entire front section of the newspaper was missing. The clerk had no idea why there should be no leading news in the newspaper. But at my destination, the reason became clear.

After arriving in the city of Shantou and checking into my hotel, I noticed that the lobby gift shop had the same newspaper on sale—only this time intact. The front page was dedicated to a sensitive bit of news, the death of former leading politician Zhao Ziyang. This was all anyone needed to know to understand why the lead story had been excised in Guangzhou.

While general secretary of the Central Committee in 1989, Zhao had called on colleagues to listen to the students in Tiananmen Square and treat them with compassion, and his soft stance as a reformer would eventually make him *persona non sinica*. I could see why some official in Guangzhou thought the news needed adjusting, but why hadn't officials in this other city arrived at the same conclusion?

Western concepts of communist authoritarianism—codified in the Cold War and inspired by fiction—have led many to conclude that the Chinese government is a well-oiled machine and that officials are omniscient. But quite the opposite is true. A great deal of speculation takes place, since top officials do not provide guidance on how to behave in every possible situation. Informalism of this kind has its advantages: Not needing explicit instructions means that individuals can act faster and more effectively. The downside of such a setup is that the right hand does not exactly know what the left hand is doing.

Chinese informalism has saved me on more than one occasion. I once had to go to the US Consulate in Hong Kong to get a new passport. Upon reentering China, I inadvertently handed the older passport to the immigration officer in Guangzhou, who did not notice it had expired—in spite of the punched holes—and stamped it, allowing me entry into the country. A week later, carrying only my new passport, I ran into trouble.

"How did you get into China?" the immigration officer asked me as she thumbed through the pages of my passport, which were completely blank.

In a flash, I saw my day going right down the toilet. China does not take border control lightly, and any suggestion of illegality at immigration typically means a lengthy interview with officials. Standing in front of this stern-looking officer, I stammered out an explanation, careful to hint that it was not me who had made the mistake but one of her colleagues. If she would just let me exit the country, I offered, this sort of thing would never happen again.

It was a long shot, and such a breathless explanation should not have had any impact at all, but she grasped the situation at once and saw her own day potentially ruined. Or maybe she worried what might happen if she embarrassed her entire department. Her eyes were hooded and she appeared tired. She considered me for the briefest moment, meaninglessly gave the passport one last flip, looked to her left, then up ahead, then down again at the booklet. Without a word, she discretely stamped the passport and slid it back to me.

In a similar way, I was once saved in Beijing. At the start of my studies there, I opened a bank account using not my birth name but my Chinese name. The clerk who processed the paperwork for the new account had asked if I had a local name and appeared relieved when I told her that in fact I did. Two weeks after setting up the account, I walked back into the same branch to make a withdrawal only to hear the teller on duty ask, "Who the hell is Meng Tian?"

The Chinese name in my bank-issued passbook bore no relationship to the English name printed in my American passport. After explaining the mix-up, I was sent to the branch manager, who said she could fix the error, but that it would take three weeks.

Three weeks? I didn't have three days!

I explained to the manager that I had no other access to money and that my hotel was insisting on a cash payment. An hour of pleading later, the manager suggested that she might be able to pull a few strings and get the matter resolved within a week. It was better than three, but still was not quick enough. After more polite begging and just before the bank closed for the day, the manager suddenly presented me with a stack of papers and showed me where to sign. Access to my account, she said, would be restored in the morning.

Relieved that the matter had been resolved, I was effusive in my praise, but also felt a burden of responsibility. On my way out, I suggested to the manager that she ought to let colleagues know what had happened. I was thinking about others who might similarly get caught in such a jam. Although this sort of gesture is a welcome sign of thoughtfulness in the West, the manager took my comment as a slap in the face.

"We solved your problem for you, didn't we?" she said.

Chinese informalism produces errors, but that same loose system also enables well-intentioned individuals to fix problems using personal power. It also creates opportunities for gaining face. The manager was proud that she was able to manipulate the system in such a way as to make an exception for me, and my way of thanking her was to request tightening up the system to make such maneuverability impossible? This attitude is precisely why Chinese have traditionally viewed foreigners as savages.

Americans are in the habit of making improvements to systems. When errors are discovered, we like to address the matter of how such an error occurred in the first place. You can solve the problem of a leaky boat by spending all your time throwing water overboard, or you can spend some of that precious time finding the leak and plugging it. In China, the emphasis too often is on a faster bailing of water. *More hands on deck!*

China's warlord era, which ran through the 1920s, is commonly portrayed as a series of military battles. In fact, few real conflicts occurred, and those that did barely qualified as skirmishes. Soldiers were untrained and undisciplined. Many did not carry weapons, but simply fell into loose formations carrying sticks or flagpoles. And when modern weaponry became available it was not always standardized, which presented its own challenge.

One writer on the scene described soldiers scavenging for bullets from an assorted mix laid on the ground. Rather than pause to set up a process, soldiers picked through the assortment, lifting one bullet at a time. If the round matched the soldier's weapon, he kept it. If it did not, he threw it back into the same grab-bag pile.

Modern-day couriers employ a similar process. Although they are successful in getting packages to where they need to go, you should see the mayhem in which they operate. The distribution centers are a war zone with packages placed randomly in heaps all over the floor (sometimes even on the curb or in the street). Delivery workers make up for the lack of rhyme or reason with their capacity for memorization and a willingness to help each other.

Chinese are keen problem-solvers, yet they show less interest in developing efficient organizations. They prefer informal to formal systems, a phenomenon observed in factory settings. Even the largest and most sophisticated operations keep few records. The accounting departments of these firms are notorious for their aversion to paper trails, and financials are quite often committed to memory.

Rumor has it that the country's largest insurance companies have only recently begun hiring actuaries, breaking their historical preference of setting rates based on intuition rather than mathematics. I am inclined to believe this particular story because it matches my own experience. Chinese factories rarely use enterprise resource planning tools; most managers simply shoot from the hip.

An American business owner dropped me an e-mail asking, among other things, how she could encourage her supplier to set up a system whereby she was automatically informed when her products were moving from one stage of production to the next.

"Good luck with that one," I told her.

American importers who want such information are rarely ever provided with it. Repeated requests to learn something as simple as when manufacturing will begin are typically ignored until the factory finally drops a note one day saying that the goods are ready and asking why no one has already arranged to have them picked up.

Chinese factories are surprisingly informal operations, but this does not mean they want to be known as such. Driving up to a plant, you are likely to see three large letters affixed to the edifice—ISO—indicating that the facility is a member of the International Standards Organization. Standing on the shop floor, you quickly recognize that no one is following any standard operating procedures and that the business of authentication is little more than façade.

Factories do not spend a lot of time or money on training, which is perhaps its own tipoff. Step into a factory that employs more than two thousand workers, and though the plant is expansive, you will see that no space has been reserved for training. There is no classroom. There are no instructors who teach new hires the basics. There is no corporate video to get anyone started. There is no procedure manual. One reason may be that Mandarin is not a particularly good language for transmitting technical information. Another is that factory bosses do not like documentation, because it is just one more thing that can be stolen and shared with outsiders.

Whatever needs to be learned in the factory is picked up from other workers, and though there is nothing necessarily wrong with this approach—an organization can build up quite a bit of institutional knowledge in such an informal way—the risk comes when the sum of the firm's intellectual capital leaves the factory each Chinese New Year.

Chinese workers like the fact that nothing is written down and that systems are not in place. It means they alone are responsible for carrying the torch. As such, the loose approach carries with it an implication of greater job security. In order to counter this power that employees have over their employers—and as a hedge against lost information through attrition—factories go out of their way to hire more workers than they need, a strategy that works only until labor costs become too high.

Americans seek to build organizations that can last beyond the involvement of any specific individuals. "If we could somehow *perfect the system*" is such an American value, and it drives the ethos of the nation. While it is an admirable quality, at times we undoubtedly suffer for it.

At a print shop in Scottsdale, Arizona, I attempted to pay a clerk for some copies I wished to make. It was late and I was the only customer in the place. He pointed to a machine against the wall and informed me that it took both cash and plastic.

"But I prefer to pay you directly," I said.

"Sorry, buddy," he said.

American managers are convinced that people prefer doing business with machines when the opposite is almost always true. Automation does not commonly generate the savings predicted by its promoters, but there is a perceived need nevertheless to continue pressing forward with its implementation. Walking through an American airport and hearing a computer-generated voice butcher someone's family name over a public address system, you recognize how this attempt to automate the world is in some instances making life worse rather than better.

Chinese use automation for different purposes. Due to the low cost of labor, few of their automation efforts are about cost savings. More often than not—especially in the technology sector—automation is done at the behest of a foreign client, who in some cases even designs the supplier's production line. In other cases, Chinese toy with automation because they are curious, or they want a new personal challenge. Or they want to see if they can support their government by decreasing China's reliance on foreign manufacturing equipment. There is also the hope that once it succeeds in conquering automation, China will have one more thing to sell to foreign buyers.

Chinese have a yen for emulating the outside world, so we cannot necessarily take their successes in robotics to mean they are excited by the prospect of an automated world. Chinese culture is more humane, whereas Americans are driven by an instinct to remove people from every process in the spirit of making it "idiot-proof." The Chinese harbor no such fantasies, as they rightly view people to be the most critical component of any organization or institution, in spite of inherent human weaknesses.

———

In the United States, when news of a plane crash breaks, we know what to expect. First, a search is made for the black box, and then we are made to wait as investigators take their time breaking down what went wrong. At the end of their investigation, which can take months or years, aviation experts almost invariably announce that the cause of the crash was *pilot error*. This explanation is actually a comfort to Americans, who cannot tolerate the notion that something might be wrong with the mechanical systems responsible for keeping planes up in the sky. If one airplane has a mechanical flaw, then others presumably do too. We prefer to forgive the foibles of a person—recognizing that everyone has bad days and because in principle we believe in second chances.

When a high-speed train rammed another that was stopped on the tracks near Wenzhou in 2011, killing forty and injuring more than two hundred, Chinese officials did not show much interest in understanding the cause. They moved backhoes into the area and buried the train cars at once. Compelled to provide an explanation, government leaders at once blamed the electronic switching systems, which were said to be faulty due to "official corruption," that trusted lightening rod.

Chinese could hardly believe that such an accident was possible. *Why didn't the driver of the train that was stopped on the tracks alert his colleagues by phone or text message?* Under normal circumstances, the Chinese grapevine was so reliable. *How could the drivers have failed to inform one another of the imminent danger?*

Chinese are not troubled by mechanical failures. Instead, they are distressed by social failures. To suggest that their informal system is flawed is to admit that there is something wrong with the nation itself, and Chinese cannot accept such a premise. Faced with such a prospect, they will look for other causes in their desperation. The train drivers in the Wenzhou case could never be faulted, because they represented the masses and their grassroots social network. Instead, blame fell on senior management—with a total of fifty-four officials listed as "responsible for the crash."

Chinese government officials were only too happy to serve as the scapegoat. Part of the legitimacy of government officials, historically speaking, is based on a willingness to play just such a role. Chinese politics is characterized by a grand tradeoff: Government officials are granted political legitimacy in exchange for preventing the masses from feelings of inadequacy resulting from the inevitable failures of their native informalism.

While informalism has its advantages, the drawbacks are substantial. Fully aware of the fact, Chinese themselves spend inordinate amounts of time and energy scrambling to cover up systemic flaws, for fear that outsiders will come to know the full extent of their defects. China is a nation held together by sheer force of will by a billion-plus, and any suggestion that their informal system is deficient draws folks together faster than you can say *"deng yixia."*

China prefers that the world not understand its lack of formal organization, but this is not to say that they are ashamed of the system they do have. Quite the contrary, Chinese are proud of the way in which they are loosely bound together. Informalism is, after all, the essence of Chineseness.

China's progression from an ancient informal system to a modern formal one is seen as an age-old challenge. In the 1930s, J.O.P. Bland highlighted the issue by quoting the English biologist and sociologist Herbert Spencer, who was inspired by evolution in nature: "Just as injurious as it would be to an amphibian to cut off its branchae before its lungs were well developed; so injurious must it be to a society to destroy its old institutions before the new have become organized enough to take their place."

Informalism is the invisible glue holding this nation together and, as such, formalism has no hope of taking hold in China. Any genuine shift away from loose arrangements to rigid, impersonal institutions removes the impetus for social cooperation. It removes an element so fundamental to the Chinese experience that it would in short order destroy the long-lived civilization.

CHAPTER 19

Brown Numbers

Over dinner with an acquaintance who works as a fund manager in Hong Kong, I brought up the Shanghai bourse's recent rout: Newspapers suggested that regulatory authorities were going to shut down ten thousand hedge funds, a number that seemed suspect for its exactitude.

"Sounds like a brown number," he said.

"You mean a round number?" I asked.

"Brown," he said. "As in a number pulled out of someone's rear end."

It was more or less what I had been thinking—that the figure appeared make-believe. In the Chinese language, there is a character for the number ten thousand—*wan*—and it is sometimes referenced as a symbol of grandeur. Chinese who traditionally called for the emperor to live ten thousand years—"*Wan sui!*"—were, for example, speaking figuratively.

Not long after our discussion, I ran across another similar reference. China's state-run media announced that a parade would be held to commemorate China's purported victory in World War Two. In order to reduce pollution that might interfere with the jamboree, Beijing was looking to close down precisely "ten thousand factories."

Looking for other examples, I found an advertisement for the loathsome Yulin Dog Festival that promised precisely ten thousand canines would be barbecued and eaten. In 1997, torrential rains caused flooding in Guangdong, which led to the closure of exactly ten thousand businesses.

When they are not busy rounding figures, Chinese authorities are in the habit of inflating them. Of all the embellishments put out by state media, none were bigger in scope than those involving law enforcement. In 2014, news outlets announced that 182,038 government officials had been punished for official corruption, a figure up slightly from the previous year's tally of 172,532. The only thing more difficult to swallow than the two-year total of 354,570 officials busted for graft was the claim that 99.9 percent of those accused had been found guilty in the court system.

Chinese police overstate their achievements to show they are getting the job done. Crystal methamphetamine made for both domestic and overseas markets had become a scourge, with media claiming that some forty percent of the 14,000 who live in Boshe—a seaside town in eastern Guangdong—were directly involved in its manufacture and distribution. Newspapers reported that "three thousand police officers" were involved in a raid on the town, but the figure beggared belief. Aerial photographs supplied to the papers showed just a few squad cars, leading one to wonder how so many police officers could have been transported so quickly to such a remote location.

China press photos rarely match their reports. In one case, journalists reported that ten million kilograms (ten thousand metric tons) of fish died in a single Chinese lake, yet the corresponding image showed no more than a couple hundred fish belly up. Another sensationalized story involved a convoy of twenty-one trucks used to haul a supposed 420,000 tons of rotten frozen meat, with some of the meat reportedly butchered as long ago as the 1950s. You would think a cache of that sort might have come in handy during the Great Leap Forward, when tens of millions of Chinese faced death by starvation.

Western journalists are notorious for accepting almost any report or statistic issued by central Chinese authorities. The Confucius Institute has claimed that it has 28,000 teachers working in 480 centers around the world, and yet no writer covering the story thought to get out a calculator to do the simple division. What center of theirs has as many as fifty-eight teachers?

Of all the "brown" statistics called upon to buoy the country's reputation, far and away my favorite is the number of Chinese said to be living in caves. In his 2002 book, *The China Dream*, Joe Studwell suggested China has forty million cave dwellers. Barbara Demick of the *Los Angeles Times* went with the somewhat more conservative thirty million figure in 2012. Reading stories like these, I always wonder, *Where in the hell are these people?* In Guangdong, you meet migrant laborers from every corner of China, but I have yet to hear any one of them tell me that her parents live in some cave on a cliff.

An American once showed me photos of his trip to the Loess Plateau in Shanxi province, and though there were definitely caves in the pictures, the scene appeared touristic: model caves framed by guard rails with signage to guide visitors. I would believe it if you told me there were as many as half a million living in such dugout abodes, but thirty million, or forty million? I have friends living in northern Arizona, an area that is home to only one million inhabitants. Although the population is small, they have region-specific magazines dedicated to architecture in the Coconino National Forest. How is it that thirty million living such a unique lifestyle do not have their own *Better Caves and Gardens*?

China has always been hung up on population, and its statisticians have the habit of putting up big numbers in out-of-the-way places. Sichuan claims to be one of the country's most populous provinces, but if you drive just a few minutes outside of Chengdu, its capital, you wonder at the desolation.

When a major earthquake hit the area in 2008, the first casualty numbers reported were not significant. But after some introspection, the government reported (not necessarily unhappily) that it had more than 100,000 dead or missing. Much was made of the nine thousand students who were reported to have perished due to the quake, which struck on a school day at 2:28 PM. The poor condition of *tofu-dregs schoolhouses* was used to explain the high casualty rate, but the statistic did not fly. The ratio of young to old among the dead—roughly one to ten—ought to have been less stark. Chinese in the countryside have not strictly followed the one-child policy, and most couples have multiple children. In addition, Sichuan is a major supplier of migrant labor to the coastal cities, which ought to have dramatically reduced the number of adults in the quake-affected towns.

As much trouble as the artist Ai Weiwei has had with Chinese authorities over political and artistic statements he has made over the years, the only time he had his head properly cracked (he was put in the hospital with a concussion) was when he attempted to draw up a list of the schoolchildren who perished in the quake. Beijing can handle a fair amount of criticism, even from high-profile figures, but what it cannot abide is a critique of its population statistic, which is considered a *state secret*.

China's population fetish is driven by a profit motive. Westerners have for the longest time gone googly-eyed at the prospect of selling some product or other to unlimited numbers of Chinese. In the nineteenth century, British firms could think of almost nothing else but targeting the supposed four hundred million who then resided in the Flowery Kingdom.

George Wingrove Cooke in the 1850s wrote about a company in Sheffield that did not hesitate before sending off a considerable quantity of forks and knives to test the Chinese market. He spoke also of a British piano manufacturer that figured China's limitless population ought to be good for at least a few sales. As the story goes, the company sent "a tremendous consignment of pianofortes" to Hong Kong figuring that, if China had two hundred million women and only one out of two hundred was interested in learning how to play, there would be quite some demand. "The Chinese remained faithful to their gongs and trumpets," however, wrote Cooke, and the end result was that the British consignees involved pressured many of the colony's foreign residents into buying two pianos each.

Modern-day foreign firms that have directed their energies toward selling something to the Chinese have received a similar sort of education. Five-year plans have been extended to ten years, with many telling themselves that they would be happy if they could only somehow break even ... ever.

CHAPTER 20

Reform, Reform, Reform

O bedience to codebook law has never been a native characteristic," wrote the British thinker Putnam Weale in 1925. Chinese common folk have historically distrusted rigid rule systems, opting instead for loose arrangements that give officials room to maneuver. Because every case is entirely unique the thinking goes, judgment should be tailored to each situation. In other words, Chinese prefer the *rule of man* to the *rule of law*.

Americans pride themselves on the rights they afford the accused. "Better that ten guilty persons go free than one innocent suffer conviction." As nice as the old saying may be, people too often fall through the cracks of the American legal system. The police officer had no choice but to make the stop, which automatically triggered the arrest. The legal defense team was constrained by procedural guidelines, as was the judge, who ultimately handed down a decision based not on his many years of experience but on a mandatory minimum sentencing law. As a result, the young perpetrator who ought to have been given a slap on the wrist ends up doing life without chance of parole.

"Chinese law is characterized by the severity of its penalties, combined with leniency in their enforcement," wrote James Bashford in 1916. Westerners assume that Chinese people distrust their own legal system since innocents are sometimes arrested without cause and tried without due process. In spite of admitted failures in this regard, Chinese still prefer their system of justice, because it more easily allows for exceptions to be made and mercy to be shown. Though some innocents are unjustly punished, the incident rate of wrongful convictions is probably actually much lower than it would be were the Chinese to adopt a system of justice like our own, which is rigid and impersonal.

China's sense of justice is built on the principle of social harmony, which is why judges in civil cases prefer rulings that assign partial blame to both parties. In the United States, there is a greater tendency to pass judgment entirely in favor of either the plaintiff or the defendant. Our preference for a clear call creates a fantasyland of implausible extremes.

When one driver rear-ends another, we say the fellow in back is entirely to blame, since he alone was in a position to prevent the accident. In dense urban areas, leaving too much space between your car and the one in front means getting cut off the entire way to your destination. Chinese understand this, which is why they drive in a tight formation and why they do not automatically insist on holding the rear-ender wholly liable. Although obviously harder to determine, Chinese police officers will take into account any claim that the driver in front slammed on his brakes. With an eye toward doing what is harmonious, Chinese prove better at apportioning blame.

The American legal system thrives on conflict, and we tend to welcome that added degree of friction. Chinese legal professionals on the other hand prefer to seek amicability, avoiding conflicts that lead to needless face loss. In the United States, when a higher court overturns the ruling of a lower court, we are inclined to think it is evidence that the system is functioning properly. In China, judges are reluctant to overturn lower-court decisions because they do not wish to take any action that might embarrass a colleague. They also rubber stamp decisions out of fear that conflicting opinions lend the impression that their legal system is somehow broken.

China's sense of justice has always been different from that of the West, so early on Chinese and Western officials agreed to run separate legal systems. The event that convinced both sides of this necessity began with a brawl led by British sailors in Kowloon in 1839. Drunk on rice wine (*shamshu*) while on shore leave, one of the foreigners was alleged to have killed a villager named Lin Weixi. The cause of Lin's death was an apparent blow to the chest, but the identity of the perpetrator in the case remained a mystery, even to the sailors.

Charles Elliot, the Plenipotentiary and Chief Superintendent of British Trade, led an investigation but failed to find the culprit. Imperial Commissioner Lin Zexu responded by saying: "Bring us any one of your men, and we will gladly put him to death." Elliot had to explain that this was not how things worked with the British and that only the culpable individual could be punished for the crime.

The British abhorred and feared China's system of shared responsibility whereby innocent individuals could be called upon to pay for the crimes of an associate. Another issue was the severity of punishments. Chinese were not only quicker to execute a man, they were also inclined to do so for even minor offenses. Their methods of execution were draconian as well and included *lingchi*, the lingering death, whereby the condemned was tied to a post and subjected to "a thousand cuts." On top of all this, Chinese distrusted witness testimony, since they believed that there was no such thing as an unbiased witness. In order to guarantee the court had its man, officials relied on confession, which was elicited through torture.

The British were given their own jurisdiction and left to police themselves. This separate legal system, referred to as *extraterritoriality,* has occasionally been misrepresented as something that only foreigners wanted. Chinese were actually happy to limit their contact with non-Chinese and to set them up in their own districts. "*Yi yi zhi yi*" was the idiom: "Use foreigners to subdue foreigners." It was yet another autopilot institution requiring minimal effort for maximum return, and for decades officials were satisfied with the arrangement.

Hong Kong has been portrayed in recent decades as some crown jewel that was stolen by the British. In reality, what the Chinese had ceded to the British in 1842 was a desolate pile of rocks set along an undistinguished coastline, and the Chinese thought they had actually done well in relegating nonnatives to what was effectively a ghetto.

By this time it was understood that foreigners could not be kept out of the empire completely. The Chinese government had essentially accepted the British notion that no major nation has a "right to isolation." China was not some small island in the middle of the ocean. It was an economy with enormous potential, and as such it was going to have to join the world one way or another. It is worth remembering that prior to the establishment of the treaty ports, the majority of China's population resided in the interior of the country. Placing the foreigner at the edge of the empire seemed like a clever compromise, a midway point between isolationism and engagement.

Extraterritoriality would eventually be considered a disaster, but only because it was such a success. Shanghai was not much of a town before foreigners turned up. Writing in 1907, W. A. P. Martin described the growing city as "formerly an insignificant town of the third order," a notion that he may have got from W. H. Medhurst, who in 1838 described "Shangh-hae" as a "city of the third rank."

Shanghai was originally swampland, which made building problematic. The American architect Harry Hussey noted in his memoir that the first big buildings in the city sank "sometimes up to six or eight feet." Despite inherent obstacles, Shanghai was developed into the city ultimately referred to as the Pearl of the Orient. What made the place a success was not the overcoming of physical obstacles, but the administration of law. Westerners did an effective job of protecting personal and property rights, and Chinese clamored to live in their districts as a result. Real estate prices soared, and foreign jurisdictions ultimately became a refuge for Chinese in times of political turmoil and war. This became an embarrassment to the Qing government, which subsequently sought to abolish extraterritoriality.

We like to think of extraterritoriality as an archaic institution, but vestiges of the system remain today. In a police station, I watched with fascination as a policeman came down hard on factory representatives who had drawn an American client into an altercation. Seated in the station's specially designated Dispute Resolution Room, the police officer gave all the impression that he was there especially to look after the foreign trader.

China's legal system appears haphazard and inefficient, yet foreign firms are increasingly claiming that they are able to find justice through Chinese courts. Turns out that intellectual property rights can indeed be guaranteed, at least they are to such high-profile foreign brands as Under Armour, Michael Jordan and New Balance.

When Americans complain about Chinese dissidents being thrown in jail, Chinese are perplexed and respond by asking, "Why do you complain about what happens in our justice system? Have you yourselves not been treated fairly by it?" Just as a few shining examples of technological progress are presented as proof that China is innovating, showcase examples from the court systems are offered up as evidence that China's legal system is functioning fairly.

The occasional story of a payout being made to some individual wrongfully convicted supports the narrative that China is liberalizing, that it is progressing. And there are other such showcases of reform.

China's new green-card program has been offered as further supporting evidence. In 2016, China issued 1,600 permits to foreigners, which from a starting point of zero may seem like an improvement. But this figure pales in comparison to the more than one million green cards issued annually in the United States.

In many instances, China does no more than mimic a policy of the United States in name only. An announcement that Beijing plans to "cut military spending," coming right on the heels of a similar announcement by Washington, is enough to make anyone think, "Hey, these guys really are becoming more like us!"

China speaks today of reform, and we are inclined to think this is a new trend. For over a century, China has succeeded in getting us to believe that it is managing incremental change. In his 1911 book, *Across China on Foot*, Edwin John Dingle spoke of how the echo heard across the land was "Reform, reform, reform," and that he was proud to be a witness to it.

In the Republican era, British writer J. O. P. Bland wrote about how the Chinese had been busy at the Washington Conference, "putting across a glowing picture of a purely imaginary Chinese Republic, successfully progressing toward orderly constitutional government by virtue of liberal ideas and democratic institutions." If this was not China's first concerted effort at making the outside world believe that it was busy with reform, it was at least the first time the stakes were so high. China was then snowing the West into believing that it was reforming in order to receive serious financial and political support from overseas.

American legal experts who specialize in Chinese law have been trying to convince us for years now that China is making headway in the area of legal reform. Beijing aids this effort by giving these law professors plenty to write about. China's Supreme Court has now established what it calls *Guiding Cases*, a farcical attempt to mimic the rulings of our own United States Supreme Court.

The problem with the cases is that they are are so simplistic as to barely serve as primers in jurisprudence. More fundamentally problematic is that China's legal system is not based on case law anyway, so it does not make use of precedence. In the United States—which does rely on case law and where most court rulings have the potential to be used as precedent—our court system logs precedents into the millions. China's top court has not produced even ninety such rulings, but because there has been some effort at mimicking our system, we are inclined to agree with Beijing that progress is underway.

Chinese lawyers and judges themselves do not know what to make of these newfangled cases. The head of Stanford University's China Guiding Cases Project, Mei Gechlick, points out that Beijing is promoting a contradiction. China's Supreme Court has on the one hand assured legal professionals that the guiding cases are "not binding," but at the same time it has warned subjacent judges and lawyers that "there will be serious repercussions" if they do not make use of these rulings. Although only five hundred lower court cases referenced the guiding cases last year, the number of references is expected to climb to one thousand this year. In a country that adjudicates millions of court cases each year, we should wonder whether the pretense is even worth mentioning.

American lawyers who work in China complain of losing cases even when the law is on their side, lending a sense that judges are issuing opinions based not on legal training, but rather on a cultural sense of right and wrong. In China, whatever a judge needs to know is learned not in law school, but at his mother's knee. In order to obscure this underlying reality, legal professionals must go through a pantomime. China calls its system of jurisprudence "a socialist legal system with Chinese characteristics," which is a way of saying it is a hodgepodge improvisation.

Chinese institutions operate at two levels. First there is the surface level, which appears rules-based. Second is the actual operating level, which is based on native tradition. One follows guidelines, the other is founded on connatural instinct. Chinese adjudicators lead with their gut and only later justify their decisions by drawing on whatever seem-ingly objective ideology is on hand. Chinese certainly tire under the burden of running two systems at once, and it is only their intellectual acuity and tenacity that allows them to keep up the absurd charade.

China watchers would have us believe that China is abandoning native informalism in favor of rules-based formalism. But firsthand experience reveals that nothing of the sort is taking place. It's not that Chinese don't appreciate formalism. Quite the contrary, China's respect for the West is rooted in an acknowledgment of formalism's many benefits. The problem rather lies in China's innate understand-ing that informalism is the system best suited to its civilization. Chinese appreciate flexibility above all, and they recognize that where it works, informalism has the benefit of creating higher levels of wealth and happiness.

CHAPTER 21

The Dynastic Cycle

N apoleon is famously said to have declared at Saint Helena: "China is a sleeping lion. Let her sleep, for when she wakes she will shake the world!" Quite a dramatic suggestion, but of course the French military leader said no such thing.

No one knows where this supposed quote originated, though it has been oft repeated, especially in recent years. The earliest reference I have been able to find comes from a volume called *John Chinaman at Home: Sketches of Men, Manners and Things in China,* by Reverend E. J. Hardy. Published in 1905, the book opens with the following epigraph: "When China is moved, it will change the face of the globe." Though less hyperbolic and lacking any reference to slumber, it appears to be the forerunner of the pithy saying.

For as long as they have been wayfaring about the Middle Kingdom, old China hands have been making predictions about the empire's revivification. John Dewey quipped in 1919 that the country's awakening had already been announced "a dozen or more times by foreign travelers in the last ten years," so he hesitated to do it again. A few years later in his book *China's Place in the Sun,* Stanley High echoed the sentiment shared by so many that the once-sleepy domain was "a nation of great potentialities."

China has always appeared to be at a crossroads with many believing the country was either bound for renewed glory or else due for a crisis. Early on during his time in China, Arthur Smith suggested that the last quarter of the nineteenth century would be a "critical period in Chinese history." At the end of his career, he brushed aside all suggestions of doom, noting that China had been "on the brink of a precipice ever since I arrived in it a half century ago."

What is it about this place that perpetually lends the impression it is either on its way to the top or else hurtling toward the abyss?

Following the dissolution of its last dynasty in 1912, China struggled with political disintegration that led to social disorder and warlordism. Much of the gloominess that followed during the Republican era was therefore understandable.

Today, few predict doom and gloom since the nation appears to be reintegrated into the global economy. China's participation in institutions such as the United Nations, the International Monetary Fund, and the World Trade Organization has convinced us that the country is now on an inevitable track toward greater prosperity and that the inertia will be for the most part constant.

Economists are fond of promoting the idea that all nations are heading toward the same inevitable future, as if the economies of the world are traveling undeviatingly along the same one-dimensional line with the lesser-developed nations proceeding from a position just slightly behind that of the other industrialized economies.

While acknowledging that some major economies have materially shrunk in the past, the presumed financial wizards of the world insist that this is not a possibility for a country like China. Similarly, while acknowledging that history is dotted with examples of nations that have regressed politically, China's only possible future is seen as heading toward a Western political model.

We have even been led to believe that Chinese themselves share in this worldview. In reality, they do not. Chinese reject out of hand the concept of linearity and opt instead for a *weltanschauung* rooted in cycles. Westerners will pay lip service to the idea that "history repeats itself," but rarely do we ever apply the concept to our understanding of current events. For the Chinese, this worldview of cycles repeating through time is as fundamental a component of nature as the law of gravity.

China has every reason to be predisposed toward such a philosophy. Having once been the world's greatest power, it wishes for a return to glory and so stakes a belief in the wheel of history. This belief in cycles runs deeper than their wish for national rejuvenation though. Chinese are deeply superstitious and believe that luck runs in turns. A family's fortune rises and falls and rises again, and this conception alters perceptions of the future. China's peasants ought to feel trapped by abject poverty, but instead they exhibit an incredible optimism. The poorer the economic condition of a family, the more convinced it is that great fortune lies just ahead.

At the other end of the spectrum, we find the wealthy living in a state of perpetual anxiety for fear that they will soon lose it all. Some of the most superstitious, joss stick-burning folks you could ever meet are not the rural poor, but rather the affluent. Nothing portends bad luck more than enjoying a spot of success, so we are not surprised to find that the wealthy as a rule wish to emigrate. These are not rats leaving a sinking ship, nor are they out seeking investment opportunities as some claim. Chinese who have made it simply want to put a few thousand miles between them and the hoodoo that portends disaster.

Chinese take their cues from history. "When a man of sufficient caliber has climbed to the dizzy height of the Imperial throne," wrote Rodney Gilbert, "his last step to the summit is the first step upon the greased chute." *The Romance of the Three Kingdoms* is one of the classics of Chinese literature, and it begins with a suggestion of cycles: "Empires wax and wane, states cleave asunder and coalesce." The fourteenth-century novel is a favorite of communist leaders, who have made a careful study of the downfall of the last dynasty.

The wheel of history preoccupies political leaders, and it is also on the minds of those who do business. I have a pet theory involving the dynastic cycle, which goes something like this: Chinese business leaders not only believe in the cycle; they actually engage in behaviors that exacerbate it.

Chinese factories that are new and small are almost always easier to work with than larger, more established ones. As a factory "evolves," it becomes increasingly difficult to deal with over time, and its owners demand more as the company expands. This is surprising given that microeconomic theory dictates the opposite. As a firm grows, it is supposed to achieve economies of scale that bring down per-unit costs, resulting in savings for the buyer.

There is an easy explanation: Emerging factories dare not play games, because they need the business. But well-established factories are better positioned to take chances with their customers. Buyers who recognize this reality will make a point of looking for suppliers that are just a bit more desperate for business, since they are seen as more reliable. And in fragmented markets especially, they will look to switch suppliers as soon as it appears the one they are dealing with has evolved beyond a certain point.

Paul Krugman and other economists have gone out of their way to admonish the Chinese for saving too much of what they earn. Although the macroeconomics of such a notion may be theoretically sound, in practice no one in China believes in the principle of saving less. Factory owners who are just getting on their feet postpone all purchases, major *and* minor, for years as they ramp up volume. Even if orders are coming in and the future looks bright, they always work first on setting aside a considerable nest egg. Some of the factory owners I have known socked away their retirement within the first four or five years of getting set up. These efforts go way beyond putting something aside for a rainy day.

The net effect of this savings strategy is to put the factory boss in a stronger negotiating position. The American buyer who flies in from New York has no choice but to return home with a deal in hand. More likely than not, his company has serious bills and debt. He might have pleased his advisors by leveraging his financial position, but in the process, the importer put his company at a disadvantage in negotiations with his overseas suppliers.

American importers are motivated to close a deal by factors that include payments on debt principal and interest, long-term leases on office and warehouse space, and significant payroll commitments. In their personal lives, they often have the pressure of a considerable home mortgage. And so, if an order nets the foreign importer only thirteen percent gross margin instead of the anticipated twenty-two percent, he has no choice but to agree to the arrangement and pray that he does better in the future.

There is another dynamic at work: Chinese factory bosses tend to grow bored with their success. The local industrialist is excited to meet his first big buyer as this event establishes him in business. If orders grow from there he remains satisfied, not so much because of the money, but because higher volumes are associated with greater levels of face. Like an addict though, he requires more in order to achieve the same high. So when sales growth flattens, he looks elsewhere for dopamine triggers. To catch a buzz, he may look to sign on his chief customer's competitor, or he may find pleasure in building a relationship with the customer's key client.

Most of the time, these factory owners get their kicks out of finding new and exotic justifications for raising prices. It's not because they necessarily need the money or because costs are rising. They do it simply to see if they can get away with it; they do it in order to tickle their egos. Having worked hard to ratchet prices from $1.55 to $1.75, they want to see if they can somehow catch $1.85. Perhaps a smaller customer of theirs accepted such a benchmark, and the operator gets it in his head that his bigger customers must, too, accept the new threshold.

Chinese industrialists who ingratiate themselves for years eventually mature into insufferable partners with chips on their shoulders. Playing the simpleton (*nande hutu*) is good for starting a business, but Confucian values dictate that eventually the tables will be turned. In cases where this happens, it typically devastates the foreign buyer.

Invited to a dinner in Guangzhou, I was seated next to a New Yorker who described difficulties with a key supplier. At the start of their business relationship he had been given the red-carpet treatment, but nowadays he found that the factory barely had time for him. "It's as if they don't even know who I am!" he said with a palpable sense of loss and confusion.

I have worked with several factories that have "gone supernova," and it's not fun by any stretch. The industrialist will surprise his buyer one day, explaining that he is no longer interested in continuing the relationship, unless it is on his starkly revised terms. In a couple of memorable instances, the piece of business involved was large enough that failure to ink a deal would have meant shuttering the factory. These factory bosses would look their biggest buyer dead in the eye, shrug and tell him that they didn't care one way or another whether they had to close the plant, because they had enough money set aside.

Seeing how they had been preparing for years to be able to deliver such a line, you were inclined to believe it was not a bluff.

Chinese office workers have a similar habit of working for many years before chucking it all and returning to their hometowns. It may be three years or five, but sooner or later they would leave. To facilitate their departure, they would push an employer in ways that all but ensured they were relieved of duty. The only way some workers can justify hanging on is by receiving more and more.

A couple of years ago, I interviewed a young man for a merchandiser role. He reported that in each of his last two jobs he had received a fifty percent pay increase to make a move and said that, in order to consider changing employers this time, he was going to need a bump of one hundred percent. The more they get the more they want, until finally the model breaks and they have to start from scratch.

China's approach to wealth is counterintuitive. In most countries, it is the poor you have to worry about. In China, it is the wealthy. This is a reality playing itself out at the macro level as well. China was a heck of a lot easier to work with when it was poorer. Now that it is a leading economy, there is less hope of smooth cooperation.

Writers in the 1920s and 1930s were of the opinion that paying Chinese laborers more than they were owed caused difficulties. "If you take pity on a rickshaw coolie and pay him too much," wrote Ralph Townsend, "he will shout that he is cheated." William Martin echoed this conventional wisdom held by the average expatriate then: "If you give the men too much they begin at once to make trouble," he wrote in 1934. In his excellent book *The Chinese*, published in 1980, John Fraser referenced an old saying, "In bad times, lie low. In good times, seek redress." Deng Xiaoping's suggestion that the Chinese should lay low and "bide their time" was a hint of an impending change in attitude, and we in the West should be curious as to what form such redress will ultimately take.

Having once found a new dry cleaner in Guangzhou, I was surprised when on the third visit their prices were raised. The owner of the shop explained that there had been no increase, but that lower prices earlier offered were merely a friendly gesture toward a new customer. Now that we were more familiar with one another, it was obvious that he should charge me the "normal" price. Chinese companies like to start nice, but then it's downhill until the customer moves on.

Chinese businesses often open to great fanfare, and though no expense is spared at the grand opening, business owners are disinclined to reinvest. There is a great deal of face that comes with a new launch, but almost none that comes with a refurbishment. So as business slows, operators seek to make up for the loss in revenue by cheapening their offering. This leads to a further loss of demand, which prompts another round of cuts.

China's economy has risen so fast that we can hardly imagine such death spirals are taking place, but cracks in the model are beginning to appear. An economy that was built on a short-term horizon, and that does not have the cultural habit of reconditioning, is guaranteed to stall. Unable to grow their way out of such a tight spot and unconvinced that good times will return anytime soon, decision makers will then seek alternative advantages.

CHAPTER 22

Nibble, Nibble...

China's masses have always led a hardscrabble existence, with frequent flooding and droughts leading to famine. In the 1930s, the British historian R. H. Tawney notably depicted the peasant as a figure who stood "up to the neck" in water so that a mere ripple might drown him. Living in such a precarious condition for so many centuries naturally shaped the outlook of the population.

Long before attending graduate school and ages before I started doing business in the Far East, I got hold of a book called *The Secrets of Power Negotiating* by Roger Dawson. Only in high school then, I found it to be an eye opener. And on occasion since, I have revisited the compendium of stratagems and maneuvers, not so much for tips on how to do business, but rather as a reminder of cross-cultural differences.

It is somewhat telling, for example, that Dawson relegates *nibbling* to the back pages of his book, as though it were a lesser gambit. The principle behind the technique is easy to understand, even if we in the West find it a bit below-the-belt. At a car dealership, a prospective buyer is preparing to sign on the dotted line, but at the last moment leans forward and asks the salesman if he will consider waiving the dealer's fee. Afraid that the buyer might be getting cold feet, the salesperson acquiesces. What about floor mats? And a full tank of gas?

The buyer keeps the transaction at the brink of conclusion while one small concession after another is exacted.

In China, nibbling is no trivial affair. It is the centerpiece of the negotiation process. Chinese managers customarily approach a transaction by offering hope that they will agree to the main objective of the other side, only to then draw the process out while accumulating as many incidental benefits as possible, some of which might even serve as a card to be traded back during subsequent discussions on the principal matter.

Tawney's observation about the precariousness of peasant existence hints at why the culture places such an emphasis on minor aspects of a deal. For thousands of years in this land, the difference between success and failure—indeed, between life and death—lay in finding a way to eke out a marginally better yield. The farmer who took the time to dream about quantum leaps in productivity was likely to go bust. But if he concentrated efforts on increasing water irrigation efficiency by just a paltry two or three percent, he might be one of the lucky souls who made it through the year.

Chinese industrialists bring that same agrarian sensibility to the production process. This understanding helps us to explain certain puzzling questions, such as why a factory boss would choose to use a poor grade of cardboard box to deliver an order worth $300,000, just to save a couple hundred bucks. I used to shake my head at such nonsense until it dawned on me that these industrialists figured themselves for farmers. Up to their knees in muddy water, they did not feel that they had the luxury of managing customer relationships on broad time horizon. They, too, were obsessed with their immediate survival.

In order to catch a piece of business, factories often bid a job at "below subsistence level," and then over the course of a few months will claw their way back to profitability. At one end of the equation, they work to ratchet up prices in modest, incremental amounts. On the other, they drive down cost by degrading the product ever so slightly, hoping the buyer won't notice. It may take a while to open up that wedge of profit, but they eventually get there. The difficulty is, they do not know how to let go of that desperate state of mind, and in going too far they often end up offending their best customers.

Chinese factories are all about finding a multitude of ways to make up for what is initially a loss-making deal. The factory might trick an importer into paying for production molds that have already been covered by another one of its customers. Or courier fees might be turned into a profit center, unbeknownst to the buyer.

A New York-based company that I worked with noted that its factory in China charged it more than $80,000 for shipping fees associated with production samples. At the start of the relationship, the factory owner refused to assume any of the shipping expense, but he offered to prepay for the shipments using his company's "special discount" with a local shipper—just as long as he was reimbursed. After a year of billings, the American importer looked into the matter and discovered that though the goods had been shipped using DHL, a major brand, some fly-by-night local agent had issued the receipts in the courier's name. Resellers of courier services—to call these operators franchisees would be inaccurate—have proliferated in China on the back of this popular scheme, wherein kickbacks are easily arranged.

To get a factory to stop nibbling in such ways, a buyer first has to notice that related behaviors are taking place. The easier part is uncovering the activity; the hard part is having the resolve to take action.

Bootlegging is an especially annoying form of nibbling. Let's say a Los Angeles company sends a proprietary design over to its supplier in China and that it buys the product from said supplier for one dollar per unit. Let's also assume the factory earns only five cents on each item produced. If the California company resells the product for two dollars, then the factory has a strong incentive to find an agent and move a few bootlegged copies at, say, $1.50 each. In this case, the factory's profit—minus the agent's commission—may be ten times its five cent margin. The factory needs to sell only one container of counterfeit merchandise to match the profit from selling ten containers of legitimate product.

Chinese factories that engage in such illicit behavior do so discreetly, of course, so clients in many cases have no hint of what is taking place until they run across bootlegged versions of their product at a trade show, on the Internet, or in market geographies where they have no active presence.

A hardware company out of Seattle discovered through routine monitoring of public trade data that its key supplier was shipping a product that it purchased—and for which it owned patent rights—to the grey market in the US. Because the hardware vendor shipped its product only to the West Coast and because evidence showed that the product was also being sent to the East Coast, it knew that it had a problem.

American importers who suspect a supplier may be cheating will typically investigate the matter only half-heartedly, because they do not want to know the truth and because they are unsure how to challenge the factory owner. Those who bravely take up the gauntlet and press for full disclosure face the grim prospect of uncovering betrayal, so they choose instead to ignore that muted, gnawing sound of a deal gone bad.

Nibble, nibble, nibble, nibble...

"Be polite," the American boss says to his manager. "See what the factory knows about those shipments."

Nibble, nibble...

"They say they never heard of them. No clue."

Nibble, nibble...

"Maybe we should tell them we have evidence?"

Nibble, nibble...

"They deny it has anything to do with their factory."

Nibble, nibble...

"Tell them we have proof."

Nibble, nibble...

"They insist it's not them."

Nibble, nibble...

"Let's show them the proof."

Nibble, nibble...

"They said it was just the one time."

Nibble, nibble...

"Is that true?"

Nibble, nibble...

"There is a record of three shipments."

Nibble, nibble...

"Just tell them to stop."

Nibble, nibble...

"They said the last time was two years ago."

Nibble, nibble...

"Is that true?"
Nibble, nibble . . .
"A container went out last month."
Nibble, nibble . . .
"Can you tell them to cut it out?"
Nibble, nibble . . .
"They promised."
Nibble, nibble . . .
(Six months later)
"Have they stopped?"
Nibble, nibble . . .
"We can't be sure."
Nibble, nibble . . .

Western firms that catch their partners cheating are inclined to believe they have uncovered some moral failure. Chinese firms tend to hold a different opinion, believing not only that they have done nothing wrong, but also that they are somehow doing their foreign partners a favor.

In the spirit of nonconfrontation, Chinese seek to minimize direct conflict. The factory could easily go to its customer and explain that it wishes to raise prices. But then the buyer may become upset or cancel his orders, because he cannot accept the higher rate. By supplementing its bottom line in an auxiliary manner, the factory need not trouble its buyer for more money.

Differences in cultural values can sometimes lead to stress, and foreign buyers who feel cheated tend to take it personally. "The accumulation of frustrations leads to a feeling of betrayal," wrote Lucian Pye. The buyer's business may not be directly affected by the cheating—like if the bootlegged product goes to a market which the buyer does not target—but news of unscrupulous behavior irks just the same. For a buyer who is already operating on tight margins, learning that a local partner has found a way to create small, secret streams of revenue may trigger an instinct to retaliate.

I've been involved in numerous cases where a foreign importer has been forced to admit that its Chinese partner has been subtly cheating. When this happens, I am typically called into a meeting, the subject of which is: *How can we stop the factory from engaging in these annoying behaviors?*

Verbal warnings do not work; this much we know. A factory that has already issued denials of any wrongdoing, even as it has quietly been nibbling away, will more than likely continue to munch even after swearing up and down that it has cleaned up its act. No matter what is said or how it is pitched, and regardless of whatever new agreement is signed in an effort to redirect the relationship, bad behavior on a deal of this kind is guaranteed to persist. The only change we might see—if we see any at all—is an added degree of discretion to prevent the buyer from losing too much face, which is the factory's preferred interpretation of the buyer's vexation.

Smaller foreign firms operating in China tend to express their frustration more readily than larger ones, in part because they have fewer reputational concerns. But all firms eventually worry less about appearances and more about financial damage. They may kick the can down the road for years, but will eventually recognize they are getting nowhere by trying to play down or wish away the problem.

The challenge in countering nibbling strategies is that there is rarely any good response. If you receive a shipment of mostly good plywood that contains some small amount of bad product taken from a shipment you rejected nine months earlier, it doesn't make economic sense to reject the entirety of the container you have just received. More than likely, you will go through this latest shipment and remove whatever bad wood you can find and argue that the factory should reimburse for the claimed rejects. But the question is, how many times are you willing to go through such a rigmarole?

Three-percent problems are not solved with three-percent solutions. Troops in a conflict zone do not respond to rocks being thrown at them by finding other rocks to throw back. At some point, you have to break out the big guns. In a business context, this might mean an undesirable extreme action, such as a lawsuit or some other move that effectively burns the bridge.

Most foreign firms do not have the resolve to tackle such issues. But where a foreign firm actually has the backbone to apply a threat backed by force, its partners in China will likely throw up their hands and say, "All right, you have our attention. Please, let's sit down and talk."

There is a pattern to these deals that is so predictable as to be comical. Suddenly, the foreign managers are in luck. Through their expression of extreme displeasure, they appear to have completely changed the attitude of their supplier. Seeing this as an opportunity, the foreign firm will insist that the local operator explicitly agree to stop all unwanted nibbling behaviors. The local firm will intimate that while it can agree to such stipulations in principle, it cannot do so under duress.

"We cannot think straight with those big guns aimed at us" is the general message conveyed. The foreigners will be asked to remove any and all threats so that the Chinese side may calmly and carefully consider their redirection. If a lawsuit has been initiated, the Chinese will insist that it first be cancelled. If the company has begun the process of moving orders to another plant, the local partner will ask that all related efforts in this area cease and that a new memorandum of understanding be signed in which the foreign side promises to devote itself more committedly to the original partnership, as if the foreign partner's lack of loyalty had been the cause of its unethical behavior.

Whatever the nature of the pressure introduced by the foreign side—and this is where we can laugh—Chinese always succeed in getting the foreigners to remove that big-gun threat, the instrument that brought the local partners to their senses in the first place.

Of course, once the threat is removed, nothing happens. The local partner sooner or later goes back to business as usual. If the foreign client finds that the supplier has reneged *yet again*, what often follows is an all-out unconstrained retaliation, which takes the relationship to the very brink.

This last feint by the Chinese team is commonly misunderstood. It is not the act of an incorrigible villain like the scorpion in Aesop's fable who cannot help what comes to him naturally, nor is it a shot at one last ill-gotten gain before inevitably severing the relationship. Instead, the local team is merely taking comfort—if not pleasure—in making a fool of their foreign counterparts one last time before settling back to a position in which they are forced into doing the right thing.

Chinese business partnerships are about the perpetual search for equilibrium. Local firms will grab as much as they can until they are met by a countervailing force. To survive in business, the foreign firm will go to great lengths to monitor its partners and put pressure to limit activity that damages its interests. The foreign firm must accept that not all unwanted behaviors can be stopped, though steps can be taken to reduce their frequency and scope.

An important part of success—and sanity—in this country is to allow for some degree of monkey business. Abbé Huc suggested that because certain behaviors in China are inevitable, a foreigner must plan for them in much the same way that one might "set aside a reserve for bad debts, or allow a margin for friction in mechanics."

CHAPTER 23

The Social Order

When expressing emotional pain, Chinese tend to misdirect. The suffering described is almost certainly real, it's just that the source is commonly obfuscated. Chinese office workers who feel over-worked or mistreated, for example, will rarely reveal to a supervisor their true feelings. Instead, they will complain of feeling tired or dizzy.

Beijing's commemoration of the so-called *Century of Humiliation* is a kind of tribute to military victimhood, a concept created by pro-pagandists in the mid-twentieth century. It is similarly an exercise in misdirection.

Before looking at sources of supposed shame, we should first probably note that there is a related tradition and that the act of self-shaming predates any modern political campaigns. In the 1890s, John Arthur Turner spoke of a drought during which government officials offered to take direct responsibility through fasting and prayer. "In accordance with custom," he wrote, "a proclamation was put out commanding the people to join with them in a season of self-humiliation."

Beijing propagandists in the twentieth century have pitched the *Century of Humiliation* as beginning in 1839 with the first firing of cannons by the British in the Anglo-Chinese War, also referred to as the First Opium War. The implication here is that the source of

China's supposed shame was England and that the ignominy was military in nature. But the claim is problematic on both fronts.

Writing in the 1930s, American journalist Nathaniel Peffer suggested that antiforeign sentiment in his day was not about military defeat by the British, but had to do with defeat by Japan in 1895 instead. China was "devastatingly shaken" by its war with Japan, whereas England did not figure as prominently in the Chinese psyche, according to Peffer, because that "monster" was in faraway Europe. Japan was close by and its proximity contributed to a sense of helplessness that "released a panic," he explained.

China's sense of historical shame may be more closely linked to Japan than to any other foreign power, but the source of raw feelings there is not necessarily military in nature. China's war with Japan lasted only eight months, ending April 17, 1895. Ten years later, according to eyewitness accounts, Chinese were actually seen cheering Japan on as it fought Russia. F. L. Hawks Pott explained then that Japan's victory against the Russians gave the Chinese hope that Asians could do well in battles against the "white man."

By the 1910s, Japan had become something of a mecca for the Chinese. An estimated 15,000 Chinese were studying there in any given year. Sun Yat-sen fled to Japan after the failure of his Second Revolution, as well as on other occasions. And, we remember, Chiang Kai-shek (who would later lead troops against the Japanese) spent four years at the Tokyo Military Academy. Chinese warlords of the 1920s who were looking to lie low almost always chose Tokyo as their hideout.

Chinese of the day were conflicted when it came to Japan. On the one hand, they had lost a war to the Japanese. On the other, they were impressed with the way Japanese succeeded in managing their own foreign barbarians by removing extraterritorial rights starting in 1900. Chinese also liked the Japanese because they felt they could more easily grasp their culture. Unfortunately for them, the Japanese displayed an equal or better facility for understanding how the Chinese thought and operated. And they would use this knowledge in the warlord era and beyond for the express purpose of manipulation.

Modern propagandists who suggest that this *Century of Humiliation* began with the First Opium War conveniently overlook the fact that the first Humiliation Day protests occurred on the anniversary of

Japan's Twenty-One Demands. The demands were an attempt by Tokyo in 1915 to capture Manchuria and take control of the Chinese economy.

Chinese were not so much upset at the idea of Japan trying to take over China as they were at the manner in which Japan went about doing it. George Sokolsky, a newspaper colleague of Rodney Gilbert, mentioned in his 1932 book *The Tinder Box of Asia* that he had knowledge through Sun Yat-sen of an explicit agreement between the Japanese and General Yuan Shikai. Japan was planning to recognize Yuan as a new "emperor" in exchange for his acceptance of a backdoor deal that gave Japan everything it wanted in China.

To the extent there ever was such a thing, China's shame has never been rooted in military defeat. Rather, the pervasive sense of national humiliation has always been related to issues of social cohesion.

Chinese of the early twentieth century viewed themselves as duplicitous, dishonest, and disloyal, and figured that such flaws made unification next to impossible. Sun Yat-sen gave speeches in the 1920s, in which he preyed on this national sense of shame. The Chinese were atomized, thinking only of their own individual interests, and thus the people were said to be "disunited as a sheet of loose sand."

Admitting to such cultural deficiencies is next to impossible in the current political climate. Japan remains hated for what was done a century ago, but the issue has been repackaged as exclusively a byproduct of military aggression. And toward the ambition of promoting such a narrative, Chinese propagandists have worked hard to inflate death tallies. While credible sources have suggested that between 40,000 and 60,000 Chinese were killed at the hands of the Japanese in Nanking in 1937, Beijing has pushed the estimates to 300,000.

In his book *China Takes Her Place*, published in 1944, Carl Crow details how the Japanese took advantage of the Chinese years earlier. Sitting on the sidelines during the warlord era, Tokyo supplied arms to competing Chinese factions, offering cheap financing so there was no excuse not to fight. William Martin, writing in 1934, went as far as to claim that "not a rifle is fired in China but its powder was paid for by the Japanese."

In its efforts to disrupt social order in China, Japan went so far as to manufacture and distribute morphine and heroin, two processed derivatives of the poppy plant, far more harmful than opium in its natural form. In other words, what the British had once been accused of—"the drugging of a nation"—the Japanese set out to do in earnest.

American politicians and policy leaders insist that we have "more to fear from a weak China than one that is strong." With so many making this claim, we should probably ask: *How do we define weakness?*

Beijing's fear of chaos, says foreign policy scholar Stefan Halper, "runs like an iron spine through the entire Chinese body politic." This is yet another great trope, and we should wonder here: *What is meant by "fear of chaos"?*

The implied threat of chaos may sound like something the communists came up with, but in fact foreigners likely originated the concern. One of the first foreigners to ever write about China and chaos theory—perhaps *the* first—was Reverend Smith, who cautioned in 1912 that change was coming to China and that "it will be well if it come not too rapidly to permit of the gradual preparation of the individual and the family to receive it. Otherwise, social and ethical chaos may be the result."

Social and ethical chaos . . .

This makes sense that perennial concerns over "weakness" and "chaos" may actually be social in nature. If this really is what concerns so many, though, why then is all of the navel-gazing on China's problems focused on its politics, its military, and its economy?

The book you hold in your hands shares its title with one published by Rodney Gilbert in 1926. Although far from perfect, Gilbert's *What's Wrong with China* offers so many on-target insights that I figured an echo of his work might be a respectful gesture. And for similar reasons, while pulling together these pages, I sought Gilbert's original title for my personal library.

Reaching out to antiquarian booksellers, I managed to get my hands on several copies, including a couple of first editions. In one such volume, purchased from a shop in London, I found an odd artifact tucked between the front cover and the flyleaf. It was a folded single sheet of sepia-tinted paper, typewritten and labeled *China News Sheet.*

It had been printed by the Baptist Missionary Society in May 1951, and marked at the top was a warning: *Strictly Confidential—For Private Circulation Only—Not to be Reproduced.*

England's top missionary in China, V. E. W. Hayward, wrote the bulk of the tract, in which he described conditions in the aftermath of the communist takeover of 1949, an event that many China watchers of the era said could never take place. The US government had supported Chiang Kai-shek and his Nationalists during this period and spent billions to guarantee that China would not be "lost" to communism. The letter is especially interesting because it touches on politically sensitive matters. The US was staunchly anti-communist at the time and suspected sympathizers were subjected to severe retribution. John Vincent Carter's diplomatic career was destroyed in the McCarthy era, for example, after he merely *suggested* that communism stood a chance.

In his secret letter, Hayward wrote, "I am personally convinced as far as internal conditions are concerned, the new regime has definitely come to stay for the foreseeable future." As shocking as that view was, he went even further by stating this was not necessarily a bad thing. "The law is now respected, which it never was before," he wrote. Previously, "it was only necessary to know an official to dodge every law ever passed. Taxes are paid by all, and paid at the right time. No shopkeeper dares not write an invoice, or write a false one. Even bus and train tickets are sold on a scrupulously fair system, which prevents anyone, even government officials, taking precedence, or getting reduced rates."

The antidote to social weakness and general chaos, it turns out, is good old-fashioned totalitarian rule. "Where trustworthiness is as scarce as it is in China," wrote Townsend in the 1930s, "it is probably better to have a government highly centralized, requiring as few authoritative individuals as possible, in order to utilize most effectively the limited amount of honesty available." Westerners today are quick to denounce Beijing's absolutist policies, but the Chinese people largely recognize the cause-and-effect relationship between iron-fistedness and social order.

CHAPTER 24

Cat's Paws and Telegraphed Punches

If there were a Mount Rushmore of old China hands, you would find the Reverend Arthur Smith up there along with Abbé Huc, and perhaps a space should also be reserved for Rodney Gilbert. And although he did not speak Chinese, British journalist George Wingrove Cooke might arguably qualify for a fourth spot in the pantheon. Somewhere near this great monument, possibly wandering the grounds as a ghost, we might also find Ralph Townsend. Though his writing was acerbic—even offensive—we miss too much if we ignore his legacy as a China watcher.

Townsend was jailed in the United States during World War Two, found guilty of sedition for taking funds from the Japanese to disseminate propaganda. Prior to that shameful episode, he had been with the US State Department, serving as vice-consul in Shanghai and Fuzhou. His career was not a particularly long one, nor was it especially distinguished. But he walked away from a few years in China with numerous insights on the country and its people, including one accurate observation that no other writer appears to have made, namely, that the Chinese have the uncanny habit of *telegraphing their punches*.

"Before the fruition of any important plot," Townsend wrote, "they manage usually to let out a few unintended hints, so that the marked victims are forewarned." He drew an analogy to boxers who convey their next moves through subtle body language. I too noticed this behavior some years ago: Factory owners who are up to some chicanery will almost always provide a suggestion of their plans.

It is a risk-hedging move. If a buyer finds out that his product has been cheapened, for example, he might become angry enough to sever the relationship. If, on the other hand, the factory owner can show, after the fact, that everything short of writing a memo had been done to signal his intentions ahead of time, then maybe the buyer would end up blaming himself, and the relationship could continue without conflict.

American parents of teenagers are familiar with the telegraphing of moves. The son saunters into the kitchen, mentioning to his mother on the way to the pantry that his friend Tommy has joined a rock band.

"That's nice, honey," says the mother, without giving it much thought.

The next night, when the boy doesn't come home until late, the mother is enraged. "But, Mom," says the kid, "I *told* you. Tommy's in a band!"

Recognizing she was given just enough information, and in the interest of maintaining a good relationship with her son, the mother chooses to blame herself for not having listened carefully and vows to do better next time. American buyers of China-made goods also often blame themselves, erroneously chalking up misunderstandings to a lack of cultural understanding. Kicking themselves, they similarly promise to be more sensitive and to listen more intently.

Among themselves, Chinese are constantly on the lookout for subtle signals. Zhang shares an apartment with Wang and mentions one day that his bicycle is broken. Wang does not even acknowledge the bicycle comment. Instead, he talks about unrelated topics for a while until he casually mentions that he has a lot of work coming up and that he will be very busy. Without this last mention of a hectic work schedule, Wang's silence on the topic might be interpreted by Zhang as tacit permission to use his bike.

During any conversation, Chinese are always wondering in the back of their minds, *"What did he mean by that phrase?"* Chinese like to "connect the dots" in ways that people from other cultures do not, which gives ironic meaning to the gentle chide one hears in casual conversations suggesting that a person is thinking too much: *"Ni xiang tai duole!"*

In a factory meeting, an American buyer mentioned to his key supplier that he was flying to Shanghai after their meeting had concluded. The wheels started spinning behind the factory man's eyes: *Flying to Shanghai? What's in Shanghai?*

The industrialist had competitors in the area, so he was maybe worried about a potential loss of business. The next morning in the hotel lobby, the factory man buttonholed me, asking in a half-whisper why his buyer was heading to Shanghai. In truth, there was no ulterior reason. It was simply his point of departure. But not wishing to waste an opportunity, I whispered back in an equally hushed tone that I was not quite at liberty to say. For reasons I never discovered, the factory owner went bug-eyed, which at the time amused me a great deal.

———

The average Guangdong driver approaches confrontation in a nonconfrontational manner. At an intersection where the right of way is up for grabs, he feigns ignorance of his surroundings in the hope that others will yield. This slick move is possible only because drivers in these parts are indeed intensely aware of their surroundings, going as far as to scan the faces of other drivers to predict their actions and gain advantage.

The driver who wishes to play thick while approaching a busy intersection will want to stare into the middle distance through his windshield without appearing even to make use of his peripheral vision. More important, he must maintain a constant rate of speed, because speeding up *or* slowing down, even a touch, reveals that the driver is indeed fully aware and able to give other drivers the opportunity to pass.

I was in a taxi whose driver was trying to play this game of chicken with a car that was approaching at a perpendicular angle. Thinking that we were on a collision course, I called out: *"Xiaoxin!"* When he made no change in speed or direction, I gripped the handle of the door, expecting to crash. At the very last moment, my driver slammed on his brakes and cursed: "You damn well saw me, you bastard!" The other fellow had also been playing thick and had won.

Road rage is not unknown to China, but it takes a culturally specific form. In the United States, where aggressive motorists can express themselves forcefully, you might get the finger, or a driver may roll down his window and tell you more directly what he thinks of your driving. Under such conditions, it is not surprising that some altercations result in personal injury or property loss.

Chinese are disinclined to act confrontationally, especially if there is a chance they might be held liable for damage caused. The smart ones prefer a nonaggressive approach, which shifts blame—and cost—to the other party. Southern Chinese who feel slighted in traffic are notorious for speeding past an offending driver, pulling ahead of him, and then slamming on the brakes.

Let *him* hit *me*, the angry but pragmatic driver says to himself. Of course the move is anticipated by most Chinese, and this ends up being nothing more than a bit of theatre, a way for the affronted party to express his frustration in a clever way.

On the high seas, the United States Navy has run into this problem on numerous occasions. In March 2009, Chinese vessels harassed the USNS Impeccable, pulling in front of the surveillance ship and slowing suddenly, forcing the Americans to perform an "all stop." Similarly, Chinese fighter jets have on several occasions forced US pilots to engage in evasive maneuvers in order to prevent a midair collision.

When these moves take place in traffic, the fellow who is "asking to be hit" will—in the rare case where an accident occurs—portray himself as the aggrieved party in order to elicit the sympathy of authorities. Chinese military officers who play the same game on the high seas and in the air are making use of a similar instinct, but have not thought through the logic of the move. In the event they actually cause an accident through such maneuvering, to what higher authority do they imagine they will appeal for sympathy? China's chauvinistic sense of sovereignty does not recognize any authority higher than the Communist Party after all. Beijing's playbook is effectively the same as the workaday citizen's. But while certain nonconfrontation strategies make sense at the grassroots level, they do not all necessarily translate to the geopolitical playing field.

———————

Mainland Chinese are belligerent without being violent. Stay in the country long enough, and you are bound to witness a few noisy altercations. The nature of these personal disputes is rarely of interest; Chinese will argue about anything and their dust-ups go nowhere. Two people standing in the street shouting abuse at one another will make empty threats and rarely is there any lasting damage. The worst that ever happens in a physical sense is that the participants grab at each other's clothing. If punches are thrown, they almost never land.

During the warlord era, militia groups rarely ever engaged in a "fight to the death." Chinese are too practical for such nonsense. Rather than carrying a battle to its maximum conclusion, fighting was usually bloodless and finished early. Arthur Ransome suggested in 1927 that warlord battles were like games of chess, except that they ended not with the trapping of the king, but rather "one move before his capture." Internecine battles and pyrrhic victories are not rational, so Chinese prefer to avoid them.

Gilbert suggested that the outcome of any given Chinese battle was actually determined at the very outset. "When two armies are face to face," he wrote, "the less numerous force retires, as a rule without fighting." William Martin was of the same opinion and suggested further details: After two armies arrived at a field and after sizing each other up, the generals from each side, now having a clear picture of who was likely to win, would strike a deal rather than go to the trouble of spilling blood. Ralph Townsend explained that as soon as the fighting begins, "peace money is passed, go-betweens commence their negotiations, opposing generals pause to seek new allies or lay plans to betray existing allies, troops desert from one side to the other as better pay is offered—and back again if promises are not kept."

Chinese companies today will occasionally resort to violence to settle a commercial dispute. But even in these cases, managers have the presence of mind to avoid a direct confrontation. Wishing to collect on a debt, the company will instead hire a group of freelance thugs to wait by the front door of the target business. Although we may view such a tactic as unethical or cowardly, we can at least appreciate the way in which risk has been reduced through outsourcing.

Beijing has a long history of farming out unwanted jobs, including military actions. In the South China Sea today, it uses its Coast Guard to chase away foreign vessels. Chinese Navy frigates will travel half a world away to pick up civilians stranded in hot zones around Africa and the Middle East. In its effort to assert territorial claims near its shores though, the People's Liberation Army Navy chooses not to get directly involved, opting instead to enlist the assistance of private fishing boats.

During the Opium Wars, China employed a similar strategy. Although the British held the Chinese Navy in contempt, they actually feared the fishermen and pirates who were sent to fight in their place. Two centuries earlier, Qing dynasty officials took credit for expelling the Dutch from Formosa in 1661. It was not Chinese sailors who did the ousting, however, but rather the Japanese-born pirate Koxinga.

In his grand tome *Far Eastern International Relations*, published in 1928, Hosea Ballou Morse noted that during the first war between China and Japan, in the 1890s, China never once scored a victory but "fled from every field of battle," surrendering one position after another. Instead of focusing on winning the war, he wrote, China wasted its energies "invoking the intervention of foreign powers." Chinese are not fighters, but prefer whenever possible to enlist a *cat's paw strategy*, which entails getting others to intercede.

Lucian Pye noted the extent to which Chinese prefer to employ such a strategy. Chinese rarely launch a direct attack, he explained, but opt instead to hang back and assess the situation. When they do move, their actions tend to be "deceitful and indirect," and those involved will try to achieve their goal by "making use of a third party."

This risk-reducing approach is so central to the way Chinese strategize that you can hardly get one of them to believe the origin of the cat's paw phrase—involving a monkey that gets a cat to pull chestnuts from a fire—is actually a fable by Jean de La Fontaine in seventeenth-century France, rather than a native idiom from Confucian-era China.

China has built a military arsenal of such size and sophistication that many are convinced we face the prospect of a traditional war. That may very well be the case, but in the interim the greater threat will be nonconfrontational in manner.

Cyberespionage is already a great risk to national security and Chinese relish the fact that such attacks can rarely be traced back to them. Unlike certain terrorist groups that seek to take credit, China is satisfied to remain anonymous.

China's love of the cat's paw suggests that we will see numerous cases of sabotage against our military, and perhaps also against our corporate interests, well before we are drawn into any traditional war. Power is subjective and China recognizes the efficiency of enlisting third parties who, for a small fee, can be made to carry out operations that cause the United States to lose face and prestige.

CHAPTER 25

The Great Absorber

Chrina has always been a great absorber," wrote Rodney Gilbert, by which he meant the grand empire had a way of swallowing civilizations whole. In the 1920s, he observed that while virulent anti-Semitism in his day had done little to diminish the number of Jews in the world, the once vibrant Jewish community in Kaifeng had almost entirely dissolved by merely associating with the surrounding culture.

Jews first settled in Kaifeng, a city in Henan, around one thousand years ago, at which time the city was the capital of the Northern Sung dynasty and arguably the most populous in the world. When the American missionary W. A. P. Martin arrived in 1866, he found that the Jewish community there had been without a rabbi for seventy years. The synagogue was "in ruins, the Jews dispersed," he wrote, and none claiming Jewish heritage spoke a word of Hebrew.

Fifteen years earlier, a Bishop Smith had visited the city, and upon hearing that the nearly defunct community was in possession of several "rolls of the law," he arranged for their purchase. Three hundred individuals gathered in the old synagogue for the proceedings, including a few of Jewish descent, and following negotiations over the sale of the six remaining Torah scrolls, a deal was struck for a mere forty *taels* of silver, or 130 British pounds.

China's reputation for absorption extends to its greatest conquerors. China's last dynasty was of course not ethnic Chinese, but was founded by a band of foreign marauders who swooped down from a territory north of the Great Wall, that long, fortified edifice built precisely for the purpose of keeping them out. Riding on horseback in the 1640s and picking up defectors along the way, the Manchu brigands made their way to the Forbidden City and declared themselves the empire's new overlords, a position they would hold for nearly 270 years.

If we forget that the Manchu were not Chinese, it is partly because they looked somewhat Chinese (more so than the Russians anyway), but mostly it is because the Manchu had by the end of their rule been fully assimilated into the Chinese culture. The new rulers only sparingly imposed their own culture onto the Chinese—most notably by requiring men to wear hair braids—and for the most part, they adopted Chinese practices and customs. It happened fast. Within a generation or two of their conquest, the Manchu ethnic identity was largely erased and their descendants were subsumed into the encompassing culture.

The empire was large and China's culture seemingly eternal. We can only imagine what it must have been like to trot into the Forbidden City and be told by sycophantic eunuchs no less that the empire was now theirs, that their chief would be called *huang-di*, the divine ruler, and that he would sit on the dragon's throne serving as the link between heaven and all that is below it. The fruits of the empire, including a rich tradition in the arts and literature, were there to be claimed. But in acknowledging the legitimacy of the Chinese tradition and in assuming leadership of the monolith, the Manchu sealed their own doom.

There is a soporific quality to the Chinese culture. Long afternoons playing cards or chess in a tea house, looking after one's crickets or birds, enjoying long strolls along the river; these popular pastimes suggest that the pace of life enjoyed by Chinese since olden times was leisured, if not languid. China is "the greatest sedative," wrote Gilbert, who also suggested that the invading barbarians underwent a kind of taming process as they adjusted to life in the empire. Beginning as warriors, these victors caught the civilization bug and determined to settle down. The Manchu desired to become sophisticated, and as they did so, they found themselves owning fewer and fewer of those "aggressive and annoying qualities" that qualify a people to rule.

Western writers of the 1920s and 1930s frequently warned: "China is the sea that salts everything that flows into it." Chinese not only unconsciously understand this to be an accurate description, they even take pride in the cultural feature, using it to prove their great resiliency. Sun Yat-sen gave speeches in the early twentieth century in which he highlighted that, though the Manchu had invaded, they were ultimately assimilated. "They not only did not wipe out the Chinese race, but were, on the contrary, absorbed by them."

When the Manchu dynasty fell in 1912, millions of Chinese packed their bags and headed into Manchuria, the homeland of their former overlords. Newspapers of the 1920s billed it as "the largest migration in human history," and though the pretext was economic opportunity in the newly opened territory, the mass population movement came to be seen also as a demographic takeover by the victorious Han Chinese.

Japan understood what the Chinese were doing in washing away the Manchurian identity. Indeed, Japan pursued a similar tactic in its own pursuit of power and influence in China. After taking the north-eastern territory by force in the 1930s, they got hold of Pu Yi—the last Manchu emperor, recently expelled from his residence in the nation-alized Forbidden City complex—and installed him as a puppet ruler of Manchuria.

George Sokolsky detailed the rest of the plan: Japan would arrange for Pu Yi to marry a Japanese princess, and their son would then also be assigned a Japanese wife. Within a couple of generations, the "Emperor of China" would be considered Japanese without question, and by extrapolation, Japan could claim authority over the whole of China. In other words, the Japanese were borrowing a page from China's own absorption playbook, a fact that did not go unnoticed by the Chinese.

Decades after the Manchu were deposed, Mao Zedong would accomplish their complete annihilation. Under communist rule, any-one with professed Manchu lineage was persecuted, causing many of them to abandon any claim to the once prestigious imperial blood-line. The obliteration was so complete, in fact, that if you wish to hear someone speak Manchu today, you have to track down a university linguistics professor.

Chinese who have some nefarious plan in mind will on occasion project their malicious intent onto a rival. Sun Yat-sen once theorized, for example, that America could use its growing population to destroy China through assimilation in the same way that China had vanquished the Manchu. He said this in the early twentieth century when the United States population was exploding due to immigration. "In another century, the population of the United States will be one billion," he speculated, "and in the meantime our population has not moved from four hundred million." Sun worried that "the Chinese would be absorbed by the Americans." The United States never did reach a billion—though China did—and of course it never had any intention to subsume any people in such a manner.

China has had no problem viewing demographics as a weapon. Mao famously said in 1957, "I'm not afraid of nuclear war. There are 2.7 billion people in the world. It doesn't matter if some are killed. China has a population of six hundred million. Even if half of them are killed, there are still three hundred million people left. I'm not afraid of anyone."

Somewhat less callously, when Jimmy Carter needled Deng Xiaoping about the way his country restricted its citizens from traveling abroad, Deng half-jokingly responded: "How many millions do you want?"

Beijing has encouraged many millions of Han Chinese to relocate to Tibet and Xinjiang, turning majorities there into soon-to-be minority populations within their own ancestral homelands. Political scientists have warned that we ought to be concerned about China's plan of "homogenization through forcible assimilation." In other parts of the world, such an ambition might be referred to as "ethnic cleansing." But because Beijing's moves are done in piecemeal fashion, and because the population shift is essentially nonviolent, we hardly comment on it at all.

In 2014, a good deal of press coverage was given to a Chinese company that organized the largest tour group ever assembled, sending more than seven thousand mainland tourists to Los Angeles at once. The following year, a group of six thousand mainlanders made a similar splash in the Côte d'Azur. The news of these spectacular events—both qualified as Guinness World Records—was accompanied by images of the tourist troops standing abreast in the streets, holding large banners, and shouting nationalist slogans. We think nothing of such a happening because we believe everyone has the right to travel. But if the situation were reversed and a similar number of foreigners had gathered on the streets of Shanghai, the Chinese authorities would not be so tolerant.

To some, such gatherings appear at first blush to be innocent celebrations. But to others they appear less anodyne and more like the storming of a beachhead. Chinese were at one time prohibited from strolling along the foreign-controlled promenade on the Bund, a stretch along the Yangtze River in Shanghai. "Later allowed in," wrote Arthur Ransome in the 1920s, "they took on an air as if they had forcibly taken the space."

Chinese are used to operating under strict controls. Freedoms of any scope usually come only after much time and effort. Not used to being allowed to rush into anything, mainlanders have become accustomed to taking an inch-by-inch approach. In the South China Sea, Beijing has made incremental moves. Throwing a bit of sand onto a few reefs, officials praised such actions so long as no one complained. As the West remained silent, buildings were added to these man-made islands, then runways, and finally hangars.

China has quietly renamed islands that for centuries were recognized as Japanese territory and has even gotten the international press to legitimize its absurd claims. Encouraged by such green lights, Beijing has gone so far as to suggest that even the Japanese island of Okinawa is a part of China's "inherent territory." That supporting evidence for this assertion is thin to nonexistent doesn't matter, so long as there is no countervailing pressure to challenge these claims. Writing in 1890, Reverend Arthur Smith cautioned: "Foreign carelessness invites Chinese annexation."

Chinese factories are also fond of the incremental approach. They quietly degrade the quality of merchandise produced. Then, when a buyer finally catches on, the manufacturer will defend itself by pointing out that "it has actually been like that for quite some time now." The factory owner is smooth and confidently cites the client's long-standing passivity as a basis for why there should be no complaint, as if it were an issue of squatter's rights. The fact that no one has noticed is presented as proof for why it should matter less. "There is nothing like getting used to things," was another warning offered by Smith to heedless foreigners.

Thomas Schelling was a modern game theorist who wrote successfully about *incremental strategies*. His analogy of a child playing along the banks of a river is an apt one for the Chinese: "Tell a child not to go in the water and he'll sit on the bank and submerge his bare feet; he is not yet 'in' the water. Acquiesce, and he'll stand up; no more of him is in the water than before. Think it over, and he'll start wading, not going any deeper. Take a moment to decide whether this is different and he'll go a little deeper, arguing that since he goes back and forth it all averages out. Pretty soon we are calling to him not to swim out of sight, wondering whatever happened to all our discipline."

Ralph Townsend had incrementalism on his mind when he relayed the story of Reverend Vance Maloney, head missionary with the Seventh-Day Adventist Church in Fuzhou. Looking to travel to the United States in 1931, Maloney left his church in the care of a fellow American missionary. While he was away, the other clergyman allowed a Chinese family to work a patch of soil at the end of the property. After a time, the family made a hole in the wall of the grounds near their patch for easier access. Shortly after that, they fenced off the plot from the rest of the compound, making it impossible to reach the garden except from outside the mission through the hole made in the wall.

The case turned into a fiasco with the family claiming rightful ownership as evidenced by their improvements to the soil and by their investment in a fence. A gang was hired by the family to threaten Maloney's assistant, and the local police chose not to intervene. Maloney was a "huge ranger type of Texan" though, and when a local gang he hired was chased off, Maloney stepped in himself and physically removed the squatters.

CHAPTER 26

Kleptoparasitism

As a fixer in the manufacturing sector, I used to pay special attention to news articles suggesting that China was "moving up the value chain," though I never saw any evidence of this actually taking place. The factory that made soap and shampoo was never going to produce aircraft engine parts or get into advanced robotics. Yes, they wanted to get ahead, but they did so by adding a hair gel to their product lineup, or else they tried (and failed) to develop a dry stick deodorant.

The manufacturers I knew "got ahead" by degrading the products they produced in order to save some small amount. Rather than looking up the supply chain, they looked outward, focusing on ways to steal business away from competing suppliers. Once these basic moves were played out, the typical industrialist would attempt to outmaneuver his key customers by directly approaching the distributors and retailers that lay behind them. There was more to be gained in *disintermediation*—cutting out the middleman—than by making material improvements to a production process or to a product.

China manufacturing is a cutthroat business. The government understands this and elects to ignore what takes place as a matter of course. Even in cases where a foreign buyer is treated in an especially egregious way, authorities rarely get involved. Beijing views factories the same way ancient emperors regarded remote villages, which were expected to operate autonomously and without supervision.

Oversight is not really necessary anyway because factory bosses are pragmatic. They might cut a few corners in production, but they rarely go so far that a customer will leave them. Chinese factory bosses have a natural incentive to cultivate long-term, repeat orders. As a result, most of the problems we have with factories are manageably small.

Rodney Gilbert had a solid grasp on the autonomous principles that drive business ethics in China, and he warned about what might happen if certain motivations changed: "If A buys regularly from B on credit and realizes a handsome profit on every turnover, it does not pay A to swindle B on a single transaction, and thereby lose a profitable connection. Under such conditions A's word is certainly as good as his bond. What is the use of writing down a pledge the breach of which would entail a permanent loss? But when the connection is no longer profitable nor promising and a breach of contract would benefit A, he has no more regard for a written bond than a verbal one if he believes B powerless to enforce collection. In China, when honesty ceases to yield returns it is a policy to be discarded at the first available opportunity."

In Guangzhou, there was a wonderful spot called Bellagio Cafe. Though it sounds like an Italian trattoria, it was in fact an eatery specializing in Sichuan cuisine. Walking in for lunch one day, I almost didn't notice anything had changed. The decor was the same, as was the menu. Had I been paying attention though, I would have caught that the sign outside displayed a different business name, even though it was still the same shade of purple.

The landlord had decided the rent he was collecting on the space was not enough. He wanted also to capture the profitability of the restaurant, so he conspired to have his tenant removed and took over the business. In another part of town, the landlord of an Irish-run sports bar similarly decided that he wanted to be more principally involved, so he too kicked out his foreign tenant and assumed control of the operation.

In ecology there are examples of animal species that either steal nesting materials or else wholly occupy a nest created by another creature. Biologists call the behavior *kleptoparasitism*, and though an ecosystem would collapse if every animal adopted such a strategy, for a select few animals, the act of free riding is a winning formula for survival.

Kleptoparasitism is common in business, and as lamentable as the practice may be, one of its advantages is that it transfers all of the risk (and much of the cost) to the one foolish enough to establish the footprint. Creating something from scratch has its drawbacks: A new product may not work, or else a company learns too late that demand for it is weak. Chinese understand instinctively that first movers are disadvantaged, and so they prefer to let others test the waters. It is not a moral issue, but a practical one.

———————

During World War One, China backed the Allied forces but decided it would stay out of the war, using the excuse that their fighting men would not be able to tell one group of Caucasians from another on the battlefield. Though not directly involved in Europe, at home the Chinese took advantage of the war—and the fact that the foreign powers no longer presented a united front—to cancel Germany's extraterritoriality rights. Soon thereafter, officials seized all German assets, including a number of banks and many businesses.

"Anti-foreignism is more often a pretext than an objective," wrote Ralph Townsend, though he was referring more directly to the violence visited upon missionaries and the attendant looting that went with it. Sun Yat-sen was so impressed with the way in which German assets had been confiscated that he actually suggested China might wish to consider doing the same with the remaining foreign powers. During the Republican era, China was looking for a way forward and Sun thought the further swallowing of foreign assets would give the struggling nation the sort of fillip that it needed. A couple of decades later of course, that very plan was put into place by the Communist Party.

In the 1860s, HSBC constructed a beautiful neoclassical building in Shanghai. The British bank (headquartered in Hong Kong) ended up losing the six-story structure in the communist takeover, but not before some unknown individuals had the good sense to cover up numerous mosaics and other architectural features that would likely have been defaced by the Red Guards.

When the economy opened back up in the 1970s, the bank building on the Bund was not returned to HSBC but remained with the new regime. Because they were eager to re-enter the country as quickly as possible, foreign firms in situations like this did not bother raising the issue of assets previously lost. Any attempt to bring up "mistakes" of the past would have only retarded the process of regaining market access and increased the likelihood that a competitor might beat them to it.

CHAPTER 27

Cleaning the Slate

C hinese factory owners like to think several moves ahead and their antennae are always up so they can monitor for shifts in business sentiment. Sooner or later, these industrialists figure, conditions will change and they will be forced to make a move. It is for good reason that Chinese manufacturers never bother securing plant equipment to the shop floor.

British soldiers of the eighteenth century noted that local troops were similarly on edge. Chinese forts all had trap doors so that soldiers could escape on short notice in an unwelcome situation, such as when they were under attack. And if it was easier to jump over the fort wall, they would take that route instead.

Beijing's central planners who seek growth across the economy are also careful to pursue strategies that minimize shocks that could trigger a cascading panic. Chinese officials lay heavy emphasis on stability, in part because they understand the skittishness of their people. In normal circumstances, Chinese are rational to a fault, but when a window of opportunity appears to be closing fast, a different mindset sometimes takes over.

Chinese instinctively understand game theory, and they are naturals at distinguishing a *continuous game* from a *discrete game*. They readily apprehend when there has been a shift in a given circumstance from one model to the other, and they will act accordingly.

A factory that is prepaid one million dollars to ship widgets is not likely to disappear with the cash if the profit margin is ten percent and the business is repeated each month. It makes no economic sense to commit fraud by stealing a million when the same amount will be realized within a year of playing by the rules. The danger of a tidal change in motivation emerges, though, when profit margins shrink to five percent and then two percent. In such cases, the incentive to take the money and run becomes more alluring.

When one factory owner in a particular industry sector succumbs to the always strong temptation to disappear with a customer's cash, it can cause all players in that sector to doubt their future. Chinese industrialists are sensitive to their credibility among foreign buyers. So if a few foreigners are cheated and the sector's reputation is tarnished, the remaining players will assume it is only a matter of time before foreigners stop placing orders. Even a normally honest exporter will ponder this situation and conclude that because his foreign buyers are about to go elsewhere anyway, he should probably take advantage while he still has the chance.

A manufacturer who assumes orders will dry up within a couple years may consider planning to withdraw earlier, say within a year. Others who worry of those planning to get out in twelve months may think that a nine-month time horizon is more prudent. Still others will figure that they have even less time to make a clean exit, maybe only six months, or three . . . and suddenly there is an immediate frenzy.

In China, people collude in a mob-like manner, figuring that so long as everyone is behaving equally badly, there is less risk to each individual. It is a rarely mentioned cultural trait that represents an unacknowledged risk.

Chinese newspapers periodically report highway accidents involving overturned commercial vehicles. No matter where the mishap takes place, or what the truck is hauling, nearby villagers will swarm to the scene and grab whatever they can get their hands on. In one case, locals ran off with ten thousand live baby chicks. In another incident where a truck of oranges spilled out onto the road, scavengers beat up the driver who attempted to stop the theft of his haul. Police are helpless to stop these mad grubbers who look upon the driver's bad luck as a sign of their own divine fortune and as a limited-time opportunity that is not to be squandered. For mainlanders, such automatic triggers provide what might be considered a temporary exemption from the normal laws of ethical behavior.

Western writers of the late nineteenth and early twentieth centuries spoke of *social typhoons*, a phenomenon peculiar to China. Coined first by Reverend Arthur Smith, the term was used to describe the excitable mobs that occasionally gather, motivated by anything from greed to displeasure to panic.

"It is a well authenticated fact," wrote Putnam Weale in 1925, "that you can do anything with any mass of Chinese if you are prepared to meet the situation at its inception, and nothing with them if the occasional madness which their peculiar nervous mechanism invites is allowed full sway."

When it takes place today, we tend to focus on those events we can label as "protests." China watchers—even the experienced ones—have in the modern era failed to understand or explain what causes the broader phenomenon. And it is precisely because we can hardly imagine something so organic and wild that we are inclined to believe that such events have been orchestrated by high government officials. But most "cyclones of passion" have nothing to do with politics or anti-foreign sentiment. Instead, they are motivated by simple greed.

Whenever you read about a stampede in India, you can rest assured that it has taken place during a religious festival. In Europe, stampedes that result in death usually happen at sporting events. In China, the mad rush of a crowd almost always has something to do with economics. A sales promotion on cooking oil and rumors of a rice shortage have both sent Chinese into frenzied action.

In 2014, a stampede along Shanghai's Bund that killed thirty-six and injured forty-nine was reportedly triggered by the release of fake US one-hundred-dollar bills that had been thrown down from a balcony as part of a nightclub promotion. And because the government issued statements vehemently denying that flying cash had sparked the stampede, you knew that the rumor was true.

CHAPTER 28

Massacred in Business

Our memories are short-lived, and this gets us into trouble. Who among us is even aware that the Chinese killed some 120,000 foreigners—Arabs and Persians mostly—in 879 AD? Or that during the reign of Henry the Eighth, hundreds of Portuguese traders were killed on direct orders from the emperor himself?

The nineteenth century saw many instances of violence against foreigners, but only a handful were recorded: the Juye Incident involved the killing of two German missionaries in 1859; ten years later, a French consul and his assistant were dispatched amid rioting; in 1870, the Tianjin Massacre took the lives of another French consul and his assistant; in 1891, antiforeign attacks took place "up and down the Yangtze River." We will never know the full extent of atrocities committed because most instances of violence went unreported. Christian missionaries were the most common targets, and they were in the habit of playing down attacks, even hiding cases of murder, because they feared making too much noise might lose them the opportunity to "win China for Christ."

By far, the most spectacular attack against foreigners in modern times took place in 1900 when a ragtag army of bare-chested, sword-wielding thugs known as the Society of the Righteous and Harmonious Fists—also known as the Boxers—murdered four hundred foreigners, mostly missionaries from the United States and England. China's head of state at the time, the Empress Dowager Cixi, was said to have personally ordered the attack.

The China Martyrs of 1900 is a sad but notable book and one long forgotten. A memorial to the Christians who were killed in the Boxer Massacre, it profiles many of those who lost their lives. Numerous images in the book show missionary couples seated with their children, and to learn that entire families were dispatched by the butchers is, even after all these years, heartbreaking. The book's many accounts of Christian teachers and doctors—all in China to aid the country's development—are poignant reminders of this great tragedy.

The event has been wiped from our collective memory though, and we should wonder whether such amnesia would even be possible had the situation been reversed. Just imagine if President William McKinley had ordered the slaughter of every Chinese on American soil, from one coast to the other, and if four hundred Chinese had been killed in the process. What monuments would we have erected to assuage our guilt? What holiday would have been created to commemorate the mass killing? Would there have been any end to the Chinese reminding us of such a horror?

The United States received an indemnity from the Chinese government following the event—cash payments as a way of saying sorry—and our response to the gesture was to tell the Chinese government after a few installments to never mind paying the balance.

The Boxer Rebellion, as it was later called, was a bit harder to forget than other outbreaks of antiforeignism, not only because of the enormity of the tragedy, but also because the threat of violence lingered. Twenty years after the massacre, Ellen LaMotte, an American nurse and journalist, wrote that while foreigners felt safe at the legation in Beijing, "they always appear to have a bag packed and a ladder leaning against the compound walls in case of emergency."

Writing in the 1920s, Putnam Weale lamented that the events of 1900 were all but forgotten and that foreigners had once again reverted to a fantastical perspective on China. In his prescient book *Why China Sees Red*, he suggested that foreigners of his day were too giddy about China for their own good and that they needed to be "violently shocked into a sane perspective" by a similar such tragedy. China's poor treatment of foreigners in the 1920s was due to a loss of Western resolve, wrote Rodney Gilbert, who figured that related problems would persist "until outrages against foreigners reach the proportions attained during the Boxer movement."

If most instances of violence were forgotten it was in part because in each case the survivors convinced themselves that the event was *uncharacteristic* of the Chinese. Western missionaries sent to replace colleagues who had been killed noted that they were greeted with warmth by some of the very same people who months earlier had participated in the rioting. So even new arrivals promoted the fallacy that whatever savagery had been exhibited was atypical.

Over the years, I have worked with numerous Westerners who have been murdered—in the business sense. What strikes me often is the way in which these people view what happened to them as exceptional. They write off bad behavior as uncharacteristic of the Chinese in general, or of their business partners in particular. It is a necessary view to take, because without such an exercise in self-delusion, the foreigner is forced to admit that he has no business operating in this marketplace, in spite of his desperate yearnings to do so.

Much of what's wrong with China is actually something wrong within us. We are too fond of this country. We are too forgiving. We willingly have amnesia on the basis that we care. That the reader should find it "impolite" to bring up an historic event such as the Boxer Massacre is proof enough of this fact. "What other country," wrote Ralph Townsend, "would have escaped so lightly after its government had calmly ordered in peacetime the slaughter of all foreigners resident in its chief city, including diplomatic representatives and their families, as did China in 1900?"

Indeed, what other country?

George Wingrove Cooke suggested that the Chinese took advantage of the foreigner's Christianity, which taught him to "return good for evil" by offering him the opportunity to prove that he held such a precept. "The two-cheek policy is an absolute failure in dealing with the Chinese," declared Townsend, who understood that the apparent uprightness of the foreigner was viewed as a defect to be exploited. Rodney Gilbert was of the same hard-boiled mind and for similar reasons he warned that "we must sooner or later revolt against the spirit of charity towards China, which is interpreted as weakness and acknowledged with contempt."

To suggest, by the way, that the Chinese have no memory of what took place a century ago is especially self-delusional. Beijing understands entirely well that no matter how badly foreigners are treated, they will eventually flock back to this illusive El Dorado. No matter how bad it gets, after some brief interval (and following sheepish excuses from the Chinese for why things went wrong), we will again be lining up—even competing with one another—for the opportunity to take yet another chance on China. This blind love affair of ours, recognized fully by Beijing, represents one of the greatest moral hazards imaginable.

CHAPTER 29

The China Watchers

China has always eluded the comprehension of outsiders. In his 1911 book, *The Changing Chinese*, Edward Alsworth Ross references a foreign engineer, who says of the place, "I have been here thirty years, and the longer I stay the less I understand these people." Sir Robert Hart, the famed nineteenth-century British diplomat, expressed a similar notion when he wrote: "A year or two ago, I thought I knew something about her affairs, and I ventured to commit my views to writing. But today I seem to have lost all knowledge. If you asked me to write even three or four pages about China, I should be puzzled to do so."

In 1862, Edward Barrington de Fonblanque suggested that long residence in China warped the judgment of certain Englishmen to such an extent that it made them unreliable witnesses: "Paradoxical as it may appear, it is the fact, that the longer a man lives in China, the less able he becomes to give information about it."

Even today, one hears echoes of this nonsensical notion—that only the newcomer is qualified to comment and that those who have been around for some time are disqualified by dint of experience. While I do not subscribe to the notion that with time comes confusion, I do believe that the China-watching community on the whole has done an increasingly feeble job as the years have passed.

It is curious that books written on China in the 1960s—Dennis Bloodworth's *The Chinese Looking Glass* is an example—should read finer than most of what is produced these days, and that even these books pale in comparison to the works of the previous generation. The trend appears to go back quite some time. In the 1930s, Ralph Townsend was convinced that his contemporaries wrote nothing as accurate as that which was produced by Arthur Smith and Abbé Huc. The writer G. F. Hudson, a contemporary of Townsend's, went further by claiming that "China was better known to Europeans in the eighteenth century than in the nineteenth, despite extensions of scholarly inquiry, simply because earlier reporters had less cause to misrepresent what they found."

It was not meant to work this way. In her turn-of-the-twentieth-century book, *China: The Long-Lived Empire*, American writer Eliza Ruhamah Scidmore suggested that "each book of the moment is an aid to comprehending the incomprehensible, deciphering the indecipherable, and working at the puzzle which other centuries may solve." Smith, who wrote also around this time, similarly thought that an accumulation of knowledge would eventually lead to an elevated understanding. "There is no apparent reason," he wrote, "now that several hundred years of our acquaintance with China have elapsed, why what is actually known of its people should not be coordinated, as well as any other combination of complex phenomena."

This was years before universities began funding departments and sponsoring chairs dedicated to the pursuit of deeper knowledge of China. Smith was right in presuming we would one day tackle the subject of China the way we objectively approach other scientific areas of study, such as chemistry. He just didn't anticipate on our failing so miserably at it.

China writers of the early twentieth century once showed great promise in advancing the cause. Author Paul French has noted that there were, between 1900 and 1937, "more magazines and non-academic journals devoted to understanding China than there are now" and that the foreign press corps during that same time frame "was significantly larger than it has been at any time since."

Although the volume of analysis from this period was impressive, much of it was written specifically to obfuscate the truth. Rodney Gilbert thought his contemporaries were guilty of reshaping facts. Competing with one another, a fair amount of one-upmanship was taking place. The fellow who dedicated himself to Chinese language studies was inclined to boast about the insight this afforded him into the great civilization. Even if he was disappointed with what he found, he was not likely to admit that he had "wasted his life burrowing into a rubbish heap." Quite the opposite, the foreigner was "inclined to persuade himself and others that his labors have been rewarded, that he has unearthed wonderful treasures."

Missionaries whitewashed their experiences because they didn't want to put their evangelical work at risk. Business representatives stationed in the Far East painted a rosy picture regarding business prospects for similar reasons, because they did not wish to be recalled or reassigned.

Economic and technological progress alone ought to have made it easier to watch China, but modernity, as it turns out, had actually a negative influence. Not only has it never been easier to travel to China, but also more of the people you meet there can speak English. The nineteenth century enjoyed no such conveniences. The average stint was four or five years uninterrupted with no vacation away from the mainland. And no one on the ground spoke any English at all, which meant that a person was forced to learn the local dialect, which was not necessarily Mandarin.

Today, by contrast, the use of English by Chinese locals has become so widespread that a foreigner can live perfectly well in Shanghai or Beijing without speaking a lick of Chinese. Counterintuitive as it may appear, the spread of English has increased misapprehension more than it has raised mutual understanding. This is because the local who speaks a fair amount of English is already a changed person, a hybrid between an ancient Chinese and a more modern soul.

China in the nineteenth century was a *tableau vivant*. Chinese were largely unaware of what went on in the outside world, which provided a clearer picture of what it meant to be Chinese. As a result, the traveler of that bygone era was given more direct access to the traditional culture.

Modernity aside, the legacy of the Mao era has added another layer of misinformation that needs to be stripped away before China as a nation can be seen for what it truly is. Although it is widely accepted that the Chinese people were brainwashed in decades past, there has never been any systematic attempt at deprogramming. China watchers of the pre-communist era got so much more right, because the political landscape was by comparison less contaminated.

I may regret putting it in such terms, but China watching was a good deal more accurate when foreigners ran the risk of dying. Westerners who lived in China during the late nineteenth and early twentieth centuries had to contend with physical threats such as rioting, a not infrequent occurrence. China is now a safer place in which to work. Threats today are less against our personal safety and more against our better judgment. We no longer need worry about being chased down the streets. Instead, we are cornered and told, "You speak Mandarin so well," even though we have uttered only a few words. At the dinner table, we can barely hold onto a morsel of food, yet our hosts compliment us on our use of chopsticks. Flattery and encouraging affection are the order of the day, and whether we are aware of it or not, we have been seduced by such fawning treatment, and this has also colored our perceptions.

———————

In 2009, Jon Huntsman Jr., ambassador to the People's Republic of China, set off a social media storm when he declared that "there is no such thing as a China expert" and that those who consider themselves as such were "kind of morons." His words, delivered in China at a press briefing held by the White House Press Secretary, upset a number of professionals who make their living by providing culture-specific expertise. I had to meditate on it before coming to the conclusion that I agreed with the guy. China is an enigma, a Gordian knot. By definition it is an unsolvable problem, and so of course there can be no deemed experts.

Knowing this to be the case, though, you have to wonder what we were doing encouraging the economy's rapid growth. Now that our future is inextricably tied with China's, it is a bit late. But if the presumption had always been that no one could ever definitively tell us what in the hell was going on, why did we start down a path that might put the global economy in a precarious position?

China watchers do their best not to think about such big questions, but focus instead on the ever more important matter of establishing their personal credibility. There may be no such thing as an expert, but certainly some are more qualified to expound than others. Those who speak the language naturally emphasize the importance of fluency. "It doesn't help much," I tell clients, because knowledge of the language rarely changes the outcome of a given transaction. Chinese factory bosses tend to follow their own game plan, and all language proficiency does is provide a small window into their maneuverings. It's a bit like being taken hostage. The terrorists had you bound and gagged with a black bag placed over your head. They were going to chop your head off no matter what, but understanding their tongue, you knew at least when and where it was going to happen.

High-level advisors such as Henry Kissinger and Hank Paulson, who do not speak Chinese, like to emphasize the number of trips they have made to China, another dubious measure of expertise. A trip is a reflection of nothing in particular. When someone says they have made a trip, we do not know what, if anything, was accomplished during what is usually only a brief stay. Americans commonly travel to China for just a few short days at a time, preferring to be back in the comfort of their own homes in time for the weekend.

Just as pilots do not measure experience by the number of takeoffs and landings they make, but rather by hours flown, a better indicator of experience is the amount of time spent inside the country. And on that account, there are numerous expatriates living and working in China today who have even the most widely traveled US-based professionals beat several-fold.

Long-term foreign residents appear to be in the perfect position to claim authority, yet even they struggle with credibility. For one thing, no matter how much time an expatriate has put in, he invariably adds a bit of fudge. Those on the ground all know someone who has been in the country only twelve years, but because he had visited eight years previously as a backpacker, he goes ahead and counts his time as starting from that earlier sojourn. My own time in the region was interrupted by graduate school, yet I have only rarely been faulted for not subtracting the intervening years from my own tally.

China expatriates are an insufferable lot, and they know it. Confucian traditions rub off on the foreign transplant, including a keener awareness of social hierarchy. In ancient China, when two mandarins approached one another on an old road, it was customary for the lesser official to dismount and for his entourage to bow in obeisance as the party of the more senior official passed. This is the sort of vibe you get from many on-the-ground foreigners. That fellow who has done eighteen years expects deference from the one who has clocked only ten, but then he dips his head in the direction of the one who claims twenty-two.

Whenever someone in China approaches me with this mindset, making a big deal of himself because he has managed to hang around for a couple decades, I say nothing since it is no real accomplishment. Samuel Isett Woodbridge, John Leighton Stuart, and Samuel Wells Williams all authored books with the exact same title—*Fifty Years in China*. And those were fifty *long* years. There was no Internet, no telephone, and no air travel. Westerners today who brag of long tenure in the country tend to leave out the part about how they shuttled back home each summer and at Christmastime.

George Wingrove Cooke was harsh on nineteenth-century expatriates and their claims of expertise, pointing out that mere on-the-ground experience was not enough. "The circumstance that a person has lived for eighteen years in China," he wrote, "is no more a guarantee that he is competent to write of the characteristics of the Chinese, than the fact that another man has for eighteen years been buried in a silver mine is a proof that he is a fit person to compose a treatise on metallurgy, or bi-metallism."

Old China hands are self-appointed. There is no examination to take, and no board exists to certify someone as a professional. As a result, all sorts of people are in the game who probably ought not to be.

A doctor can have his license yanked for malpractice if he gives bad medical advice. An incompetent lawyer may be disbarred. Nail salon technicians working in Los Angeles County have more rights to claim expertise in their field—they get a plaque at least—than consultants whose careers are based on explaining China to the outside world.

Ten years ago, when I sat down to write my first book—a farcical critique of China—you could not *find* a condemning voice on the subject. Now the whole crowd is on the other side of the equation. China consultants who advised their clients to jump feet first into the market when they ought to have recommended caution have nothing to say about their faulty counsel. The same thing can be said of foreign journalists who have similarly backpedaled from predictions of peace and harmony in regards to our relations with China. Asked now to answer for themselves, they shrug and say, "What do you want from me? I was just being optimistic."

———

Because there is no objective measure, China watchers and old China hands aim to convince the lesser initiated that they know China by projecting an air of serenity and a sense that they appreciate certain esoteric aspects of the culture. They assume a tranquil disposition; their eyes will appear softly focused when they speak. "You have to understand the importance that the Chinese place on etiquette," they remind, and if you do not immediately nod your head in agreement, you run the risk of being labeled ignorant.

In order to show that he understands China and the Chinese, the foreigner makes a spectacle of his conscientiousness. He will be careful in your presence to express criticism of neither the place nor the people, because to do so would be to hint that he might not appreciate the subject, which is perilously close to not understanding it. Those who pretend to have the greatest insights into the Chinese culture have trained themselves to hardly speak of it at all. Their rhetoric is limited to the grossest cultural platitudes and the latest Beijing-backed political opinions.

To show that you *know* China, you do not *speak* about it. And as preposterous as that may sound, it is the ethos driving modern-day conversations on the subject. It is another reason why you will find more insights in a book written one hundred years ago than in something written last month.

China watchers walk on eggshells, and any apparent courage displayed is limited to a discrete list of preapproved subtopics. You may speak about pollution now, if you like. That one is on the approved list. The great amount of wealth disparity in the country is now also allowable, as is the subject of official corruption. Even though these are direct criticisms of the government, Beijing welcomes such chatter. It enables everyone to blow off steam while furthering the impression that China is liberalizing. China watchers who congratulate themselves for having the temerity to "take down" a big, authoritarian government by focusing on such topics are doing nothing more than playing in state-approved discourse sandboxes.

One of the more courageous China analysts the field has known, Lucian Pye criticized the China-watching community for being too reluctant to dive into discussions on prohibited cultural matters. Following World War Two, he pointed out, academics went to great lengths to understand the German character and how it gave rise to Nazism, and a "theory of Japaneseness" was likewise presented and debated in an effort to study the Japanese. But there has been only cowardice when it comes to applying a similar treatment to the Chinese. "There is no reason why psycho-cultural studies should be seen as inherently unfriendly toward the societies that are their subjects," he wrote. But in fact, any analysis offered on the Chinese people, unless it is overwhelmingly positive, is considered an affront and is countered with great vigor.

China watchers are natural apologists, and they often feel duty bound to defend the nation. Should an ill-mannered detractor mention some national fault, he is likely to hear from one of them, in a professorial tone: "China's population is quite large, as you well know." Everything from draconian government policies to the worst cultural traits of China can be forgiven and dismissed by citing this single impersonal element: the nation's vast population. Assigning blame to demographics is among the more fashionable intellectual cop-outs.

It is not surprising to see foreigners defend China, since any self-selecting group of people that immerses itself in a foreign environment is going to be predisposed toward its new homeland. What does surprise, however, is the way in which these outsiders adopt their hosts' own nonconfrontational style of defense through avoidance. Mainland Chinese are not in the habit of admitting a problem—not at work and not in life. Their preference is to enlist a denial strategy while secretly resolving the issue out of sight. Chinese business managers will deny a difficulty up to the very moment they declare it has been resolved, which makes for some awkward conversations along the way.

China watchers themselves—grown adults—are loath to discuss certain issues unless given the wiggle room to simultaneously insist (in the very same breath) that while there are issues, things are not all *that* bad. "China has problems, but it's getting better," has been a preferred way to frame the discussion. Whenever some well-meaning booster tries to stump me with that line, I always tell them that I wouldn't mind conceding that it *is* getting better, so long as we could have at least some dialogue on what *it* is exactly.

CHAPTER 30

Isolationist Past

In the early twentieth century, Qing officials encouraged foreign nations to invest in railroad projects in order to help build up the national economy. Westerners of the era were made to believe that they were operating in a free market and that their rights would be protected. But they soon came to find that the Chinese had different ideas. James Whitford Bashford, an American missionary, noted a changing attitude starting in the 1910s. Chinese were beginning to grumble about the land rights granted along rail lines, which were seen as "limiting the sovereignty of the Chinese nation."

Walking around a large mainland city such as Shanghai today, it is hard to believe that Chinese are not bothered by so significant a foreign presence. Step into any high-end shopping mall and you find nothing but imported brands—Louis Vuitton, Michael Kors, Tory Burch. Foreign retail outlets are ubiquitous and the signage is usually in English only. It makes you wonder where Chinese chauvinism has gone.

Wall Street business analysts mistakenly presume that certain US companies are successful simply because they have a strong presence in China. In many instances, associated brands have entered the market by way of a joint venture in which the local partner retains a high percentage of profits. Chinese officials did a slick job of encouraging growth through this model, which not only enriched many local operators but also lent the appearance that China was now up-to-date.

One hundred years ago, Chinese officials were similarly satisfied that they had struck good bargains with foreign powers wishing to invest in railroads. They played the Russians off the Japanese, and the French off the Americans, picking up commissions on deals along the way. So long as they succeeded in running such gambits, they figured China was doing all right. Not long thereafter, though, they looked around and saw themselves surrounded by "symbols of imperialism" and convinced themselves that they could have built the railroads on their own.

The joint ventures of today will be subjected to a similar policy shift in the near future. But lucky for the foreign firms involved, before any major shift in policy occurs, we will receive some telegraphed hint of moral justification. Beijing will echo the rhetoric on national sovereignty of that bygone era, reminding us that the only people who should be allowed to "exploit" China through profits should be the Chinese themselves.

In an interview with Mike Wallace for *Sixty Minutes*, Deng Xiaoping once spoke of the realities of finance, saying that he understood no foreign investor would risk going to China "unless he got a return on his investment." In my experience, Chinese factories that tell prospective buyers that they "understand" the customer's need to earn a profit are among the most rapacious partners. And eventually more in the West will come to understand the insincerity of such expressions of empathy.

Decades ago, Chinese Communist officials who allowed foreign firms to earn excessive profits ran the risk of being jailed for treason. Suddenly encouraged by Deng Xiaoping's "Opening-Up and Reform" program, Chinese business leaders came to recognize the need to dangle a profit incentive in order to get foreign firms to contribute capital, technology, and business know-how. Now that the economy has matured to a significant extent, leaders feel they have less need for these external inputs and can easily revert to a more traditional stance of "China for the Chinese."

When the crunch comes, the approach will not be as broad as it was during the communist takeover. This next time, efforts will be targeted at specific industries. It is hard to see what is taking place in entertainment, for example, and not imagine that Beijing will soon hint at an enlightened consciousness.

Chinese companies have convinced major Hollywood studios to spend billions of dollars to set up shop in China. Mainland executives figure they have done well, because not only did they catch the money, but they even got American studio heads to promise that they will teach the Chinese how to make Hollywood-quality films. Hollywood is a singular institution with a unique and long history though, and even with a budget of a trillion US dollars the phenomenon cannot be replicated.

Chinese film companies have shown that they do all right when it comes to animation and computer graphics, but they do not have the same tradition of storytelling (as evidenced by dozens of film adaptations of *Monkey*, the sixteenth-century classic). China has its own beloved actors to be sure, but they do not bring a level of craft comparable to America's own top talent in the field. Music, an integral part of the film experience, is another area where China falls short. The United States is home to dozens of top musicians capable of scoring a movie in its entirety—names like Hans Zimmer and John Williams come to mind—plus it has a voluminous catalog of popular music that stretches back decades. Licensing a few tracks from the 1970s or 1980s is easy and there is much work to choose from. In other words, Hollywood is bigger than the sum of its component studios.

There ought to be a word to describe the way in which Chinese chauvinism is inverted into a loss of national face. Chinese hate nothing more than appearing foolish, and when they realize this attempt to clone Hollywood in Beijing was sheer folly, they will lash out.

We will see variations on this theme in multiple sectors of the economy where the Chinese have leveraged foreign greed in an attempt to replicate foreign successes. In their own way, they will "nationalize" foreign investments, ejecting foreign joint venture partners, while denying them further market access. Chinese leaders will then congratulate themselves once more on having outmaneuvered us.

The West has consistently been an active supporter of China's resurgence over the past few hundred years, and if we had high hopes, it was partly due to our expectation that economic cooperation with the nation would be mutually beneficial. China has not always shared the view that trade is good, however, and throughout much of its history it has sought isolation.

In the fifteenth century, the Ming dynasty closed its doors to the world. It wasn't until three hundred years later—and even then only under threat of violence—that China finally agreed to trade again. The next age of openness proved short-lived as the doors shut once more in 1949. China's most recent reentry into the international economy has been slow and reluctant.

China has expressed a willingness to join the international system, but only so long as it is offered a leading position. Understanding that China is thin-skinned in this way, global leaders pander to Beijing. We fully recognize that if China does not get its way, in numerous regards, we run the risk that it will take its ball and go home. In the 1920s, foreigners spoke about the great effort to have China take "her rightful place in the comity of nations," and a century later we appear desperate still to find a way to convince Chinese leaders that this is something they should desire, without guarantees.

China has not signed onto globalism in any meaningful way, leaving us to wonder whether the soft-boiled approach works. Beijing barely acknowledges the nation-state system, as evidenced by its willingness to jail and mistreat ethnic Chinese who hold passports from foreign countries. China has even sent bounty hunters into Australia, Canada, and the United States on secret missions to track down mainlanders suspected of having committed crimes back home. And how has the international community respond to such outrages? By allowing Beijing to appoint its own man, a former paramilitary officer, to head up Interpol, the world's largest international police organization.

Many of the rights and privileges afforded China in recent years have not been deserved. Our expectation has been that in offering such honors, Chinese leaders would see that we were sincere, and we hoped that it might bring them around to our way of thinking of the world. China has failed to reciprocate, opting instead to hold off and see what else we put on the table as an additional incentive.

China has been given the prestige of a superpower without having made the necessary commitments. As such, China is the only superpower in history that ever attained such status on a credit basis.

Not long ago, the International Monetary Fund announced that it would shove aside more established currencies to make room for the renminbi in its benchmark currency basket. In announcing the policy change, IMF managing director Christine Lagarde offered that the move was partially in recognition of "progress made" and with the implied understanding that Beijing would continue "deepening" reforms in the future. Most critics would agree that the Chinese by this time should have been much further along with financial reform, but we appear to have been unable to motivate them to any material extent. And so in our frustration, we have done the only thing we can think of, which is to indulge them even further.

It is as if we have been supervising a child who only pecks at his dinner. Responding to his entreaties, we have effectively agreed that the boy may move on to his chocolate cake with the understanding that he will later return to his broccoli and carrots. In what world does a dessert-first policy ever work?

Rodney Gilbert warned that our spirit of charity toward China would backfire. We are generous and forgiving when a wiser policy might have been to stand resolute and insist upon holding China to the same standard we hold other nations. China has ultimately been harmed by our indulgence, not helped by it. China in the Republican era was spoiled and capricious, Gilbert wrote, because it had been "consistently overpraised and overrated" when it "should have been spanked." The opportunity for tough love has passed us now, and we are likely to experience regret as old-fashioned analogies of children and spankings are ultimately replaced with serious talk of a belligerent superpower that threatens world peace.

In some ways, China appears to be reliving the tail end of the Qing dynasty and its aftermath. China's stubborn insistence on coal as a leading fuel source and an emphasis on railroad building are both echoes of that period. China's current effort to get developing nations hooked on Beijing-backed credit is, as well, a page torn out of the playbook of foreign nations who at the turn of the century—purposefully or unwittingly—turned China into a "semi-colony" through burdensome debt.

There is yet another echo that lingers from that era. In 2014, China created a new holiday to celebrate its "martyrs," defined by Beijing as any citizen who ever died in war. Other nations who wish to commemorate their soldiers will set aside a "Memorial Day" or "Veteran's Day." The point of establishing a Martyrs' Day is, I believe, an effort to dilute the memory of the true martyrs who died on Chinese soil, namely, the American and British Christian missionaries murdered by the Boxers.

Given the sordid history, Beijing would have been better off not mentioning anything about "martyrs," but they could not help themselves. In creating the secular twist on what is traditionally a religious notion, Chinese leaders have all but alerted us—through unconscious telegraphing—that we have forgotten a meaningful event, a lesson from our own past. That we barely noticed the propaganda ploy is shameful to say the least, but it is not too late to recognize that China silently has such things on its mind.

───────────

Rodney Gilbert had the sense in the 1920s that China yearned once more to be secluded from the world, which is why he spoke of the "right to isolation" and whether or not it existed. China's interest in pursuing an isolationist strategy in the years leading up to the communist takeover undoubtedly had much to do with the hope of "nationalizing" foreign assets—*kleptoparasitism*—but a more influential factor was national face. China was falling apart, and the Chinese did not want outsiders observing the disorder firsthand. "The craving for isolation is never anything but a confession of weakness," wrote Gilbert, "of incapacity to deal with the results of bad government and of that same fear of social intercourse which grips the man whose house will not bear inspection."

Should the Chinese economy slow dramatically in the coming years, or should the Chinese face another round of political uncertainty, we must recognize that they again may not want witnesses.

Whenever we convince ourselves that a certain kind of event could not possibly be repeated is precisely when we find ourselves in trouble. And to the extent that evaluating political risk is a serious component in any business, and given that a political calamity in China would mean catastrophe for the world, we must put this subject on the table for discussion. Chinese prefer not to speak of their isolationist past, precisely because it reveals a shameful instinct.

China watchers, who mimic the Chinese and who aim to ingratiate themselves with them, provide active support to this avoidance scheme. The fact that we are mute ourselves on China's isolationist past when it was such a prominent feature of the nation's history strikes me as wrongheaded.

"Johnny knows what he's done," is what adults say just beyond earshot of the naughty little boy who has done the unspeakable. We can hardly bring attention to his actions without shaming the youth, so our preferred method of discipline is eschewal. It's a bad approach. Glancing over at the boy as we work to change the subject, we manage to catch a glimpse of his put-on sheepishness, which not only hints at his complete awareness, but also confirms that we can expect the same undesirable behavior from him in the future.

CHAPTER 31

The Benefit of the Doubt

Chinese have finally begun to admit to mistakes being made during the Cultural Revolution (and in the surrounding years, collectively referred to as the Mao era). While these acknowledgments of past wrongs are long overdue, the focus has been limited almost exclusively to acts of violence. China's greatest sin during this period, however, was not premeditated bloodshed—prodigious though that was—it was isolating itself from the world in an attempt to bring about *autarky*. While an estimated one million Chinese died of physical brutality, at least twenty million died of starvation. China's isolationist policy caused massive economic contraction, a crisis made worse by the nation's refusal to accept overseas aid.

Chinese civilization is the experience of the nuclear family writ large, and just as extended families are expected to look after their own survival, China has long felt that it ought to be self-sufficient. Mainland Chinese may not treat the topic of isolationism as a strict taboo, but they do not like to discuss the matter all the same. On the surface, they understand that the world frowns on reclusiveness, but deep down, they view interdependence as a weakness.

China watchers have a tendency to cherry-pick history. They predict that China will become the wealthiest economy in a globalized world because at times in the distant past it was rich.

These prognosticators ignore that during much of the periods of affluence, China was also essentially isolated. There was a Silk Road, to be sure, but links to Europe were tenuous. Although a fair amount of trade took place in the Ming dynasty, it was not what we would call true internationalism, which did not begin in earnest until Great Britain took up the mantle of global hegemon in the nineteenth century by offering sterling silver as a stabilizing currency of exchange and the British Navy as a global policeman to guard against piracy. China actually had to be coerced into joining the global system. Strange that some insist the wealth will return, but never any interest in isolation.

China may have been a wealthy nation during long stretches in history, but for even longer periods it was a poor place. Abject poverty was the primary impression of foreign travelers in the nineteenth century anyway. Yet while the masses lived hand-to-mouth, they were nevertheless proud. For hundreds of years, this was China's default existence: impoverished, cloistered from the world, and sustained psychically on a diet of past glories.

The *Middle Kingdom complex* had the Chinese believing they were a magnificent nation, even as they struggled to eke out a subsistence. A shared sense of prominence and honor carried the people and gave them hope for survival. But there was a downside to this cultural feature. At least to outsiders, Chinese were insufferable. "Many who know the Chinese well," wrote Lucian Pye, "lose the feeling for their historic greatness in exasperation with their arrogance and self-satisfaction."

———

United States military strategists and foreign policy experts are currently preoccupied with answering a rather specific question: "What can we do to prevent war with China?" It is an unfortunately worded query, not only because it presupposes we are not already at war, but also because it presumes the burden of the two-party problem rests exclusively on *our* shoulders.

Harvard professor Graham Allison has recently popularized a hypothesis he calls the "Thucydides trap," in which he argues that incumbent political powers are predisposed to wage war against rising nations that threaten their political standing. "It was the rise of Athens," wrote Thucydides, "and the fear that this inspired in Sparta that made war inevitable." To make his point that the United States and China are on a collision course, Allison brings up numerous examples from the past couple hundred years. The problem is that none of the cases he references describes a direct confrontation between China and a major Western power. This is odd given that his purpose is to show that China and the United States are on track for a major conflict.

To my mind, the Opium Wars are sufficiently analogous and provide meaningful lessons. England went to war with China twice, we note, and in neither case was this because the British Empire felt somehow threatened by China. The reason behind the wars was simple: The British were exasperated by the Chinese, and in their frustration, they figured it would be easier to resolve differences "by ball and bayonet."

China historians who work in American universities are conspiring to convince the White House that they alone can advise on the matter of avoiding conflict with China. It is an unlikely proposition, given that this group widely believes the Anglo-Chinese War and the Arrow War were exclusively about narcotics—hence, the repackaging of these conflicts into "Opium Wars." Historians portray England as a drug lord in the mold of Pablo Escobar, and this narrative has been accepted because it lets China off the hook. At the same time, it makes Western civilization come off as the bad guy, which allows American sentimentalists the opportunity to indulge in feelings of guilt by proxy.

"Most aggressions against the Chinese," wrote Ralph Townsend, "have followed intolerable provocations." This one word— provocations—is coming up increasingly in press mentions related to the South China Sea, and we should expect it to appear with even greater frequency in the coming years as China continues to pursue strategies that annoy and ultimately inflame.

Specifically on the matter of opium in the run-up to the Anglo-Chinese War, the effort to limit opium traffic could have been handled in many different ways. But the Chinese elected to promote policy change by kidnapping the entire British trading community in Canton, along with Charles Elliot, England's top diplomat in this part of the world. The capture of the trading community at Canton ended only after the British agreed to round up some 20,000 chests of opium (an amount greater than what they had at sea), in order that it might be destroyed by Chinese authorities. To further signal its displeasure—and to apply additional pressure—China prevented British ships from obtaining supplies, including fresh water. This provocation alone was cause enough for war, given the importance of water and the great distance the British fleet would have had to sail to find an alternative source.

Chinese prefer what they believe to be nonconfrontational approaches to dispute resolution. Rather than launch an all-out attack, they seek to apply pressure. They have no qualms about kidnapping, so long as it does not result in physical harm. This belief, which persists in modern China, stems partly from a different cultural attitude toward personal time and freedom. The kidnapped British may have had no immediate complaints, but those on board ships who were deprived of fresh water were incensed, since the threat to their lives was imminent.

Vexed by a lack of options, Chinese who feel disadvantaged in a transaction will often seek to project their frustration onto those they believe are responsible. Imagining themselves unable to resolve issues related to the opium traffic, Chinese wished for their counterparts to understand their annoyance at least. Ultimately though, the greater motivation in holding another party's feet to the fire through *frustration tactics* is a strong desire to force the other side to "do more" toward resolving a matter.

Under normal circumstances, Chinese are cool and pragmatic. They not only know the value of every commodity, but they also understand the weighted benefit, or cost, of every action. The Qing government's insistence that such a large value of opium be destroyed—a product that had been traded legally for decades—showed a callous disregard for the value of property. And the withholding of water similarly showed on the part of the Chinese a lack of concern for the value of life.

Chinese who pursue nonconfrontational tactics believe that they are behaving ethically. The problem is that foreign groups may often be infuriated by some of their moves and see them, quite the opposite, as disturbingly confrontational. Westerners do not typically share the phlegmatic disposition of the Chinese, and their resulting moral outrage will often compel them to respond in an extreme fashion.

There are those who think the best we can do is train ourselves not to react to provocations made by the Chinese. Another way to go—and it is probably in everyone's best interest—is to get the Chinese to understand how certain undesirable approaches have served as root causes in past conflicts with a major power in the West.

––––––––

American importers do not mind the occasional nibble, and understanding this to be the case, Chinese factory owners will take care to limit the size of the bites they take on any given deal. Incrementalism, after all, is about reducing the risk of confrontation. Because in the normal run of things Chinese take a careful approach, we are understandably surprised whenever they act in a manner that is hurried and dramatic, and which calls our attention.

Beijing's motivation for building islands in the South China Sea is clear. A large percentage of global trade moves through that sea, so China wishes to protect the area from any threats that might limit the flow of commerce. In addition, there are vast reserves of oil and gas under the seabed that could help satisfy the country's voracious appetite for energy.

The question was never *why* China should want to build islands in the middle of the South China Sea but, rather, *why so fast?* The United States might have been able to ignore the reclamation work had it proceeded slowly. But Beijing moved rapidly, guaranteeing that the world would take notice and increasing the chance that America would insist that it stop its expansionist efforts.

There is an economic analogy here. Beijing's levels of borrowing and lending money have in a short time reached levels that have attracted the attention of the world. Economists and fund managers have told us for years that the constant credit injection was about preventing a "hard landing," but no major slowdown appeared to threaten. The economy is not currently in desperate need of fiscal support, and yet debt levels are soaring. China watchers are universal in decrying the trend, though none has provided an adequate explanation for why Beijing insists on keeping its foot on the gas pedal.

Beijing appears to be in a hurry, but for what?

Economists are warning that the nation is piling on too much debt. Beijing has not countered the accusations, nor has it chosen to reign in lending. In its silence, it all but acknowledges that a potential economic calamity is on the horizon, and if that is the case, how interesting to see that Beijing is choosing to meet this event by sending more fuel to the engine.

When the United States voiced its concern over reclamation activity in the South China Sea, Beijing did not respond by cooling down related activity. Quite the opposite, project crews began working around the clock. Beijing figured that it would be better to have built 3,200 acres on seven islands rather than just a few hundred acres on two.

In moving fast, Beijing was guaranteeing that the international community would apply greater pressure. But by its own calculations, the window of opportunity was going to close one way or another anyway, so why not put as many points on the board before it did so? In a similar way, political leaders figure that if the Chinese economy is going to enter a period of stagnation, they might as well secure as many successes for the nation before that event takes place.

I have long been curious about a specific cultural difference having to do with language: In the United States, there is tendency to judge a person's education level by mistakes made in speech, filtering out the good parts. Chinese, quite the opposite, tend to give a speaker the benefit of the doubt and focus only on high-water marks. In the United States, a basic grammatical error might be interpreted as a sign of poor education. In China, mistakes matter not at all. You can trip all over yourself in the linguistic sense, yet be redeemed by tactfully dropping a bit of erudition—an obscure idiom or a line from Confucius usually does the trick. Related to this culture quirk, Chinese in general lay heavy emphasis on showcase achievements at the expense of overall performance.

China is about to hit the wall as a result of too much lending, and its response to the prognosis has been to announce a one-trillion dollar Belt and Road Initiative, which will have it funding infrastructure projects around the world. China may yet go bust, but not before it has created some incredible lasting landmarks, and not before a host of nations from around the world has groveled at its feet seeking to win contracts for rail lines, highways, and ports. What a feat: an achievement for the ages.

Much of what Chinese leaders do bemuses. Beijing hosted the Olympic Games in 2008, and we were told this was the nation's "coming-out party." Then two years later, we were treated to another such celebration when the World Expo hosted in Shanghai was also billed as a cotillion. The world has since seen numerous more arrivals. China's success at putting a rover on the Moon elicited cheers, as did its triumph in reaching one—and then two, and then three—trillion dollars in foreign reserves. China craves these milestones in a way that is almost pathological.

———————

Many are convinced that the current mad pace of growth is about an effort to "rule the world." But global domination does not suit the Chinese well, since they perennially prefer not to take the lead. Indeed, no nation that desperately seeks to avoid confrontation—and which holds the cat's paw strategy in such high esteem—can ever stand to be out in front for long. And anyway, China does not in its wildest dreams believe that the world would ever allow it to rise to the stature of global hegemon. No, this foolish rush is about something else, something simpler. It's about ringing the bell. It's about seeing just how far China can take things before that great window of opportunity shuts.

China's sense of the dynastic cycle sets the expectation among its people that good times don't last. Convinced that they are soon heading back to square one, Chinese are busily making the most of these watershed years. Beijing's ruling class understands that the dynastic cycle portends paradigmatic change, and in its arrogance it figures that it can beat history and somehow survive the turn intact.

China's belief in dynastic cycles is a self-fulfilling prophecy. In the political sphere, a government that fears disorder seeks ways in which to limit freedom, and in its draconian approach it inflames public sentiment, thereby triggering social unrest. In the economic domain, business owners who collectively worry that an opportunity may soon be limited rush to take advantage while they still can, and in their frenzied scramble, they trigger the panic that all but ensures their fears come true.

Modern China is a fantasy novel written by Philip K. Dick. Beijing is the mad scientist who has invented a time machine that can peer into the future. Having seen that he will soon die, the inventor works hard to avoid that which has been portended. But every action that he takes following his enlightenment serves only to fulfill the conditions that assure his predetermined demise.

Beijing is not in control to the extent it wishes to be. Although it purports to have dictated all of the nation's recent accomplishments, internally, leaders recognize that events are influenced more by cultural trends than political edicts. The time to call for a rain dance is when you see clouds are brewing. "When a dog runs at you, whistle for him." This is another trick. It confuses the animal into thinking that he is somehow following a command. Beijing is not looking to prevent the inevitable. It only wishes to get out in front of it.

In future, Chinese will not delve into the distant past and recount the achievements of antiquity. Instead, they will brag about the nation's more recent accomplishments, such as going to space and rising to become the world's largest trading partner. China may not have the biggest navy in the world, but it does have the bomb. And it has built supersonic missiles capable of taking out American aircraft carriers. Not that China ever needed to use such weaponry, because its leaders had been smart to play one nation off the other, and to manipulate others into doing its dirty work. Chinese leaders proved skillful global players. Beijing tricked foreign economies into suffering trade deficits, yet the leaders of these other nations pleaded for a chance at closer ties. Chinese children will eventually be called upon to memorize a long list of more recent national glories, and along the way they will be especially made to remember which regime made it all possible.

Living on the glory of the past is one of the most fundamental aspects of Chinese culture. Beijing political leaders believe in the dynastic cycle, not as an abstract concept, but as a reality—and they sense change is coming. They know they cannot prevent the turn of history's wheel, but they figure that they can convince the Chinese people that they ought to remain the legitimate rulers of the country for an additional cycle. Beijing's secret plan is not world domination. It is to create as many new symbols of national pride as possible, to establish tomorrow's myths of yesteryear.

KEEPING IN TOUCH

The author is available on Twitter, Facebook, and LinkedIn
Business and media inquiries: paulmidler@gmail.com